MICHEL MONTIGNAC

Preface by Professor Leonardo Santi

DINE OUT
AND
LOSE WEIGHT

THE FRENCH WAY TO CULINARY "SAVOIR VIVRE"

*Translated from the original French version
"Comment maigrir en faisant des repas d'affaires"
and specially adapted for the U.S.A.*

MONTIGNAC U.S.A., INC.

First published in FRANCE under the title, *"Comment maigrir en faisant des repas d'affaires",* 1987.

EDITIONS ARTULEN
46, avenue d'Iéna
75116 PARIS FRANCE
Tél. 40.70.91.47

MONTIGNAC USA, INC
2980 Beverly Glen Circle
Suite 203
LOS ANGELES CA 90077
USA
Tel. 1-800-932-3229

ISBN 2-906236-17-9

TABLE OF CONTENTS

BIOGRAPHY

Michel Montignac has been in charge of personnel since the beginning of his professional career.

In 1981, he became Area Personnel Director for the European headquarters of an American pharmaceutical company.

In addition to his main responsibilities, he was regularly called upon to entertain the company's foreign visitors, and to dine in the best restaurants of the French capital.

Within three months, Montignac, who was already 13 pounds overweight, gained an extra 15 pounds. Moreover, obesity was not uncommon in his family.

He soon reached a point where he had difficulty in accepting his physical condition, and therefore decided to embark on an in-depth exploration of dietetic and nutritious phenomena. He began to study on his own—reading, interviewing experts, and conducting research in the scientific environment where he worked.

He met with doctors, physicians and researchers who were already familiar with the topic. He also conducted experiments on himself, his family and friends.

Within a few months, Montignac lost 28 pounds which, to this day, he has not gained back.

9

In 1987, he published his book in France and has sold nearly half a million copies since. The rights of his book have been sold throughout Europe.

Today, the principles presented in Montignac's book have been recognized by a significant majority in the French and international medical establishment. A medical team that works closely with the author is currently training other doctors in the context of his discoveries.

Montignac holds seminars especially designed for business professionals. The first of a chain of Montignac restaurants is currently being launched.

The author is 46 years old, married, and the father of three.

PREFACE

BY PROFESSOR LEONARDO SANTI
"DINE OUT AND LOSE WEIGHT"

Certain readers might be surprised that the preface of a dietary book would be written by a doctor whose specialty is in an entirely different field.

The reason for this is not really all that shocking once one realizes that the diet plays an essential role in human health.

It is often forgotten that nutritional factors constitute the best prevention against even the most serious diseases. They are responsible for neutralizing the toxic agents, or at least, preventing them from altering the cell's fundamental mechanisms.

It is well known, even among the general public, that an unbalanced diet constitutes the principal risk factor for most diseases. This is why it is important to correct bad eating habits and to adopt new, healthy ones, that provide the best prevention against health problems.

When writing for the general public, it is always wise to assure a good comprehension of the dietary technical information. While stressing that it is in one's personal interest to change the

11

bad eating habits that are ingrained in dietary habits, the information should, nevertheless, be conveyed in such a way as to avoid moralistic sermons and overly aggressive messages that could cause fear.

It would not be very reasonable to place the entire blame of an unhealthy diet on an individual's socio-cultural environment, nor on the ways and customs of his region or country. Food, and the ritual that is attached to it, is not only one of the parameters of our modern day society, but also, one of the bases of our cultural heritage. This is why certain people are obliged, due to their social or economic status, to conduct their business affairs over lunches and dinners.

Businessmen and women should not have to be obsessed with the fear that food will cause them to be overweight and/ or lead them to have poor performance. This obsession will often lead to deprivation which can jeopardize one's professional effectiveness and general health. That is why, on behalf of all of those, who like myself, worry about the well-being of their contemporaries, I recommend Michel Montignac's book "Dine Out and Lose Weight" as a helpful aid in learning how to reconcile socio-professional obligations with the well-being of one's health.

Professor Leonardo Santi

President of the International Society for Preventive Oncology (I.S.P.O.), New York Scientific Director of the National Institute for Cancer Research, Genoa, Italy

12

FOREWORD

The principles of nutrition which I recommend in this book were originally intended for the French public whose eating habits are quite different from those of a country like the United States of America.

I wrote this book for my compatriots to warn them that the more they abandon the culinary traditions of their country, the more they would suffer the secondary effects of bad diet, as is the case in the Anglo-Saxon countries.

Such is the image of gastronomic delight which French cuisine inspires in the American imagination; the mere mention of it to an American will make his or her face suddenly light up with pleasure.

But this initial reaction of pleasure is quickly followed by a more cynical attitude, as the average American is also convinced that French cooking is much too rich, according to dietary beliefs in the U.S.

In Paris, I once met a young American woman of 25 with the figure of a model. I asked her if she had always looked that way.

"No," she replied, "when I arrived in France I was 14 pounds overweight which I'd put on during my studies at the University."

"What did you do to lose them?"

"Nothing!" she told me. "I've been living with a traditional French family in Paris for a year and all I had to do to get rid of the extra kilos was to eat like the French."

On the other hand, I often get desperate calls from French parents whose children have spent a few months in the U.S. and who return with a worrying weight problem.

It should be noted that apart from Japan, France has the lowest average weight of all Western countries. Obesity is rare (about 4 times less than in the U.S.), and when it does occur it is fairly limited. It is also rare for a French person to know his or her cholesterol level, as the rate of cardiovascular disease is very low in France (3-4 times lower than the U.S. according to the WHO). Only Japan does slightly better.

The reason for this is not genetic. The difference is quite simply dietary habits, including two main factors:

First, we must examine the nature of food itself. The French diet is more varied. The French eat more green vegetables, and therefore fiber. They do not eat sandwiches or hamburgers and most of all they consume less sugar (77 lbs per person per year compared to 138 lbs in the U.S.). They drink wine (10 times more than in the U.S.) which has been proven to have exceptional nutritional qualities when taken in moderation. In particular, it protects against cardiovascular disease which is definitely not the case of beer and soft drinks (cola, sodas, etc.) where the reverse is true.

The second reason is that the method of eating is different in France. French people eat 3 meals a day and do not snack in between them. Lunch is a full meal over which time is spent. A full meal consists of an appetizer, a main course and a dessert, usually cheese.

In French schools there is always a cafeteria which serves a normal meal; the ritual of the peanut butter and jelly sandwich in a lunchbox does not exist. At the workplace there is a proper lunchbreak and the food provided is not only varied but usually fresh and cooked at the last moment.

Homecooking is also important; it only takes a few seconds to make "French" dressing, mayonnaise or tomato sauce.

Every evening the whole family gathers for dinner around the same table to share a meal including a starter, main dish and dessert.

Butter, charcuterie, oil, foie gras, fresh cream, cheese and wine are all part of the French daily diet and yet the French suffer from neither obesity nor heart disease.

Many American observers, journalists in particular, are beginning to make the same remarks and address their questions to American medical experts:

Why should we continue to restrict the calorie intake of our citizens, to remove cholesterol and fat from their food and to exhaust them with physical exercise, to achieve only poor results, or, as in the case of obesity, even worse results?

Would it not be wiser to first try to understand why the situation is better in France where pleasure and gastronomy dominate everyday nutrition?

I believe this book partially answers these questions.

I wrote this book originally for the French so they could be made aware of the risks they run in letting themselves be seduced by the American example of fast food and soft drinks, and the advantage of conserving traditional French nutritional habits.

At the same time, it can show Americans the real reasons

why they have reached crisis point with regard to their eating habits.

If they wish to achieve long-lasting results, which is easy if the recommendations found in this book are followed, they should accept two principles:

First, they should realize that it is the disorganized way in which they eat, rather than the quantity they may eat, which is at the root of their weight problem. They should also admit that all the sauce, mayonnaise and other pre-packaged foods constitute "polluted" foods, if only because of the astronomic amounts of sugar, starch and preservatives they contain.

They should then agree to change their eating habits. Nibbling and frequent prepackaged meals and sandwiches should be dropped.

New habits such as respect for lunchtime and the systematic checking of food labels to identify undesirable ingredients should be developed.

Experience has proven that the principles of nutrition contained in this book are quite compatible with the American way of life.

During my stays in the U.S., I have personally verified that all restaurants and even fast food chains and coffee shops include on their menus a possible choice of meal which corresponds to the rules of the method we propose.

We have also shown that all the products and foods particularly recommended can be found in all American shops from the East Coast to the West.

The adoption of these principles of nutrition is therefore completely compatible with typical American family and professional life.

The only real effort to be made is "gastronomic".

NOTE

The method described in this book is to be distinguished from the common "diet." It is based on the metabolism's natural equilibrium and on the physiological principles of digestion. If the method, which does not call for quantitative restrictions, is fully understood, no nutritive deficiencies should result. However, the method is designed, first and foremost, for a healthy subject, and if you are undergoing special treatment of any kind, it is necessary that you check with a doctor before you apply the principles presented here. Nevertheless, it is highly recommended that everyone go in for a medical check-up before altering their diet, in order to be certain of a healthy condition and to be able to monitor the positive results that will follow.

LIBERTY BANQUET

1919

Liberty Banquet, February 8, 1919. New York.

AUTHOR'S NOTE

Since the early 80s, I have never deprived myself of anything. I drink red wine with every meal, and the amount of chocolate I eat is really quite impressive.

I realize that this "mysterious" behavior sometimes elicits a sense of jealousy and frustration among my close friends, my family and especially my colleagues at work.

Their frustration often stems from what they think is provocation on my part.

They all knew me when I was 28 pounds overweight and have a difficult time understanding how I am able to maintain my weight and continue to pay homage to the best restaurants of Paris on a regular basis. They think I am keeping a "secret" from them.

This "secret," if we can speak in those terms at all, is revealed in this book both to them and to you.

Michel Montignac

A GOURMET'S LIBRARY

"Gourmet's Almanach," by Grimod de la Reyniere

INTRODUCTION

I hesitated a long time before finally choosing the title of this book, "Dine Out and Lose Weight." At first, it seemed too commercial for a work that I had intended to be extremely serious. But I kept this title to evoke the true purpose of the book rather than to impress my readers. Losing, or not gaining, weight is what really interests you, right?

Over the last few years, every time I was asked how I was able to lose weight and maintain that loss, I would answer that "I ate out and conducted business meals." People smiled but were never fully convinced.

You are also probably confused over this apparent paradox, especially if you blame your belly and love handles on the professional obligations that call for you to honor "haute cuisine" a little too often. At any rate, this is what you have led yourself to believe.

Like most people, you have probably tried to apply those so-called "golden rules" of dieting and countless weight-loss methods which have by now become part of everyone's common knowledge. Nevertheless, you have noticed that the methods often contradict each other, and usually only produce temporary results or even nothing at all. Moreover, you may have found it practically impossible to fit these diets into the framework of your professional lifestyle.

So today you are still in a frenzy over what we will modestly call your "excess weight."

In the early 1980s, when I was well into my thirties, my scale read 176 pounds—about 13 pounds above my ideal weight. Nothing too alarming for a man over six feet tall and approaching his fortieth birthday.

Up until then I had led a rather regular professional career, and my excess weight had apparently stabilized itself. I hardly ever overate, and when I did, it was usually in a family setting. When you come from the southwest of France as I do, gastronomy is inevitably part of your heritage, culture and education.

I had already given up sugar, at least the dose I put in my coffee. I never ate potatoes under the pretext that I was "allergic." And I hardly ever drank any alcohol, except for wine, of course.

I gained those 13 extra pounds over a ten year period, a rather moderate and progressive gain. When I looked around to gauge my portliness, I never felt above the norm, and most of the time I was in better shape than the average middle-aged man.

Overnight, however, my professional lifestyle changed. I was assigned to the general headquarters of the American multinational company where I worked, and was suddenly given international responsibilities.

I spent much of my time traveling to visit the company's affiliate branches to which I was assigned. These business trips were always interspersed with a series of business lunches and dinners.

In Paris, since I was in charge of internal public relations, it was my duty to accompany mostly foreign visitors to the best restaurants of the French capital. I must admit that this was not the most unpleasant part of my job.

I remain nevertheless convinced that restaurants, meals, the dinner table, all pleasures aside, are the best place for discussion and communication. As a specialist in Human Relations, I can assure you that, for me, the best place for conducting negotiations (whether they be with the president of the company or with a new recruit) has always been in a restaurant setting, at the coffee shop across the street or at the company cafeteria downstairs.

Three months after I was promoted to my new position, however, I had already gained a few more pounds and weighed no less than 28 pounds above my ideal weight. The three week training trip I took to England did not help much either.

It finally became urgent that I do something serious about my less than flattering corpulence.

Like everybody else, I had more or less tried the usual weight-loss methods that never led to anything, as we all know.

But, soon thereafter, as chance would have it, I met a general practitioner who was impassioned by nutritional problems. He gave me some fundamental guidelines which seemed to question the basis of traditional dietetics.

I quickly obtained some promising results and decided to look into the matter more thoroughly. Since I worked for a pharmaceutical company, it was relatively easy for me to gain access to the scientific information I needed.

A few weeks later, I had collected most of the French and American publications on the topic. Even if certain rules "worked," I wanted to understand the scientific explanations behind them. I wanted to know how the rules caused me to lose weight and how efficient they actually were.

From the start, I told myself that I would not eliminate anything from my regular diet except for sugar, and that had already been accomplished. When it is your duty to accompany visitors to restaurants and "entertain," you simply cannot allow yourself to count calories and order only "a hard boiled egg and an apple" at every meal. I needed to find another solution.

So I lost 28 pounds conducting business meals everyday, and you will soon learn how. Since this weight-loss method asks you to choose your foods, to mix and match, where else besides a restaurant do you have the liberty to do so?

But understanding the principles and applying them are two different things.

After a couple of months, my friends and colleagues asked me to explain my "secret" to them. I summarized the essential principles of my new weight-loss solution on three typewritten pages.

I tried, whenever possible, to spend at least one hour with each interested person explaining the scientific basis for the method. But my subjects were inevitably influenced by false preconceptions on how to lose weight that did not always jibe with what I proposed. Consequently, they often made involuntary and blatant mistakes which offset any good results. A more complete explanation thus became imperative.

This book is a guide. For the sake of my readers, I have worked toward the following objectives:

- to present indispensable scientific information for the reader to understand nutritional phenomena;
- to forever rid the reader of preconceived ideas;

- to present simple rules and support them with basic scientific and technical explanations;

- to make this a practical guide that the reader can always use as a reference.

Within the last few years, under professional guidance, I observed, researched, tested and experimented. At this point, I am thoroughly convinced that I have discovered and established a simple and efficient way to weight-loss.

You will learn, as you read on, that "one does not gain weight from eating too much, but from eating badly."

You will learn to manage your diet like you manage your budget.

You will learn to reconcile your professional obligations with personal pleasure.

You will learn to improve your eating habits without taking the spice out of your meals.

This book is not a "Diet Book." It introduces a new way of eating that allows you to maintain your weight while you continue to indulge in culinary pleasures.

You will be surprised to find that once you adopt this new way of eating you will rediscover a physical and mental well-being that you may have thought long gone.

You will learn that certain eating habits are often at the root of a lack of dynamism and, subsequently, physical or professional under-achievement.

You will also learn that by adopting certain fundamental nutritional principles which are easy to apply, the fits of fatigue you probably experience will be eliminated and you will rediscover optimum vitality.

For the above reasons, although your surplus weight may be only a modest sum, or even non-existent, it is still important that you assimilate the principles to adopt for the proper management of your diet. This method is a passport to discovering new energy for you and your enterprise and guarantees improved professional efficiency.

You will also notice that any gastro-intestinal worries you may have had will disappear forever because your digestive system will establish a new equilibrium.

Although I may defend good French cuisine, especially wine and chocolate, I do not intend to plagiarize the excellent gastronomical guides I am sure you have on your shelves.

I admit, nonetheless, that I am often tempted to do so since it is very difficult for me to disassociate nourishment from pleasure, and simple cooking from gastronomical cuisine.

I have been lucky enough to have visited some of the world's finest restaurants. For me, a handshake from a great chef is as sacred as a benediction from the Pope.

Great cuisine, and often the simplest, has truly become an art—one that I would place before all other forms of art.

CHAPTER I

WHAT IS THE SOLUTION?

Every year, after your annual medical check-up, you go home a little bit more desperate. Once again, you have gained weight over the last year. Although you suspected as much, you did not want to admit it.

When you look at yourself in the bathroom mirror, you automatically suck in your stomach as if you were trying to impress someone on the beach. As long as you can't see it, it isn't a problem, right?

It is not easy to admit that this is one area in life where you can never win. And it is all the more difficult to accept that fact when you are by nature a "winner"; someone who never shies away from a challenge.

Over the years, you may have fought with your boss or with members of the board. You fought to move up, to get a promotion, to realize your goals and maybe even your dreams. You fought to become who you are today.

You know how to solve problems, find efficient solutions, make decisions, lead and organize. You may even be a model of inspiration for your colleagues at work.

But when the doctor says "you have gained weight again!," you want to crawl under the examining table, ashamed and embarrassed.

And like a child who has not done his homework, you desperately try to find an excuse.

"But doctor, I don't understand," you manage to sputter. "I watch what I eat and I try not to eat too much. It's true. I can assure you that I eat much less than before. Of course, you understand, I cannot avoid business meals and social affairs. They are somewhat of an obligation in my field. However, I am being extra careful. I even exercise. I started jogging, and I run miles every week. But when I see the results, it isn't very encouraging. Maybe it's the all too frequent change in foods; you know, today New York, tomorrow Paris, and Hong-Kong the day after. Maybe it's jet lag... No, it's true. I've noticed that jet lag makes me bloated... And if you saw what they are serving on planes nowadays... It's garbage!"

Your doctor begins to smile. He has heard this same old song too many times.

"Well," he says as he gets up from his chair, "you must be careful or the situation can become dangerous. An active person such as yourself, under constant stress at work, is already a prime candidate for a cardiac arrest. So don't make it any worse on yourself by adding fat to your worries."

"Then doctor, tell me what I should do!"

"Eat less, drink less, and exercise! Start a diet!"

A diet! You have tried everything. Your extra weight is enough of a problem by now that you know a great deal about diets already. Your spouse, your friends, even your secretary at work talks enough about this subject for you to have become almost an expert in the field.

28

How many times have you stumbled upon an article in *Elle* or *Mademoiselle* that promised quick weight-loss?

You learned to chew well, to eliminate bread, not to drink while you eat, to have meals consisting only of fruit, to avoid fats and, of course, to count your calories. You are repeatedly told not to consume too many rich foods and to exercise. But you have tried all that. You cut down on alcohol. You bought a bike, and even took up jogging.

Results: nil! You may have lost a few pounds, but quickly gained them back.

So, since you never despair, you rid yourself of any guilty feelings following your medical check-up.

You reassure yourself that the people around you accept you just the way you are. In other words, you have become somewhat of a fatalist.

But deep down inside you cannot continue this seemingly losing battle. You are winning all the others. You and your colleagues are always looking for new information that could lead to the ultimate solution.

I think I have found the solution.

I have found it!

It has worked successfully for me and a number of people I know. Now it is your turn to discover it and be just as successful.

Best Wishes and Good Luck!

GARGANTUA A SON GRAND COUVERT.

GARGANTUA DINES

Carnavalet Museum

CHAPTER II

FOOD CLASSIFICATION

Personally, I find this to be one of the most worthwhile chapters. The technical explanations of the different food categories outlined in this section are crucial to following my weight-loss method. You will discover how to make eclectic choices of the various food groups and to distribute them accordingly during each meal.

I urge you to read this chapter attentively so as to fully absorb the importance of its meaning. Please remember that you should return to it as often as necessary in order to completely understand how the method works, or everything may fail.

Foods are edible substances that contain a number of organic elements such as proteins, lipids, carbohydrates, minerals and vitamins, as well as water and non-digestible matter.

PROTEINS (or PROTIDS)

Proteins are the organic cells that make up living matter: muscles, organs, the brain, the skeletal structure, etc. They are made up of simpler bodies called amino acids. Some amino acids are produced by the body, but for the most part, they are introduced into the system through different ingested foods. Protein comes from two sources:

- *Animal sources*: meats, fishes, cheese, eggs and milk.
- *Vegetable sources*: soybean, almonds, hazelnuts, peanuts and certain leguminous plants.

Foods from plant sources, except soybean, generally contain a low amount of protein. They therefore cannot fulfill our physiological needs alone.

On the other hand, a diet low in protein can lead to serious consequences: muscle deterioration, wrinkling of the skin, rupture of certain organs, etc.

It is necessary to consume about three ounces of protein per day. Protein is necessary to produce globules, secrete hormones, produce scar tissue, and maintain muscle tone. If the amount of proteins consumed is too great when physical activity is low, unburned residue will remain in the body and turn into uric acid which is usually the cause of gout and arthrosis.

CARBOHYDRATES

Carbohydrates are molecules composed of carbon, oxygen and hydrogen. They can be reduced to three simple sugars; glucose, fructose and galactose.

Glycemia

Glucose is the body's principle "fuel." It is stored, in reserve, under the form of glycogen, where it is found in the muscles and in the liver.

Glycemia represents the blood's glucose level. On an empty stomach, the glucose level is usually one gram per one liter of blood. After glucose has been absorbed (on an empty stomach) by the ingestion of bread, honey, cereal, sweets, etc., the variation of the blood's glucose level can be examined.

In the first phase, the glycemia increases (more or less according to the nature of the carbohydrate).

In the second phase, after an insulin secretion from the pancreas, the glucose level decreases and the glucose penetrates into the cells.

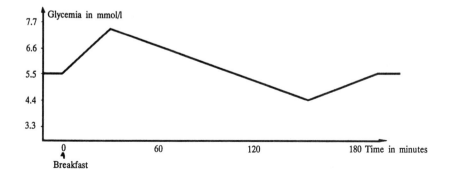

33

In the third phase, the glucose level reverts back to its normal level (see chart on previous page).

For a long time, carbohydrates were placed in two distinct categories: "quick sugars" and "slow sugars." These two classifications correspond to the assimilation rate needed by the body to absorb these sugars.

"Quick sugars" are really "simple sugars", such as saccharose and fructose. They are found in processed sugar (extracted from sugarcane or beets), honey and fruits.

The name "quick sugar" was originally employed because it aptly described the carbohydrate's molecular simplicity which allows for a rapid assimilation rate by the body after ingestion.

Conversely, in the "slow sugar" category, the sugars have a more complex molecular structure which must chemically convert them into simple sugars in order for the body to absorb them. Starchy foods are a good example of slow sugars, for their digestive process is slow and progressive.

The classification of these carbohydrates as quick sugars and slow sugars is today considered outdated because it is based on an erroneous belief. Recent experiments have shown that the carbohydrate's molecular complexity does not play a role in the rapidity or speed in which glucose is freed and assimilated by the body.

These studies have even shown that the glycemic peak of both quick sugars and slow sugars, (that is to say, their maximum absorption level), taken independently on an empty stomach, occurs during the same lapse of time (around half an hour after their ingestion). Rather than spending time explaining the rapidity of carbohydrate assimilation, let us move on to a more pertinent subject: carbohydrates and the increased glycemic effect they produce in the body.

Scientists and others in the nutrition field admit that the

carbohydrate classification as "quick sugars" and "slow sugars" should really be defined by the hyperglycemic potential as shown on the glycemic index.

The Glycemic Index

The glycemic potential of each carbohydrate is defined by the glycemic index which was first used in 1976. This index corresponds to the triangular surface of the hyperglycemic curve induced by carbohydrate ingestion.

Glucose is arbitrarily given an index of 100 which represents the triangular surface of the corresponding hypoglycemic curve. The glycemic index, taken from other carbohydrates is thus calculated according to the following formula:

$$\frac{\text{triangular surface of the tested carbohydrate}}{\text{the carbohydrate's triangular surface}} \times 100$$

The glycemic index rises corresponding to the level of hyperglycemia. Thus, the higher the glycemic index, the higher the hyperglycemic rate will be.

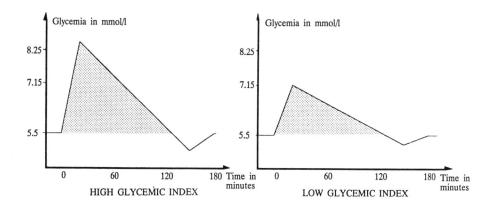

HIGH GLYCEMIC INDEX   LOW GLYCEMIC INDEX

35

It should be noted that chemical processing increases the glycemic index. For example, corn flakes have a glycemic index of 85, while corn in its natural state has a glycemic index of 70; instant potatoes' glycemic index is 95, while boiled potatoes have a glycemic index of 70.

We know that fiber quantity can produce a high or low glycemic index. However, fiber quality also plays an important role in the glycemic index. For example, white bread has a glycemic index of 70 while whole wheat bread has a glycemic index of only 45. The same applies to white rice whose glycemic index is 70 while whole rice has a glycemic index of 50.

GLYCEMIC INDEX CHART

HIGH GLYCEMIC INDEX		LOW GLYCEMIC INDEX	
Maltose (beer)	110	Whole rice	50
Glucose	**100**	Whole wheat bread	50
White bread	95	Whole wheat pasta	45
Instant potatoes	95	Fresh white beans	40
Honey/jam	90	Oatmeal	40
Cornflakes, popcorn	85	Whole rye bread	40
Carrots	85	Green peas	40
Refined sugar	75	Whole cereals	35
Corn	70	Dairy products	35
Beets	70	Wild rice	35
White rice	70	Fresh fruits	35
Cookies	70	Lentils	30
Boiled potatoes	70	Chick peas	30
White flour pasta	65	Dried beans	30
Bananas	60	Dried peas	30
Raisins	60	Dark chocolate	22
		Fructose	20
		Soya	15
		Green vegetables	< 15

In order to simplify matters for our personal use, I propose that carbohydrates be placed into two categories: "bad carbohydrates" (carbohydrates having a high glycemic index) and "good carbohydrates" (carbohydrates having a low glycemic index). This classification will enable you to discover in the following chapters, the reason, among others, for your being overweight.

Bad Carbohydrates

Bad carbohydrates have an assimilation process which provokes a glucose increase in the blood (glycemia). For instance, glycemia occurs when table sugar is ingested (in no matter what form, be it pure, cakes, candy, etc.). This holds true for all processed foods as well: refined flour, rice, potatoes, corn and even alcohol (especially distilled alcohol).

Good Carbohydrates

Contrary to previous thought, good carbohydrates are responsible for a small increase in the blood's glucose level. For example, whole cereals, unrefined flour, whole rice and certain starchy foods, such as lentils and beans, provide good sources of good carbohydrates. Fruits and most vegetables (leeks, turnips, lettuce, green beans, etc.) are also found in the good carbohydrate group.

LIPIDS OR FATS

Lipids, or fats, are complex molecules. There are two large lipid categories:

— *Lipids of Animal Origin :* Lipids found in meat, fish, butter, cheese, sour cream, etc.

— *Lipids of Vegetable Origin :* Lipids found in peanut butter, margarine, etc.

Lipids are also classified in two categories of fatty acids:

— *Saturated fatty acids* that are found in meat, cold cuts, eggs, and dairy products (butter, cream, cheese).

— *Unsaturated or Polyunsaturated fatty acids.* These fatty acids are the fats that remain in liquid form at room temperature (safflower oil, rapeseed oil, and olive oil) as well as certain others that can harden by hydrogenation (margarine fabrication). It is necessary to also include all fish fats in this category. The transformation of fats by the metabolism is relatively slow (slower, however, than the transformation of unsaturated fatty acids).

Lipids are essential dietary elements, for they contain a number of vitamins (A, D, E, K) and essential fatty acids such as linoleic acid and linolenic acid. These fatty acids aid in the proper functioning of diverse hormones.

When fats are mixed with bad carbohydrates, their energy becomes trapped, producing an interference in their assimilation process. The end result is that the once trapped energy changes itself into fat reserves.

In the traditional diet, lipids generally have had a bad reputation for two reasons. The first reason is that they have been thought to be the reason for being overweight. (This is not entirely true).

The second reason is that they have been believed to be linked to cardiovascular diseases. (Another myth that is not totally correct). It is true, however, that they do carry some dangers, but definitely not all the ones that they have been attributed to producing.

What is correct is the following: lipids are responsible for an increased cholesterol level. There are two types of this cholesterol, the "good" and the "bad." The objective, of course, is to try to maintain the cholesterol total at the lowest point possible. It should be done in such a way that all the proper conditions are united so that the proportion of good cholesterol remains the most significant [1].

It is necessary to realize that not all lipids favor the increase of "bad" cholesterol. On the contrary, some lipids are even capable of decreasing the cholesterol level to a certain degree.

In fact, in order to be totally objective, it is necessary to categorize these fats into yet another three classifications:

1) *Fats that increase the cholesterol level.* These are saturated fats found in meat, cold cuts, butter, cheese and lard;

2) *Fats that have no reaction whatsoever on the cholesterol level.* These fats are found in skinless poultry and safflower oil;

3) *Fats that are responsible for lowering the cholesterol level* and helping to prevent fat deposits. All fish oils (especially fish richest in fat—tuna, mackerel, sardines) but also olive oil, corn oil, soy, rapeseed oil and safflower margarines.

---

1. See chapter VI on cardiovascular disease prevention.

The weight-loss method that I propose to you rests, in part, between the choice of the "good" and the "bad" carbohydrates. Along these same lines, it is necessary for you to make the choice between the "good" and the "bad" lipids, especially if you have a tendency to have a high cholesterol level, or if you simply would like to avoid such a possibility.

ALIMENTARY FIBERS

Alimentary fibers are substances found particularly in vegetables, fruits, and whole cereals. It is true that these fibers have no energetic value, but what is important, is that they do play an extremely important role in the digestive process. The cellulose, the pectin, and the gums that they contain assure a good intestinal route and their absence is the cause of most constipations. These fibers are also rich in vitamins and trace elements (mineral substances) without which grave deficiencies can occur.

Certain fibers activate the secretion of the bile salts which control fats and regulate the intestinal transit. They also impede the digestive absorption of the lipids, thereby diminishing the atherosclerosis risk [2].

Alimentary fibers also have the advantage of limiting the toxic effects of certain chemical substances, such as additives

---

2. An entire chapter has been dedicated to hypercholesterolemia as it relates to cardiovascular risks. See page 267.

I encourage you to pay close attention to this chapter in order for you to make wise and informed decisions in your diet and to benefit as much as possible from the Montignac method.

and artificial colors. According to gastroenterologists, certain alimentary fibers could even be capable of protecting the colon from a number of risks, notably digestive cancers.

During the past decades, the increase in the standard of living in industrialized countries has led, unfortunately, to a diminution of fiber consumption.

Americans, in general, have a daily dietary fiber intake below the recommended daily intake of 40 grams. A study done by the CSFII in 1985-86 showed that women aged 20-49 years received approximately 11 grams and children aged 1-5 years received approximately 10 grams of dietary fiber per day. A report from the CSFII 1985 indicated that on the average, the dietary fiber intake of men is higher than that of women by about 17 grams per day. (Nutrition Monitoring in the United States: An Update Report on Nutrition Monitoring 1989, pg. 55).

The food base for Italians has always been pasta. Even 30 years ago, the essentials of their diet were vegetables (rich in fiber) and whole pasta. That is to say, the pasta was made with whole flour containing wheat fibers.

Today in Italy, however, with the increase of the standard of living, meat has become the popular replacement of vegetables. The pasta is made with processed flour (which means the absence of fiber). Italian medical authorities have not only noted the increase of obesity cases but also the alarming rate of digestive cancers due to this change of dietary intake.

In addition, it has been proven that fibers have a beneficial effect on obesity. Their introduction into the diet has had a diminishing effect on the glycemic as well as insulinemic levels. This means that the insulin secretions, which we will see in the following chapter, are responsible for fat reserves.

FIBER SOURCES
AND THEIR CONCENTRATION
FOR 10.5 OUNCES

CEREAL PRODUCTS		DRIED OILY FRUIT	
Bran	4.20 oz	Dried Coconuts	2.55 oz
Flour	3.20 oz	Dried figs	1.90 oz
Whole fiber		Almonds	1.50 oz
flour (without bran)	.95 oz	Dried raisins	.75 oz
Whole rice	.53 oz	Dates	.95 oz
White rice	.10 oz	Peanuts	1.40 oz
White bread	.10 oz		
Whole wheat bread	1.10 oz		
DRIED VEGETABLES		**GREEN VEGETABLES**	
Dried beans	2.65 oz	Green cooked peas	1.28 oz
Lentils	1.30 oz	Parsley	.95 oz
Chick peas	2.43 oz	Artichoke	.40 oz
		Leeks	.40 oz
FRESH FRUITS		Cabbage	.42 oz
Raspberries	.85 oz	Radishes	.32 oz
Pears with skin	.32 oz	Mushrooms	.26 oz
Apples with skin	.32 oz	Carrots	.21 oz
Strawberries	.20 oz	Lettuce	.21 oz
Peaches	.20 oz		

Among the four large food groups, proteins are absolutely necessary. Their amino acids are the most indispensable to our body since we cannot make them ourselves. The same applies to certain lipids that contain two essential fatty acids (linoleic acid and linolenic acid). Our cells are also incapable of producing these fatty acids independently. Only the carbohydrates could be considered as the least necessary because our bodies know how to make glucose from our fat reserves.

What is interesting to know, is that lipids and proteins

are often combined in the same foods; for example in meats. On the other hand, only carbohydrates and lipids are energetically important. That is why, for the clarity of this report, we will not waste time stressing the importance of protein. Therefore, each time that we speak of a food, we will define it in the following terms:

- *carbohydrates* (more specifically glucides) that are "good" or "bad."
- *lipids*
- *alimentary fibers*

When a food contains both carbohydrates and lipids, in the case of peanuts, for example, we will call this food a "lipidic-carbohydrate."

SUMMARY

Proteins are substances contained in a number of foods having an animal or vegetable origin. They are found in meats, fish, eggs and dairy products. Proteins are indispensable to the human body and their residual energetic potential is very low.

Carbohydrates are substances that transform themselves into glucose. They are found in foods whose origins are either from sugar (fruits and honey), or from starches (flour, cereals, etc.). The absorption of "quick" or "slow" carbohydrates on an empty stomach occurs during approximately the same lapse of time after initial ingestion. Their classification is made according to their glycemic potential, as measured by the glycemic index. One can therefore make the distinction between the "good carbohydrates" and the "bad carbohydrates" according to how they rate on an elevated glycemic index.

Lipids are substances whose sources come from either animals or from vegetables. They are found in fats (meats, cold cuts, fish, butter, oil, cheese, etc.). Some of them can increase the cholesterol level (meats, dairy products) and others, on the contrary, contribute to the reduction of the cholesterol level (fish fats, olive oil, etc.).

Alimentary fibers include all green vegetables (lettuce, leeks, spinach, green beans). However, certain dried vegetables, fruits and whole cereals, also contain a significant quantity. They should be consumed regularly because their insufficiency can lead to grave deficiencies.

CLASSIFICATION OF LIPIDS, CARBOHYDRATES, CARBOHYDRATE-LIPIDS AND FIBERS

LIPIDS*	CARBO-HYDRATES	CARBO-HYDRATE-LIPIDS	FIBERS
MEAT	FLOUR	MILK	ASPARAGUS
- LAMB	BREAD	WALNUTS	LETTUCE
- BEEF	COOKIES	HAZELNUTS	SPINACH
- VEAL	POTATOES	ALMONDS	TOMATOES
- PORK	RICE	PEANUTS	EGGPLANT
POULTRY	PASTA	LIVER	SQUASH
RABBIT	SEMOLINA	SOY FLOUR	CELERY
FISH	COUSCOUS	WHEAT GERM	CABBAGE
CRAB	TAPIOCA	EGG NOODLES	CAULIFLOWER
SHRIMP	BEANS	CASHEWS	SAUERKRAUT
PRAWNS	PEAS	COCONUT	STRING BEANS
LOBSTER	LENTILS	CHOCOLATE	LEEKS
EGGS	CHICK PEAS	OLIVES	ARTICHOKES
COLD CUTS	SUGAR	CHESTNUTS	CARROTS
BUTTER	HONEY	WATER CHEST-	BELL PEPPERS
CHEESES	ALCOHOL	NUTS	ENDIVES
OLIVE OIL	CORN	SCALLOPS	MUSHROOMS
PEANUT OIL	FRUIT	OYSTERS	TURNIPS
	DRY FRUIT	AVOCADO	SALSIFY

* All foods in this column (except butter and oils) also contain protein.

CARBOHYDRATE CLASSIFICATION

BAD CARBOHYDRATES	GOOD CARBOHYDRATES

CANE SUGAR
BEET SUGAR
BROWN SUGAR
HONEY
MAPLE SYRUP
SWEETS
MOLASSES
JAMS, JELLIES
SOFT DRINKS
BLEACHED FLOUR
  (French bread, rolls)
CAKES
  (made with white flour and sugar)
PIZZA
COOKIES, CROISSANTS
QUICHE
PASTA
  (spaghetti, ravioli)
WHITE RICE
POTATOES
SWEET POTATOES
POTATO STARCH
CORN STARCH
CORN
CARROTS
SEMOLINA, COUSCOUS
REFINED CEREALS
- CORN FLAKES
- PUFFED RICE
ALCOHOL
  (especially distilled)
CHOCOLATE
  (with less than 60% cocoa)
	WHOLE CEREALS
	  (wheat, oats, barley, millet, etc.)
	WHOLE WHEAT FLOUR
	WHOLE WHEAT BREAD
	BRAN
	BROWN RICE
	WHOLE WHEAT PASTA
	WHEAT GERM
	BEANS
	LENTILS
	CHICK PEAS
	FRUITS
	CHOCOLATE
	  (with more than 60% cocoa)
	
	EXCELLENT CARBOHYDRATES
	(less than 15 glycemic index)
	
	ALPHALPHA SPROUTS
	BROCCOLI
	CELERY
	TURNIPS
	SOY BEANS
	BAMBOO SHOOTS
	HEARTS OF PALM
	SALSIFY
	EGGPLANT
	SQUASH
	CUCUMBERS
	TOMATOES
	RADISHES
	MUSHROOMS
	CABBAGE
	CAULIFLOWER
	STRING BEANS
	LEEKS
	ARTICHOKES
	BELL PEPPERS
	LETTUCE
	SPINACH
	SPLIT PEAS

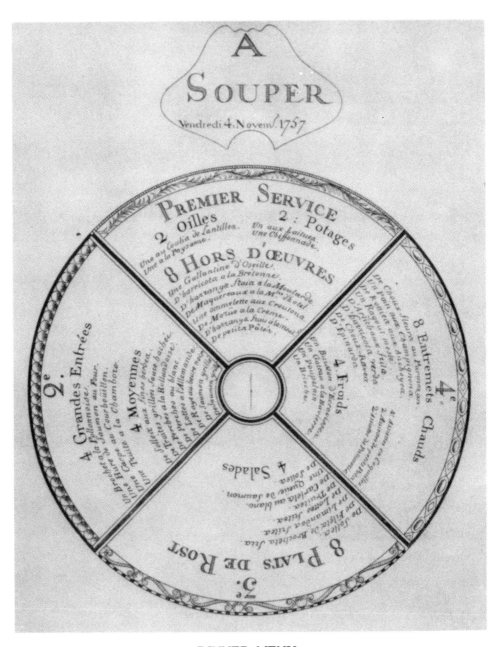

DINNER MENU

Friday, November 4, 1775
Dinner menu for the King and Mrs. Pompadour at the castle of Choisy.
The royal dinner consisted of 4 separate parts and 9 different courses.
Each course consisted of 2 to 8 dishes.

CHAPTER III

THE CALORIE MYTH

The calorie theory is probably the greatest "scientific swindle" of the twentieth century.

It is nothing more than a trap, a deception, a simplistic hypothesis, not based on any validated scientific data. And yet it has dictated our eating habits over the last fifty years.

Look around and you will see that the plump, the portly, even the obese are those who religiously count the calories they consume.

Everything that has been called a "diet" since the beginning of this century, with a few exceptions, has essentially been based on the low calorie approach.

What a shame! No long term or serious weight-loss can ever be reached through this method; not to mention the dangerous side effects that can occur.

At the end of this chapter, I will get back to the scandalous "socio-cultural" effects of the calorie theory that are a direct result of what can be referred to as "collective conditioning."

ORIGINS OF THE CALORIE THEORY

In 1930, two American doctors, Newburgh and Johnston of the University of Michigan, put forth the theory that "obesity stems not from a deficient metabolism, but from a diet too rich in calories."

Unfortunately, their study on energy equilibrium was based on limited observations and had been conducted over a period of time that was much too short to establish any serious conclusions.

But despite these weaknesses, the publication of their study received much acclaim and was immediately accepted as an irrefutable truth. Their word has since been considered gospel.

Several years later, however, Newburgh and Johnston, somewhat troubled by the public excitement over their discoveries, quietly published some serious reservations they had on their findings. But nobody paid any attention. Today, the conclusions of their initial study are integrated and enshrined in the curriculum of most Western medical schools.

THE CALORIE THEORY

One calorie is equal to the amount of energy or heat needed to raise the temperature of one gram of water from 14 to 15 degrees centigrade [1].

---

1. See more complete definition in Technical Appendix p. 274.

The human body needs energy, first and foremost, to maintain its body temperature at 98.6 degrees Fahrenheit. When the body is active, additional energy is required to move, to speak, or simply to remain standing in a vertical position. Then, more energy is needed to eat, digest, and carry out the basic activities of daily life.

The body's daily energy requirements vary with age and gender, and from one individual to another.

The calorie theory is as follows

If an individual needs 2,500 calories a day and only consumes 2,000, a 500 calorie deficit results. To compensate for this deficit, the body will draw from its stored fat reserves to find an equivalent amount of energy, and weight-loss will follow.

If, on the other hand, an individual regularly consumes 3,500 calories whereas 2,500 would suffice, the excess 1,000 calories will automatically be stored away in the form of fat.

The theory is therefore based on the assumption that there is never any loss of energy. The theory is purely mathematical, directly inspired from Lavoisier's theory on the laws of thermodynamics.

In light of this theory, we may ask ourselves, how did prisoners in Nazi concentration camps survive for nearly five years on only 700 to 800 calories a day? If the calorie theory was indeed correct, the prisoners would have died once their fat stocks expired—in other words, within a few months.

Similarly, we can ask ourselves why hearty eaters who consume about 4,000 to 5,000 calories a day never grow fatter (some even remain desperately skinny)? If the theory held true, these hearty eaters would weigh over 1,000 pounds after only a couple of years.

Moreover, how does one explain that certain people put on weight even though they restrict their diet and reduce their daily ration of calories? Ironically, they will continue to gain while they are starving themselves to death.

Statistics have also proven that more than 50% of the obese eat less than the average.

THE EXPLANATION

Why does weight-loss fail to occur despite a reduction in one's caloric intake?

Actually, weight-loss does occur, but only temporarily. The reason why Doctors Newburgh and Johnston erred is because they conducted observations over too short a period of time.

The phenomenon works like this

Let us imagine that an individual needs 2,500 calories a day and consumes accordingly. If, suddenly, the ration of available calories falls to 2,000, the body will then use the equivalent amount in stored fat to compensate, and weight-loss will result. Now, if the individual continues to consume 2,000 calories every day instead of 2,500, human survival instincts will cause the body to adjust its energy needs according to the amount of available calories. Since the

50

available ration is no greater than 2,000, and the individual can consume no more than that amount, the body will stabilize its energy expenditures by lowering its daily requirements. Weight-loss will quickly be interrupted. But the body does not stop there. Its survival instincts will drive it to take even greater precautions and create a stock to store potential energy. In other words, if the body is only given 2,000 calories, well!... it will reduce its daily needs to, say, 1,700 and preserve 300 calories every day in the form of stored fat.

So, we obtain the opposite results than we had hoped for. Paradoxically, even though the individual eats less, the body continues to store fat and progressively regain weight.

A human body, constantly driven by its instinct to survive, behaves no differently than the dog who buries his bone when he is starving. A dog who is not being well fed usually acts on his primal instincts, and hides his food to create reserves in order to keep himself from starving to death.

How many of you have fallen victim to this unscientific theory on caloric equilibrium?

Most members of the medical profession today are hiding their heads in the sand. They realize that their patients are not losing weight, and accuse them of cheating.

You have surely seen obese people who are dying of hunger, especially women. Too often, psychiatrists' offices are flooded with women with neuroses because they rely on the calorie theory to lose weight. They become slaves to a vicious circle they cannot escape, for fear of gaining back any lost weight.

The number of weight-loss therapy groups—of the type "Over-eaters Anonymous"—is another socio-cultural phenomenon created by the calorie theory. Members are applauded for a couple of pounds lost and put to shame for a couple of pounds gained. The psychological cruelty of these practices harks back to the Middle Ages.

Many doctors will hardly ever question their rather rudimentary knowledge of nutrition, since the scientific basis of their understanding is rather slim.

In fact, physicians, in general, are not particularly interested in the subject. I have noticed that, among the twenty or so doctors with whom I worked before writing this book, all had taken a specific interest in nutrition, and conducted research and experiments, because of a personal weight problem.

What I find most disheartening is that the calorie theory, an unproven theory, was able to develop and propagate itself among the general public in such a widespread manner. Today this theory has unfortunately become an accepted fact, one of the cultural "givens" of Western societies.

The calorie theory is so anchored in our minds that many cafeterias or local restaurants, so that no one will feel alienated, post the amount of calories in each dish. Every week, at least one women's magazine headlines a new weight-loss method based on the calorie theory and designed by a group of professional nutritionists. These diets usually allow you a tangerine at breakfast, half a cracker at 11 o'clock, one chick pea for lunch and one olive for dinner.

We may wonder how the hypocaloric approach created a delusion for such a long period of time. There are two answers to this question. First, a hypocaloric diet always procures results. Food deprivation, the basis of the approach, inevitably leads to weight-loss, but the results, as we have seen, are always temporary. A return to the starting point is not only systematic, but in most cases the gain is superior to the loss. The second reason is that "low-calorie" products are an important economic stake today.

The calorie exploitation, under the guidance of "qualified nutritionists," has turned into a tremendous market, one that primarily lobbies to and benefits the food industry as well as a few distraught chefs who have lost sight of the true definition of gastronomy.

The calorie theory is false and now you know why. But do not think you have overcome the most difficult part. The theory is so ingrained in your mind that you will inevitably continue to eat according to its basic principles for some time.

When we begin to explain the new method of eating I have presented in this book, you may feel confused because the information here will seem to contradict what you think you already know.

If this is the case, reread this chapter until everything becomes perfectly clear [2].

---

2. See also Technical Appendix, p. 274.

THE ROYAL BANQUET

17th century

CHAPTER IV

WHERE DO THOSE EXTRA POUNDS COME FROM?

As we saw in the last chapter, the difference between "calories gained" and "calories burned" does not explain our excess weight. In other words, the calorie theory does not explain how body fat is stored. There is another explanation, and that is the subject of this chapter.

INSULIN

Since the procedure of creating or not creating stored fat is directly linked to the secretion of insulin, we will briefly discuss this hormone. Insulin is a hormone [1], secreted by the pancreas, that executes a vital role in the human metabolism.

---

1. Insulin is a hormone created by small masses of cells in the pancreas called Langerhans' Islets.

It acts on the glucose (i.e. sugar) in the blood stream in such a way as to enable it to penetrate the body's tissues. In the tissues, glucose is either used as energy for the body's immediate needs, or, if there is a substantial amount, it is stored away in the form of fat.

We will now look at different hypotheses to determine under what conditions, with what foods, and in what amounts stored fat is formed.

INGESTING A CARBOHYDRATE

For example, let us look at a piece of bread eaten alone. Bread is a carbohydrate whose starch is broken down into glucose which then passes directly into the blood stream. The body is suddenly in a state of hyperglycemia [2] (an increase in the amount of blood sugar). The pancreas then automatically secretes insulin in order to:

1. establish glucose in the body's tissues, either for immediate use (glycogen) or as stored fat for long term use, and to

2. decrease the sugar level in the blood stream (see chapter on hypoglycemia).

———————

2. See Chapter VIII on Hypoglycemia.

INGESTING A CARBOHYDRATE AND A LIPID

For example, when you eat a piece of bread with butter, the metabolic procedure is similar to the one described on the previous page.

A carbohydrate is broken down into glucose; the sugar level in the blood increases, so the pancreas secretes insulin.

However, herein lies a fundamental difference. In this case, the lipid is transformed into a fatty acid. If the pancreas is in perfect condition, the dose of insulin secreted will be exactly proportional to the amount of glucose to be treated. If, on the other hand, the pancreas is defective, the quantity of insulin released will be greater than the amount necessary to treat the glucose and subsequently a part of the lipid's energy will be abnormally stocked away in the form of fat reserves.

We can now comprehend that the difference between he who tends to gain weight and he who can eat anything without gaining an ounce lies in the state of the pancreas. The former has a tendency toward hyperinsulinism [3].

The body will again create two types of reserves—a "moderate" one for the body's vital needs (glycogen) and a "substantial" one in the form of stored fat.

Insulin will thus trap not only the carbohydrate's energy, but the lipid's as well.

---

3. See Technical Appendix from page 282.

INGESTING A LIPID ALONE

For example, let us take a piece of cheese eaten alone.

The decomposition of a lipid alone has no glycogenetic effect. In other words, no glucose is released into the blood stream, so the pancreas hardly secretes any insulin.

In the absence of insulin, there is practically no risk that the energy will be stored away as fat reserves.

This is not to say that ingesting a lipid alone is of no consequence. During the digestive process, the body extracts all the essential substances from the lipid, particularly the vitamins, the fatty acids and the minerals (such as calcium), for its energizing metabolism.

This demonstration has been purposely narrowed down. Even if prominent scientists helped me establish it, many may smile at its simplicity. I am sure you have already guessed that actually the process is slightly more complex.

But this sketch does emphasize the essential aspects of the nutritional phenomenon that are of interest to us. It explains the fundamental rules that will guide us through the weight-loss method. Although I find this chapter to be of the utmost importance, especially because it defines how stored fats are created, there is not enough information here for us to fully grasp how it is possible to continue eating "normally" yet "differently," to lose those extra pounds, and maintain your weight at a desired level.

NOTE

In reality, the abuse of carbohydrates of a high glycemic index incites frequent cases of hyperglycemia which result in a pancreatic dysfunction. The hyperinsulinism that consequently arises, provokes an abnormal retention of fatty acids in the fat reserves.

It is thus ascertained that a highly hyperglycemic diet, associated with the consumption of fats, will culminate in a progressive weight gain by the intervening hyperinsulinism.

"Dinner for the King at the Hotel de Ville, Paris 1688,"
Carnavalet Museum

CHAPTER V

MANAGING YOUR STOCKS

In the last chapter, we saw how stored fats are created. Now we will look at "why we gain weight."

You already understand that the carbohydrate-lipid combination will generate excess pounds in the case of a defective and malfunctioning pancreas. In fact, instead of carbohydrates in general, I should have specified "bad" carbohydrates because, as we saw in Chapter II, it is the quality of the molecule rather than its mere presence that will affect the metabolic process.

You may have already heard all this, but probably never understood the scientific explanation for the phenomenon.

What you probably do not know, (otherwise you would not be reading this book), is how to apply these basic nutritional principles in order to reach and maintain your ideal weight.

Let us imagine that you weigh 190 pounds, and, taking into account your height[1], your ideal weight is about 160

---

1. See the calculation of the ideal weight p. 273.

pounds. So, you are 30 pounds overweight. Some people have always been slightly more corpulent than average, you may argue. Nevertheless, this does not mean that the method will not work.

Like many people, you were probably at a comfortable weight in your early twenties. And little by little, without realizing it, you gradually took on a few extra pounds.

The reasons are apparently more or less the same for everyone: a sedentary lifestyle and frequent changes in diet.

The first notorious change in diet usually comes right after marriage and with a drastically different social life. But it is essentially the eating habits that you cultivate in your professional lifestyle that will lead to the love handles around your waist.

Eating habits at the work place are usually very irregular; you eat either too much or not enough. We will get back to why these habits are unhealthy later on.

Meanwhile, you weigh a couple of pounds above your ideal weight and need to find a way to slim down.

First, since a rational mind always seeks to understand "how," we will look at the purely technical aspects of the method.

The basic idea behind this new way of eating immediately rules out the bad carbohydrate and lipid combination, and encourages ingestion of good lipids to avoid cardiovascular diseases.

The lipids should be consumed with different vegetables of the lowest glycemic index (we will see which ones later in further detail).

Listed below, are a few examples of balanced meals without bad carbohydrates:

1. *Sardines* (protein + « good » fats)
    Mushroom omelette (protein-fats + fiber)
    Tossed green salad (fiber)
    Cheese (protein-fats)

2. *Smoked salmon* (protein + « good » fats)
    Lamb chop with string beans (protein-fats + fiber)
    Tossed green salad (fiber)
    Strawberries (fiber)

3. *Tomato salad* (fiber)
    Tuna with eggplant (protein + « good » fats + fiber)
    Tossed green salad (fiber)
    Cheese (protein-fats)

None of these meals contain any bad carbohydrates. Of course, the meals should *not be served with bread*, and if you choose the cottage cheese, *no sugar* should be added, unless it is an artificial sweetener [2].

But let us not stray from the technical explanation so we can continue to unravel the mystery behind this weight-loss method.

As was explained in the previous chapter, if the food does not contain any carbohydrates, the pancreas will not secrete insulin and subsequently no fat reserves will be formed.

Since the human body needs energy to maintain equilibrium (to keep its temperature at 98.6 degrees Fahrenheit to execute movement, etc.), it will draw from the stored fat reserves to release the amount of energy it needs.

---

2. Be sure to read the ingredients on the product. Some cottage cheese brands may contain sugar. Also, preferably choose well drained cheeses so as to avoid the whey which contains a carbohydrate: lactose.

So, as you continue to eat in a healthy way (i.e. ingesting vitamins, minerals, etc.), you will lose surplus pounds by burning the previously stored fat reserves.

If you are a business manager, you already know the rules for administering stocks: "last in/last out," "first in/first out."

When bad carbohydrates are present, however, the basic "stock market rule" is never applied. Energy from bad carbohydrates, as we saw in the preceding chapter, is stored only for *immediate* use (last in/first out). Any surplus energy is stored away in the form of fat, and will remain there for a significant period of time.

If we exclude bad carbohydrates from our diets, then our bodies will automatically look to the fat stocks as a source of energy.

You are probably asking yourself what happens when the body has exhausted its fat stock.

Well, when you are "out of stock," so to speak, your body creates "a minimum buffer stock" that it will replenish as the need arises.

The human body, like the most sophisticated computer, will establish a top-notch management program for its stored fats. But beware—the program is sensitive and easily upset by bad carbohydrates.

Nevertheless, you must not jump to conclusions and immediately assume that once you adopt these new eating habits, you will never taste pastries or other sweets again.

Bad carbohydrates will eventually be integrated into your diet, as long as you consume them moderately and are aware of the dietary imbalances they create. In the next chapter, we will learn how to sensibly indulge in these guilt-ridden pleasures.

You will see that once your system has completely reabsorbed your fat surplus, you will be able to reintegrate lipids containing bad carbohydrates into your diet, as long as you make your choices prudently.

Medically speaking, it is possible that your body does not tolerate glucose (i.e. sugar) well. This is, in fact, the only difference between the normal eater who cannot help gaining weight, and your skinny neighbor who eats like a pig and still remains thin as a rail.

If you are a member of the first category, you are going to have to raise your body's tolerance level to sugar, because your threshold is, at the moment, very low. In other words, the smallest carbohydrate you ingest, especially if it is a bad carbohydrate, stimulates the pancreas to secrete an excessive amount of insulin.

Maybe you attribute your low tolerance level to hereditary factors [3], but even in this case you are inevitably one of the many victims of our civilization's deplorable eating habits.

In all industrialized countries, particularly the United States, the tendancy to priviledge bad carbohydrates has been strongly emphasized during the past forty years.

You are probably addicted to (I will even go so far as to say *intoxicated* by) bad carbohydrates, and it will take some time for you to resume proper eating habits.

Everything started during your childhood—soft drinks, porridge, cookies, candy and lollipops. At snack time you ate enriched white bread with butter, peanut butter and jelly, a chocolate bar, donuts, or grandma's chocolate chip cookies. In college, it was potatoes, pasta, rice and pizza on a regular

---

3. A study published in the "New England Medical Journal" (Jan. 23, 1986), conducted with 540 adults who were adopted during childhood, demonstrated that obesity is primarily due to hereditary factors.

basis—so much easier to prepare than a vegetable soup, and you needed nourishing foods that were filling and cheap. Of course, you always took a lot of sugar. Sugar is good for your muscles, you were told.

For four years you lived on notorious "dorm food," or went to the fast food place across from campus. Little get togethers with friends at your "pad," or the weekend take-out dinners usually turned out to be "carbo-feasts."

And since you started your professional lifestyle, although the quality of your meals may have improved, you are still a victim of bad eating habits.

At home, with the kids, it is never-ending French fries, rice, and macaroni and cheese dinners—so much more practical in our day and age with microwave technology.

At work it isn't any easier for an upwardly mobile professional such as yourself. The morning meeting drags on, so you ask your secretary to bring up a couple sandwiches, heavy on the mayo.

Since you are always desperately trying to save time, you schedule meetings during your lunch hour and are forced to skip lunch altogether. You tell yourself that you'll get something from the vending machines later. As well, to keep going late at night and early in the morning you cannot do without your coffee.

And as if it's not bad enough, you will add an extra dose of sugar to your coffee since it is so good for your muscles, even if you are not using them.

Beyond that, there are the infamous business meals. You clear your conscience by telling your secretary on your way out the door, "I surely could have done without this one. What a hassle! But I can't refuse. Our business depends on it and I can't back out now."

So, with the help of your wonderful restaurant guides, you pick one of those "nouvelle cuisine" places that specializes in light cooking. But you immediately wolf down the mini rolls with a generous slab of butter.

And then there are the cocktail parties. Another "hassle," but that does not stop you from tasting all the sausage rolls especially catered for the affair.

Saturdays and Sundays it's the barbecues with friends, the country club brunches, and traditional family dinners. On these occasions, there are the French fries or the sirloin steak that tastes so much better with a side of mashed potatoes. And so that is the story of how, like the Michelin man, you grew a tire around your waist—a spare tire that you are more than willing to spare.

This is how you have become addicted to bad carbohydrates that decompose and release a sizeable amount of glucose into your blood stream.

It has finally come time for a disintoxication cure that will happily coincide with the loss of any excess fat.

The amount of insulin produced by your body is no longer proportional to the amount of glucose released into the blood stream. Since the dose secreted is greater than your metabolism requires, part of the retrieved fatty acids will be stocked in the form of fat reserves. Your body is merely in a state of hyperinsulinism [4].

But these bad eating habits you have become accustomed to over the years do not have the sole effect of causing you to gain weight. They are also responsible for fatigue and digestive problems. We will study these two consequences in further detail in the chapters on hypoglycemia and on digestion.

---

4. See Technical Appendix p. 282.

At this point, I want to reassure my readers that this weight-loss method will not leave you weak and tired like many other diets tend to do.

On the contrary, as I made clear in the introduction, you will see that the guidelines presented to you in this book are not only simple to apply, but practical as well.

Even at first, when you will have to categorically eliminate certain foods or food combinations from your diet, you will see that this is much easier to do in a restaurant, within the framework of your professional lifestyle. You may even find it more troublesome to apply the principles of the method at home, since it is not easy to change the eating habits of an entire household overnight. But when your spouse sees your results, (maybe even reads this book) and understands how these eating rules can be applied, your whole family may turn over a new leaf and eventually adopt your new style of eating.

As a general rule, any theory is relatively easy to accept. The difficult part is applying that theory. Perhaps you are already familiar with the concepts presented to you here, but because you lacked a true and complete guide, you never knew how to efficiently apply the principles in your day to day life. I suggest that you study Chapter VII carefully and you will see that you will not only win the war against fat, but you will also rediscover a remarkable physical and mental well-being.

But, before beginning to practice the nutritional principles of my method, I suggest we examine together the very serious problem of cardiovascular disease.

By remaining conscious of the common beliefs on this subject, we could then learn to make the appropriate choices concerning fats.

CHAPTER VI

CARDIOVASCULAR DISEASE PREVENTION

Cardiovascular diseases are the number one cause of deaths in industrialized countries.

In 1982, 55% of all deaths in the United States were due to ischaemic cardiopathy and 16% were due to cerebro-vascular disease.

The impressive awareness campaigns put into place since 1963 have helped to lower cardiovascular diseases by 40%. However, the lowered mortality rate from cardiovascular diseases has not reflected a general decrease in the national mortality rate itself.

We can, however, notice that the diminution of the mortality rate from cardiovascular diseases is inversely pro-portional to the level of education, family revenue, and profession. What has been seen, in the end, is that the lower the income level, the higher the vulnerability to coronary heart disease. With the highest birth rate being among lower income families, we can only expect to see a steady increase of cardiovascular diseases in the 21st century.

It is important to realize that the gravity of cardiovascular diseases varies from country to country in relation to the diet. It must be stressed that cardiovascular diseases have multiple causes and are not only linked to the cholesterol level, as people so often want to believe.

The different cardiovascular risk factors are the following:
1) *excess cholesterol*
2) *hypertriglyceridemia*
3) *hyperinsulinism and insulin resistance* (fat diabetes)
4) *free radicles*
5) *alcohol*
6) *smoking*
7) *stress*
8) *coffee*

EXCESS CHOLESTEROL

The cholesterol level has become a real obsession in the United States, almost to the point of paranoia. Contrary to popular belief, cholesterol is not an intruder in our body. In fact, more than 100 grams can be found in the human organism. Cholesterol is an indispensable fat of which only an excess can prove to be dangerous.

Cholesterol is essential to cell functions. It favors the fluidity and permeability of the cellular membrane. Cholesterol is a substance capable of converting itself in the liver into bile salts (important for digestion), in the surrenal glands into hormones (necessary to counteract stress) and, in the skin into vitamin D (needed for healthy bone development).

70

Excess cholesterol is dangerous because it stimulates the tendancy for fat deposits (atheromas), weakens the arterial walls and shrinks the blood vessel's diameter.

When this happens, the blood flow is slowed down. This creates vascular resistances capable of giving rise to different cardiovascular affections: angina, cerebrovascular disease, hardening of the arteries, high blood pressure, and in extreme cases, myocardial infarction (this is when the collapse of the vascular system suddenly obstructs the blood circulation).

It is important to know that human cholesterol has two origins: 70% is synthesized by the liver, that is to say, it is made by the organism itself, and the other 30% comes from foodstuffs.

For instance, someone can have a diet consisting of only carrots and water and still find himself with a critical cholesterol level due to other reasons. Professor Apfelbaum, one of the most well-known nutritionists, says that "alimentary cholesterol and blood-cholesterol are rarely related, and, for certain individuals, there is no relationship whatsoever..."

The absorption of alimentary cholesterol varies between 30% and 80%. The lower the exterior cholesterol intake, the higher the hepatic synthesis. What this translates into is the formation of gall stones which increase the risk of hepatic colics.

Good and Bad Cholesterol

Cholesterol is distributed in the blood by the lipoproteins, which are, in some ways, types of transporters. It is here that one distinguishes the low-density proteins that diffuse the cholesterol to the cells and to the arterial walls, which are often the victims of fat deposits. The LDL-cholesterol is, for this reason, called the "bad cholesterol."

On the other hand, high-density lipoproteins, which transport the good cholesterol (or HDL-cholesterol), are responsible for cleaning the fat deposits out of the arteries. Hence, they are called the "good cholesterol."

The actual cholesterol make-up is as follows:

- the LDL-cholesterol should be lower than 1.30 g/l.
- the HDL-cholesterol should be higher than 0.45 g/l.
- the cholesterol total should be lower than or equal to 2 /l.
- the ratio of the total cholesterol level on the HDL-cholesterol should be less than 4.5 g/l.

We know that the risks of cardiovascular diseases are twice as high if the cholesterol level surpasses 1.8 to 2.2 g/l and four times as high if the cholesterol level is higher than 2.60 g/l. However, the total cholesterol level, as we have already seen, is not sufficient to make a noticeable difference in potential cardiovascular risks. This is why 15% of myocardic infarctions are present in victims having a total cholesterol level between 1.5 and 2 g/l.

Fifty-three percent of American children (in comparison to 21% of French children) ages two to twenty years have a cholesterol total higher than 2 g/l where the normal cholesterol level is 1.60 g/l.

The autopsies done on American GI's killed in Vietnam revealed that 40% of them had serious arterial lesions.

Women of childbearing years are protected from cardiovascular risks by hormonal secretions. However, vascular risks are multiplied nine times if the woman is taking birth control pills. It is even more significantly increased if the woman smokes.

On the other hand, some studies have shown that the mortality rate for men and for women is a lot higher when the cholesterol level is too low. In this case, the risk of cancer is multiplied three times.

Alimentary Cholesterol

Foods contain varying quantities of cholesterol (see chart below).

FOR 3.5 OZ OF FOOD	CHOLESTEROL IN OUNCES
3.5 oz of egg yolk	.300 oz
2 eggs of 1.75 oz	.340 oz
beef kidney	.015 oz
caviar	.012 oz
shrimp	.010 oz
butter	.008 oz

It has been popularly believed, for a long time, that the daily cholesterol intake should not exceed 300 mg (as recommended by the World Health Organization). In fact, it has been shown, since, that a daily supplementary cholesterol intake of 1000 mg only produces an approximate five percent increase of cholesterolemia.

It has also been proven that the consumption of 27 eggs per week, does not act upon the blood cholesterol. This could be due to the egg's high lecithin content.

Only the reduced consumption of saturated fats contained in foods can have an effect on the cholesterol level.

We have seen in Chapter II that fats should be classified in three categories:

— *Saturated fats* that are found in meats, cold cuts, poultry, milk, butter, dairy products and cheese.

These fats indirectly increase the total cholesterol level, especially the LDL-cholesterols. Let us also remember that only poultry skin contains a significant percentage of saturated fats. Therefore it is quite healthy to eat poultry (without its skin).

While it is true that cheeses are high in saturated fats, their effects are not as negative as those of butter and whole milk. Professor J.M. Bourre stresses the fact that saturated fatty acids could produce insoluble salts with calcium, thereby interfering in their intestinal absorption.

— *Monounsaturated fatty acids* lower cholesterol. The best example is certainly oleic acid, found particularly in olive oil. It can also be said that olive oil wins hands down in all the categories as far as its beneficial action on cholesterol. Oleic acid is the only acid that has succeeded in reducing the bad cholesterol (LDL) while at the same time increasing the good cholesterol (HDL).

— *Polyunsaturated fatty acids* from animal sources.

These acids are primarily found in fish fats. It was thought that the Eskimos, who consume a lot of fish, were not victims of cardiovascular disease for genetic reasons. We finally realized that it was the nature of their diet that was responsible for this prevention factor.

The consumption of fish fats helps to lower the LDL-cholesterol level and triglyceride level. What is most important is that it aids in the blood's fluidity, thereby reducing the slightest risk of thrombosis. Their consumption in the form of gelatin capsules, however, is much less effective. Too strong a dose could even induce a cerebral hemorrhage.

— *Polyunsaturated vegetable fatty acids.*

These acids are in corn oil, safflower oil and wheat germ. They reduce the total cholesterol level, the LDL-cholesterol level and to a lesser degree, the HDL-cholesterol level. Some polyunsaturated vegetable fatty acids carry the essential fatty acids (linoleic acid, alpha-linolenic acid) and vitamin E.

HYPERTRIGLYCERIDEMIA

An excess of 1.50 g/l of triglycerides in the blood can also be a factor of cardiovascular lesions. This excess of triglycerides can be directly linked to alcohol abuse, or the consecutive overconsumption of bad carbohydrates, (sugar, white bread, carbohydrates, corn, potatoes, sodas), as generally is the case in industrialized countries.

HYPERINSULINISM AND INSULINORESISTANCE

As we have already examined in the preceding chapters, the nutrients causing hyperglycemia in our fellow citizens (too much sugar, too many white flours, too much corn, too many potatoes, etc.) have led to an overextension of the pancreas.

This translates into the first step towards hyperinsulinism (bad tolerance to glucose) which can later evolve into fat diabetes, which is most often associated with obesity.

In addition, we know that insulin resistance is highly pathogenic for the arteries. The increase in blood platelet aggregation decreases the blood's fluidity, thereby making it more susceptible to blood clots which block the arteries.

As a consequence, the arterial walls become less flexible and the chances of the LDL-cholesterol to form atheromas increase.

It is understood that for there to be an effective treatment of hypercholesterolemia, one must also adopt correct eating habits. To think otherwise is totally illusionary.

We realize then, that bad contemporary dietary habits, particularly those in the United States, are not only at the root of obesity, but are also the cause of cardiovascular disease. Thus, it is erroneous, as well as dangerous, to designate only fats as responsible.

FREE RADICLES

Free radicles are substances that stimulate cell degeneration. Cell degeneration is often the cause of cancers and is capable of producing vascular lesions. Free radicles can be traced to a deficiency in selenium (whole cereals, fish, etc.), in vitamin E (safflower oil, wheat germ oil, walnuts, hazelnuts, fish fats, etc.), in beta carotene (vegetables) and in vitamin C (fresh fruits). Free radicles increase the action of LDL-cholesterol and its accumulation in the arteries.

ALCOHOL

An excess of alcohol reacts negatively on the cardiovascular system and provokes arterial hypertension. However, it has been shown that a low alcohol consumption (from 0.35 to 1.23 oz. per day or from one to three glasses of wine), could have a beneficial effect on lipid metabolism, notably increasing the good cholesterol level (HDL-cholesterol).

Professor Masquelier has proven that wines rich in tannin (such as red wines) containing procyanidine, decrease the cholesterol level. Numerous studies have stressed that the population of countries that drink wine regularly, as in France, Spain, Italy, and Greece, had fewer incidents of cardiovascular diseases than found elsewhere.

TOBACCO

Tobacco is the cause of 25% of cardiovascular disease and is responsible for reducing the good cholesterol level (HDL-cholesterol). Thus, continuing to smoke when one already suffers from cardiovascular illness is truly suicidal.

SALT

— Daily Needs

Our bodies need 3 to 4 g (.10 to .14 oz) of salt per day. However, on an average, we consume 10 to 13 g (.35 to .45 oz) daily.

— Salt and Obesity

Obesity results from an overload of fat where salt interferes only in water metabolism.

There is, therefore, no evidence that obese people have a salt-free diet, especially when women complain about swollen hands or feet.

However, it is not advisable to have a diet with too much salt as an excess of salt increases the carbohydrate absorption at the intestinal level.

— Salt and Cardiovascular Disease

Too much salt has been blamed for arterial hypertension. This is true, but only 40 % of people suffering from high blood pressure get better by following a strict salt-free diet (less than .14 oz per day).

As individual sensitivity is changeable, the effects of a salt deficient diet are not constant.

On the other hand, very low-salt diets (less than .03 oz) can be dangerous because they favor an increase in the total cholesterol (+ 11 %) and in the LDL-cholesterol (+18%), which may enhance cardiovascular risks.

STRESS

Stress from modern day life is responsible for the reduction of good cholesterol (HDL). It is important, therefore, that one utilizes effective stress management and/or relaxation methods.

COFFEE

Although the exact reason is still controversial, studies have shown that the ingestion of coffee (surpassing six cups per day), whether it be regular or decaffeinated, increases the cholesterol level from five to ten percent.

UNEQUAL CARDIOVASCULAR RISKS ACCORDING TO DIFFERENT COUNTRIES

One would be tempted to believe that among all the industrialized Western countries where there is an elevated standard of living, there would be approximately the same percentage of cardiovascular disease. This, however, is not the case because there are considerable cultural differences, especially dietary habits. In the table below, it can be seen that Japan has the lowest percentage of cardiovascular disease, immediately followed by France.

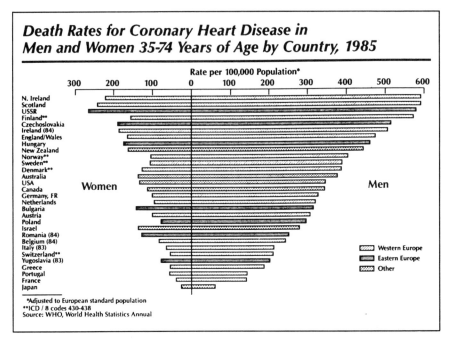

Death Rates for Coronary Heart Disease in Men and Women 35-74 Years of Age by Country, 1985

Rate per 100,000 Population*

| 300 | 200 | 100 | 0 | 100 | 200 | 300 | 400 | 500 | 600 |

N. Ireland
Scotland
USSR
Finland**
Czechoslovakia
Ireland (84)
England/Wales
Hungary
New Zealand
Norway**
Sweden**
Denmark**
Australia
USA
Canada
Germany, FR
Netherlands
Bulgaria
Austria
Poland
Israel
Romania (84)
Belgium (84)
Italy (83)
Switzerland**
Yugoslavia (83)
Greece
Portugal
France
Japan

Women   Men

Western Europe
Eastern Europe
Other

*Adjusted to European standard population
**ICD / 8 codes 430-438
Source: WHO, World Health Statistics Annual

With the short-sightedness of Americans in what concerns cholesterol and the pseudo responsibility of fats in cardiovascular illness, the difference observed according to the different countries may seem paradoxical. This phenomenon, however, is linked directly to diet. This fact can be easily illustrated by comparing the Irish dietary habits and the French dietary habits.

When an alimentary analysis is made on the Irish diet (a country which incidentally has one of the highest percentages of cardiovascular diseases) compared to that of France, it is clear that it is not the fat quantity that makes the difference, but the nature of the fat and an insufficient intake of vitamin C and fibers.

The Irish eat few green vegetables, a lot of potatoes, use butter in their cooking, and are beer drinkers (beer is rich in maltose whose glycemic index is 110). The French,

80

on the other hand, consume more green vegetables and fresh fruits, use oil (especially olive oil), instead of butter, in their cooking, and drink red wine.

Countries that have the lowest percentage of cardiovascular disease are those that consume olive oil, fruits, vegetables (lentils and beans) and that drink wine. This is especially the case for countries near or around the Mediterranean periphery.

The populations, on the other hand, that have the highest percentages of cardiovascular disease, are those of Northern Europe (Denmark, Sweden, Norway, etc.) and Anglo-Saxon countries (United States, Canada, England, etc.). They are usually large consumers of hyperglycemic foods (sugar, white flour, potatoes) and of beer. Their consumption of olive oil and of wine is very low as well as their consumption of green vegetables and fruits.

The different awareness campaigns in the United States between 1962 and 1980, as studied by various health authorities, showed a significant amelioration of the situation, as cardiovascular incidents had dropped by nearly 40%. While the Americans continue to focus on the responsibility of fats to cardiovascular illness, they ignore, at the same time, that the lack of the very fats they strive to eliminate from their diets could lead to grave deficiencies in essential fatty acids and vitamins A and E. Such an approach does not deal with the real problem—a high cholesterol level.

Americans' attitudes towards fats in the diet, have led some food industries to eliminate all fats from certain foods via industrial processing. However, one day Americans might realize that to go to such extremes is dangerous because certain fats are recommended in dietary intake to help decrease the cholesterol level.

If the French do not have high cholesterol levels and still eat foie gras, cheese, olive oil, and drink wine, why indeed should these good foods be eliminated from the diet if this is what God, in his great wisdom, decided to give to us?

Conclusion

One should realize that, despite common belief, cardiovascular problems, especially those related to cholesterol, are not always what we had thought. To assign sole responsibility to fats is not only erroneous but also dangerous. Such a reductionist view can only serve to throw off-balance the patient's diet, without offering an effective solution. Having one believe, through the various anti-cholesterol campaigns and advertisements, that the problem can be solved by the simple suppression of fats, is totally irresponsible and abusive.

What is necessary, then, to remember from this chapter is the following:

- Cholesterol is not the sole reason for cardiovascular illnesses. There are other factors such as hypertriglyceridemia, insulin resistance, diabetes, free radicles, alcohol, tobacco, salt and stress.

- Food-cholesterol represents only 30% of the total cholesterol level. Seventy percent is synthesized independently by the liver from foods.

- The cholesterol content in foods is to a little, or to no extent, assimilated by the organism (in eggs, for instance).

- Saturated fats from nutrients are the real reason for a high cholesterol level. Thus, it is in this area that action must be taken.

- On the other hand, there are certain fats that help lower the cholesterol level. Monounsaturated (olive oil) and polyunsaturated fats (fish fats or grain oils such as safflower oil and wheat germ oil) are examples of these oils.

The best way to lower the cholesterol level is thus to change dietary habits:

- Reduce saturated fat consumption (meat, cold cuts, butter, whole dairy products).
- Eliminate the consumption of hyperglycemic carbohydrates such as sugar, white flour, corn and derivatives of corn, and potatoes (whose glycemic index is higher than 50).
- Consume monounsaturated (olive oil) and polyunsaturated fats (fish fats, grain oils).
- Augment consumption of whole cereals especially whole wheat bread.
- Increase vegetable consumption (lentils, beans).
- Increase fish consumption (minimum of 11 ounces per week).
- Consume fibers regularly (fruits, vegetables).
- Strive for a sufficient intake of vitamins A, E, C, and selenium.
- Limit coffee consumption to a minimum.
- Eliminate sugared sodas and beer.
- Stop smoking.
- Decrease salt consumption.
- If possible, drink red wine (a maximum of half a quart per day).
- Control stress level by utilizing an effective relaxation method.

A business meal in a private office in the 19th century
Drawing by F. Miery

CHAPTER VII

THE WEIGHT-LOSS METHOD

We have finally reached the heart of the matter. The preceding chapters gave you a detailed overview of the technical explanations but you are now probably impatient to know "how do I apply this weight-loss method?" So, without further ado, we will now see how to apply the guidelines that will help you achieve your goal: *to lose weight forever without disrupting your social and professional life.*

However, I will not cease to stress the importance of the preceding chapters. It is crucial that you understand the nutritional mechanisms described and rid yourself of popular notions on weight-loss, such as the calorie theory, which have inevitably influenced your logic.

The weight-loss method takes place in two stages:

1. *Actual weight-loss*

2. *Maintaining that loss* or stabilizing your new weight.

WEIGHT-LOSS
PHASE I

I do not think I have to teach many of you "managers" the importance of setting a goal for yourself when you undertake a new project, especially an ambitious one.

First, you should determine how many pounds you want to shed. Maybe you already have an idea of how much you would like to lose. I know that many of you will be satisfied with a 10 pound loss when you actually need to lose 20 to 25.

I will encourage you to be more ambitious in the goals you set for yourself. You are determined and enterprising at work, so I urge you to be the same way with your own body. Would you be satisfied with 4 or 5 percent of market shares if your sales potential and marketing team are capable of reaching 12 percent? Of course not! So be the same way when it comes to your personal well-being.

A quantitative goal is perhaps not enough for some. A time limit must also be set. You want to lose x pounds. Fine! But how much time will you allot yourself?

It is important to know that every organism is different and the degree of sensitivity varies from one individual to the next due to a number of factors: sex, age, alimentary and nutritional history, heredity. It is therefore difficult to say how many pounds you will lose per week. Some may lose 2 to 4, others a little less. Moreover, in many cases the loss may be significant at first and then gradually slow down. Do not worry if it takes you longer than your associates or friends.

FOODS TO BE MONITORED CLOSELY

I know from experience that, psychologically, it is not always best to begin anything on a negative note. For a long time, I tried to start my exposé by listing the foods that are permitted before cautioning against what is not. But it would be foolish for me to proceed in this manner, because the list of allowed foods is never-ending. It is better to start with the short and important list of foods one should avoid, so as not to lose any more time.

SUGAR

In this list, sugar takes the cake. It should always be labeled with a skull and crossbones symbol since it is a dangerous product when consumed in large amounts—and such is unfortunately the case in our day and age, especially for our children.

I have set aside an entire chapter on sugar so that you are absolutely convinced of its nefariousness; it is not only responsible for your excess weight, but it can also generate fatigue (see chapter on hypoglycemia), diabetes, gastritis, ulcers, cavities and coronary problems.

You may think that it is impossible to do without sugar. Well, it is not. Just think that for millions of years sugar was not available to Man and he was not any worse off. Less than 200 years ago, sugar was still a luxury product not accessible to the majority of the population. Today, sugar is everywhere, and it is just as dangerous as alcohol and drugs combined due to such widespread consumption.

You are probably wondering how you will maintain a minimum level of sugar in your blood stream if you completely eliminate it from your diet.

Good question!

The human body does not need to receive sugar from outside sources (this is how the glycemic level becomes upset). It can produce its own sugar in the form of glucose and is much happier that way. Glucose is, in fact, the organism's only fuel.

The body is able to determine how much sugar it needs and consequently produces the required amount from stored fats. The fats are then transformed into glucose whenever the body deems necessary.

So, no more sugar! You can either forget sugar completely, and I would congratulate you, or, if you have a sweet tooth, you can replace it with an artificial sweetener [1].

BREAD

I could have taken up an entire chapter on bread alone because there is so much to say about "good" bread, so rare in this day and age, and about the deceptive product most commercial bakeries are selling.

Ordinary bread (not to mention all the packaged frozen

---

1. See Chapter X on sugar.

dough) is made with bleached flour which is devoid of everything upon which a healthy metabolism needs to thrive.

In the refining process, flour loses all the essential elements that are necessary to ensure a healthy digestion.

The whiteness of the bread indicates to what extent it has been bleached. The whiter the bread, the worse it is for your metabolism.

Whole wheat bread [2], or bread made the old-fashioned way with unbleached flour, is more acceptable than white bread because it contains fibers. The quantity of glucose released is markedly inferior to the amount released when white bread is ingested so whole wheat is therefore deemed less fattening. Despite the value of whole wheat bread, it will temporarily be eliminated during your meals, but on the other hand it should be eaten often at breakfast. We will see why in fuller detail later on.

Are you worried about giving up bread? Let me reassure you.

If you eat white bread on a regular basis, like over 95% of the population, you have nothing to lose (except excess pounds) when you give it up. Since refined flour is so bad for your health, you will be making a wise decision and actually come out ahead.

On the other hand, if you are used to eating *only* whole wheat bread or bread made from unbleached flour (which proves you already have good eating habits), you may lose the benefit of the fibers when you eliminate the bread from your diet.

But rest assured, not only will you continue to eat bread at breakfast, but you will be encouraged to eat fibrous

---

2. See Technical Appendix p. 247.

vegetables, as a substitute for whole wheat bread, to ensure a proper flow through the intestine.

STARCHY FOODS

Starchy foods are, for the most part, bad carbohydrates and must be excluded from your diet.

Potatoes

The number one starchy food is the potato. A historical fact for your personal knowledge: when the potato was brought back from the New World, the French did not even deem it good enough for pigs. They refused to eat it even though the Germans, the Irish and the Scandinavians took to the potato completely. One must not forget that these Nordic populations did not have much else to eat, and thus, did not really have a choice.

For two centuries, the French continued to scoff at what they called a "tubercule a cochon"—a pig root. The vegetable was primarily used to feed pigs since it had been noticed that it helped fatten the animals.

It was not until 1789, during the French Revolution, when Parmentier, upon demand from the revolutionary leaders, published his *Treatise on the Uses and Cultivation of the Potato,* that the French finally decided to accept it. The famine at the time no doubt influenced their change of mind.

It was later discovered that, although the potato contains vitamins and mineral salts, it loses most of its nutritive qualities when it is peeled and cooked.

Recent experiments have proven that the potato releases a large amount of glucose when it is digested because of the poor quality of its fibers.

Traditional nutritionists have always incorrectly categorized the potato as a "slow sugar." On a scale of 100, it has been shown that the amount of glucose released by the potato is about 70 [3]. So, despite the complexity of its carbohydrate molecule, the potato remains a bad carbohydrate (see Chapter II). It has also been verified that industrial treatment of the potato (instant mashed potatoes) raises the glycemic index to 95.

Look upon the steaming potato in your neighbor's dish with the utmost contempt!

Remember—potato also means French fries, and I can feel you slipping already.

The fried potato is a carbohydrate-lipid, somewhat like the buttered bread. The consumption of French fries is automatically linked to the risk of gaining weight since the oil used for frying can be stocked away in the form of fat reserves.

So, think of burger and fries as a heresy!

Rid your mind of that satanical combination! The lipid from the meat and the bad carbohydrates in the fries constitute an unnatural combination.

I know it is not easy to give up this all-American meal, but it is a small price you must pay in order to reach your goal. Believe me, when you do reach your ideal weight, you will not regret the sacrifice.

You will understand in further detail the dangers of mixing meat with carbohydrates when you read the chapter

---

3. See Technical Appendix p. 246.

on digestion. You will become more conscious of the digestive problems and secondary effects that can occur.

I, for one, never knuckle under when I am faced with a steaming plate of French fries. Once or twice a year, however, I deliberately decide to indulge in an order of fries (when you no longer have a single ounce to lose, you can decide anything)—but not just any fries. Since this only happens rarely, I want to savor them to the fullest.

If you do not know where to go, consult one of your fine restaurant guides. I am sure the best fries in the country or in the state have already been selected for you. And if you want to keep damage to a minimum, order a salad with your fries. An excellent choice; especially because the fibers in the lettuce trap the starches, limiting the amount of glucose released and slowing down the rate at which the glucose is processed.

In Phase II, I will explain what should accompany the potato in order to reduce the glycemic index.

When you order meat in a restaurant get into the habit of asking what will be served with your dish. There is always something other than potatoes. Ask for string beans, tomatoes, spinach, eggplant, celery, cauliflower, squash, etc. And, if sadly enough, only bad carbohydrates are available, simply order a salad.

Beans

Some may expect me to condemn beans in a most unrelenting way, given what was just said about the potato. Well, they are mistaken!

92

In the first version of this book in 1986, I ruled out beans, even when cooked to make a noble cassoulet [4].

I have since surprisingly and happily discovered the virtues of the bean. Henceforth, this food should be categorized as a good carbohydrate given its very low glycemic index [5].

Nevertheless, I recommend that it be avoided in Phase I unless it is consumed at breakfast as a substitute for whole wheat bread.

We will later return to this food and learn that it can be eaten in reasonable amounts in Phase II.

Rice

Rice, as it is traditionally eaten in Asia, is an unrefined grain that, by nature, contains all the essential elements needed to survive.

But white rice, as it is eaten in the Western World, is industrially refined. It is refined to the point that nothing remains that is of nutritive value except the one thing we could happily do without: starch.

Ordinary refined rice should be excluded from your diet, because like refined flour, it is a bad carbohydrate that releases large amounts of glucose [6].

Brown rice, on the other hand, will be allowed in Phase II only as long as it is not ingested with lipids (i.e. cheese or butter). Brown rice, served with cooked tomatoes and onions,

---

4. Cassoulet is a bean stew made with duck or goose preserves, comparable to pork and beans.

5. See Technical Appendix p. 246.

6. The amount of glucose released by rice on a scale of 100: - white rice: 70; - brown rice: 50.

constitutes a healthy and balanced meal that everyone in the family will enjoy.

Unfortunately, it is very difficult to find brown rice in restaurants.

Maybe it is because of its unaesthetic gray-brown color or because it can take longer to prepare. Another problem with brown rice is that it takes a long time to chew—which can be quite inconvenient if you are conducting business over your meal.

Corn

Corn has been raised for centuries, yet humans started to consume it on a regular basis only in the last few decades.

Forty years ago, not a single can of corn was to be found within Europe. It was cultivated exclusively for the purpose of feeding animals. In the United States, corn was used to fatten the livestock until 1929, when the drought that year decimated the herds and ruined the Midwest farmers. A true famine followed and, for lack of bovine meat, the hungry people decided to eat the farm animals' food instead, or at least what remained.

That is how America took to corn, a habit exported to Europe during the post-World War II American occupation.

We should not be surprised to learn that corn has a high glycemic index (making it a bad carbohydrate) in light of the fact that for centuries it served to fatten bovines.

It is interesting to note that industrial processing of the vegetable considerably raises its glycemic index. Popcorn and corn flakes therefore have hyperglycemic properties.

Pasta is by nature a bad carbohydrate. Even if pasta is fresh from the chef's kitchen, it should be excluded from every meal, because most of the time it is made from bleached flour. After that, lipids are often added: butter, eggs, cheese, oils, etc. Despite numerous advertising slogans, rich pasta is a carbohydrate-lipid that only delays weight-loss.

During the past few decades Italian food has become more and more popular in the United States where it is responsible, in part, for changing eating habits. Business meals are often organized in such restaurants. I know it is unpleasant to even think about giving up pasta, especially when it is fresh and deliciously well-prepared. However, you should stay clear of it and resist the temptation to order it.

If, unfortunately, you are served pasta (in any circumstance), try to refuse while you are still in Phase I—the weight-loss phase. When you are cruising along at your ideal weight in Phase II, order only if you are sure it is worth the sacrifice and if your diet is full of fiber.

Whole wheat pasta, noodles made from unrefined flour, will be incorporated into the Phase II eating habits. I will later explain how it should be prepared and tell you at what point in the day it is best to eat.

Whole wheat pasta is, in fact, categorized as a good carbohydrate since the glycemic index is only 45.

It is, however, regrettable that this product should be wrongly sold as a health food item and therefore two to three times the price of normal pasta - a scandalous swindle indeed since the costs of producing whole wheat pasta do not include the expense of industrially bleaching and refining the flour. In Germany, whole wheat pasta is sold at the same price as normal pasta. Let us hope that all countries will soon follow the German example.

Other bad carbohydrates

I purposely elaborated on the bad carbohydrates that you are probably most used to eating, and that you will have to temporarily give up.

There are other carbohydrates to be avoided and you can find a full list at the end of Chapter II. It is worth your while to become familiar with this list, so if you ever run into a bad carbohydrate on a menu or on your dish, you can avoid it. To list just a few examples: semolina and the refined breakfast cereals, often made with fats, sugar and other caramels, that we eat "just for the sake of feeling healthy."

Lentils, chick peas and other split peas are different in that they only release small amounts of glucose during digestion [7]. We will look at them more carefully later on. Nevertheless, they should be excluded in Phase I, and will be reintegrated into your diet during the stabilization phase.

For the time being, there is a special carbohydrate that I would like to examine separately: fruit.

FRUIT

Fruit is a taboo subject, and I know that if I dared ask you to eliminate it from your diet, you would probably close the book immediately.

---

7. See Technical Appendix p. 246.

96

Fruit is a symbol in our culture; a symbol of life, health and prosperity. Fruit is a source of many vitamins—at least that is what we think.

First let me assure you that we will not eliminate fruit. But you will have to learn to eat it differently in order to benefit fully and avoid the disadvantages. Fruit is harder to integrate into your diet than you are likely to think.

Fruit is a fiber but also a carbohydrate containing sugar in the form of fructose. And, we must pay careful attention to fructose because it transforms itself into glycogen (immediately available energy). Fortunately, the amount of sugar is not very great and is released in weak amounts into the metabolism because of the fiber contained in the fruit. Therefore, the amount of energy that results is not very alarming. And the energy released is always used for immediate needs. The important rule to remember here (and if you remember only one rule in the book, retain this one) is that *fruit should never be combined with either lipids, proteins, or other carbohydrates.*

This rule of thumb should be followed not only for weight-loss purposes. It is based on chemical observation and laws of digestion. When fruit is consumed with other foods, it upsets the digestive process of those other foods. Moreover, the fruit loses all its nutritional value (vitamins, etc.). This is why the biggest mistake one can make is to eat fruit at the end of a meal.

I know you must be very skeptical at this point, but I will explain this phenomenon more thoroughly, although these explanations should be part of the chapter on digestion. Starch, in order to be digested, must be in the presence of an enzyme called ptyalin, which is secreted in the saliva. The presence of fruit will deteriorate this enzyme, so the starch will no longer be digestible. Consequently, the fruit-starch, the heat and the humidity ferment and produce flatulence and stomach pains. Perhaps I have shed some light on these familiar symptoms.

When fruit is consumed with lipid-proteins—meat or cheese, for example—it will remain blocked in the stomach instead of going directly into the intestine where digestion normally occurs. Meat, on the other hand, is able to undergo the most important digestion phase in the presence of all the essential enzymes, while it is still in the stomach.

So the fruit remains imprisoned in the stomach where it ferments and eventually produces alcohol. The regular digestion process is upset, the fruit loses all its nutritional value, and—when it rains it pours—lipid metabolism will also be upset which can lead to an abnormal storage of fat reserves.

Fruit must always be eaten alone!

This is one rule we should have all learned in school. If we had, our children would not have upset stomachs as often as they do—although at their age their bodies have other natural mechanisms to react accordingly. But for an adult, and especially a senior citizen, fruit at the end of a meal can be a veritable poison.

So when can we eat fruit?

On an empty stomach. In the morning, for example, before breakfast. You will have to wait 20 minutes before eating a carbohydrate breakfast (such as cereal).

You can also eat fruit late at night, at least two or three hours after dinner. For those who habitually suffer from insomnia (which can also be cured through the eating method described in this book), be sure to avoid oranges before you go to bed, since vitamin C is a stimulant and can keep you awake.

Fruit can also be consumed some time in the afternoon. Make sure that it is well after lunch (about three hours) and still far from dinner time (at least one hour).

You can even eat a meal consisting only of fruit, as long as you eat nothing else.

I will conclude my discussion on fruit by emphasizing one last detail. If possible, always eat the skin of the fruit. Most of the fibers, that benefit the intestinal tract, (and even some vitamins) are found in the skin.

Eat fruit with the skin to reduce the glycemic index. You will lose more weight (or gain less) if you respect this last rule.

Among the last foods to be monitored closely we will study the beverages in this category. To begin, let us look at alcohol.

ALCOHOL

Alcohol is fattening! You have often been told that you can attribute every extra ounce to alcohol. Let us study the question more objectively.

It is true that alcohol is fattening, but much less fattening than sugar, white bread, potatoes or rice. This is why, very soon after having lost your excess pounds, you can reintroduce wine into your diet in moderate amounts.

Alcohol is fattening because it is a carbohydrate that is rapidly stored in the form of fat when insulin is secreted. This is especially true when it is imbibed on an empty stomach. When the stomach is already full, particularly with protein-lipids (meat and cheese), alcohol is metabolized at a slower rate and combines with other foods. Subsequently, less fat reserves are produced.

The aperitif must be categorically given up. If you feel obliged to follow your guests, choose a non-alcoholic drink like tomato juice or sparkling water.

The only noble aperitif, in my mind, is champagne. But I beg of you, never let them put "liqueur de cassis"[8] or any other added substance in your champagne. It is usually done with the intent of camouflaging its mediocre quality.

So, if you have no choice, accept a glass of good champagne, but above all *do not drink it on an empty stomach.* Nibble on the hors d'œuvres first.

However, learn to recognize appetizers that are free of carbohydrates: olives, cheese, cold cuts (dry salami, for instance) etc., but stay clear of cheese and cold cuts if you have cholesterol problems.

Beware of chips, peanuts, crackers, etc.

In Phase I, try to rule out the aperitif completely. It is necessary to abide by the stringent rules of these first few weeks in order to achieve noticeable results.

AFTER DINNER DRINKS

Cross these drinks out. Cognac, Armagnac and many pear liquors are delicious, but they are also very bad for your metabolism from every point of view.

---

8. "Liqueur de cassis" is a syrup, made of blackberries and full of glucose. It is often added to white wine or champagne for flavor.

Maybe you like to think that these after dinner drinks (they are called "digestifs" in France) will help you digest your meal. Well, rest assured, once you become used to the eating habits suggested in this book, digestion problems will be the least of your worries—even after the most copious meals.

BEER

One must take care to drink this beverage in moderation. Just as you may know people who wolf down carbohydrates by the ton and never gain an ounce, you have certainly met heavy beer drinkers whose stomachs remain incredibly flat (like one of my best friends' wife).

It is not necessary to have visited Germany to know about the secondary effects of drinking too much beer: bloating, weight gain, bad breath, and indigestion, despite the presence of diastases—small enzymes that are specifically designed to help the digestion process. In the absence of diastases, the digestion process is less smooth.

We should be wary of what beer contains: alcohol (although in small quantities), gas, and especially a substantial amount of maltose, a carbohydrate, with a glycemic index of 110; in other words, higher than glucose. Furthermore, the alcohol-sugar combination favors hypoglycemia and, consequently, fatigue and under-achievement (See chapter on hypoglycemia). Beer therefore contains a high level of potential energy that can be stored as fat. If you are a heavy beer drinker, give up the habit, especially between meals. If you really cannot resist, every now and then, indulge in one or two mugs of quality beer at one of your city's finer bars, but never on an empty stomach.

In Phase I, eliminate beer completely. In Phase II, since we will reintegrate a moderate amount of wine, if you prefer, you may instead choose to drink beer with your meal (no more than 32 centiliters).

WINE

I saved wine for last because it is the only drink that I am not completely against.

I must first make a slight distinction between white wine and red wine. If you have the choice, I would advise you to choose red over white, particularly because, as we saw in previous chapters, red wine has a more positive effect on cholesterol. If not, it does not matter much, but I urge you to be slightly more restrictive with white wine. I appreciate Sancerres, Chablis and white Burgundies as much as you. But they are sometimes a bit more toxic relative to reds. Furthermore, be aware of the quality of white wine you drink. A low quality white wine, depending on the sensitivity of the individual, will often provoke headaches or insomnia (especially for women) [9]. Red wine, especially Bordeaux, can be introduced into your regular diet as long as you do not drink excessively (no more than approximately a half liter a day).

---

9. Bad champagnes have the same effects. Only drink top quality brut. Severe headaches usually result from the alcohol's interrupted fermentation process, when sulfur anhydride is released (SO_2). This is particularly true of rosés.

In addition to Bordeaux, I also recommend any other red wine, including the Californian, as long as you are assured of its quality.

It is better to stay away from wine as much as possible in Phase I. In Phase II, you can consume it on a daily basis and not worry about gaining weight. You should drink wine taking into account the amount of other carbohydrates you consume. I am thinking specifically of chocolate and other desserts that we will study in further detail later on.

In Phase I, the restrictive phase, it may pose problems to attend a business lunch without drinking a sip of wine. Others are usually bothered or ill at ease if you tell them you do not drink.

Try this method: let your glass be filled. Hold it in your hand as often as possible and, without ever actually drinking, let your lips taste the wine every so often. Participate in choosing the wine, the region, the vintage year, etc. to express your interest vis à vis your dining companions.

I have tried this method many times over several weeks, and believe me, nobody ever noticed I was not drinking.

In the same way, no one has ever noticed that I never eat bread. I always take a roll from the basket, break it in half, and leave it next to my dish.

COFFEE

Really strong coffee, Italian espresso that could wake a dead man, is absolutely forbidden. Drink decaffeinated or light drip-filter coffee. You can find "decaf" anywhere, and it is usually rather tasty. Even serious coffee drinkers cannot tell the difference.

If you are used to drinking very strong coffee, you probably feel you need a strong stimulant to wake you up.

If you regularly get tired at around 11 o'clock in the morning or after lunch, you are probably hypoglycemic (see chapter on hypoglycemia).

Caffeine is forbidden in this method because, even though it is not a carbohydrate, it stimulates insulin secretion from the pancreas. If you have just finished a meal free of bad carbohydrates, and all excess energy is being dispensed of, it would be foolish to drink a strong cup of coffee, cause the pancreas to secrete insulin, and trap the energy from the food you have just consumed. If you are a habitual coffee drinker, you will have no trouble switching to decaffeinated coffee. Soon enough, you will be surprised to find that you have forgotten about coffee completely. Regular coffee drinkers (caffeinated or decaffeinated) should especially beware of an additional risk: an increased cholesterol level.

SODAS

Colas, sodas and other soft drinks are usually made from synthetic fruit or plant extracts, and all contain a lot of sugar.

They should be excluded from your diet, not only because they contain sugar, but because they also contain artificial gas that causes stomach aches, gastritis, and aerophagy.

Even if the extracts are natural, the soda, unless it is sugar-free, is still toxic. In the natural acidic fruit extracts, there are often important traces of noxious substances like terpene.

The worst soft drinks are sugared colas. Like cigarettes, they should carry a label that reads: "This product is hazardous to your health."

According to Doctor Emile-Gaston Peeters [10]:

"Today, every bottle (approximately 19 centiliters) of cola, contains about 21 mg of caffeine and 102 mg of phosphoric acid. Caffeine is a strong stimulant and phosphoric acid is very acidic. The high phosphoric concentration can upset the calcium:phosphorus ratio in the food, which can lead to a serious calcium deficiency in the bones. Finally, one must be certain that the phosphoric acid does not contain any important traces of toxic heavy metals. The conclusion is simple: *Children and adolescents should be encouraged not to drink cola.*"

As far as diet sodas are concerned, they are obviously less harmful because of the absence of sugar. But what was said about colas, sugar-free or not, still holds true.

MILK

Milk is a carbohydrate-lipid containing both fats and carbohydrates. It is better to drink only skimmed milk.

Carbohydrates are found in whey. In the cheese-making process, they are lost and only lipids and proteins remain.

Non-fat cheese only contains proteins and other substances that are not of interest to us.

---

10. *Le Guide de la Diététique*, published by Marabout.

FRUIT JUICES

I will not deal with fruit juices at length because the previous discussion on fruit also holds true here. They are carbohydrates and should be treated as such.

I will, however, advise you to choose fruit above fruit juice so as not to lose the benefits of the fibers in the pulp. In sum, only homemade fruit juices made from fresh fruits are acceptable. Never consume the commercial pseudo-fruit juices, which are overly acidic, completely void of vitamins and, for the most part, sweetened with sugar.

APPLYING PHASE I
WEIGHT-LOSS

Phase I of this method is not necessarily difficult, since it simply consists of eliminating certain foods from your diet. But in order to truly succeed, you need to have a thorough understanding of the *basic principles* presented to you in this book.

I know from experience that this is where many fail. I am not doubting your intelligence or your ability to assimilate new concepts, but in this particular case, it is important that you rid your mind of any preconceived ideas, so deeply ingrained in your subconscious that they have become part of a "cultural inheritance." The simple ideas presented, based on elementary scientific and medical principles, unfortunately have not yet broken any cultural barriers. So, you cannot count on the people you know to help you in your venture.

For instance, do not forget that if you eat a proteic-lipidic meal (meat or fish with a side of vegetables), you can eat "crème fraîche" or sour cream [12], (in moderate amounts, of course), with a guilt-free conscience and without breaking any of the new eating rules you have learned.

Now if you want to eat cheese during a carbohydrate meal, you may only eat non-fat cheese.

What follows is a guide to help you apply the principles of Phase I.

BREAKFAST

Breakfast #1

A *carbohydrate* breakfast:

- *fruit* (at least 20 minutes before the rest of the meal),
- *whole wheat bread,*
- *non-fat cottage cheese,*
- *decaffeinated coffee or light tea,*
- *skimmed milk,*
- *artificial sweetener* (if necessary).

The breakfast suggested here contains no lipids and is made up only of good carbohydrates with a low glycemic index.

Let us take a closer look at what it does contain:

---

12. This stands true only if your cholesterol rate is normal (see Chapter VI and Technical Appendix). A light crème fraîche or sour cream will do the job.

Fruit

You may choose any fruit. Personally, I would recommend an orange, two tangerines or even kiwis because vitamin C is very efficient on an empty stomach.

If you choose an apple, eat it slowly with the skin.

A banana, too rich in carbohydrates, is not a good option.

Be sure to wait 20 minutes between the fruit and the rest of your breakfast. I would suggest you eat the fruit when you get up, wash and dress, which should take you at least half an hour, and then sit down for the rest of your meal.

Fruit in Phase I is optional, and your weight-loss does not depend on it. If you never eat fruit, which is really too bad, do not go out of your way because I mention it here. If, on the other hand, you are used to eating fruit every day and do not want to give up this habit, as I remarked earlier, one of the rare moments you can eat fruit is in the morning on an empty stomach. You can, if it is convenient, eat only fruit for breakfast. If you pick breakfast #2, the proteic-lipidic breakfast, you should eat your fruit at least one hour beforehand.

Whole wheat bread

Only buy whole wheat bread. (Most bakeries sell quality whole wheat bread. Commercial brands are often made from 25-30% whole wheat flour only). To recognize a good quality bread, look for a rough texture. Do not judge solely by the loaf's exterior color. You can also buy black bread, what Germans call "schwartz brot," if you like it. It is generally dark and has a rough and grainy texture.

Whole wheat bread absorbs gastric juices faster than white does. So you will feel full soon after you finish your meal. Since I have not specified the quantity of food you should eat, I would be tempted to tell you to eat as much as you want. But, in fact, I will advise you to eat in moderate amounts. You can also eat whole wheat crackers or grilled toast. Many brands exist, but you must be sure the product contains no added sugars or fats. Similarly, if you buy rusk make sure it is made from whole wheat flour and contains no sugars or fats, although it is rare.

What do you put on your bread? In Phase I, it is forbidden to spread butter or margarine on your bread like you will be allowed to do in Phase II. Honey and jam, bad carbohydrates containing a lot of sugar, are also prohibited. They are to be permanently banned unless you are able to find a special jam that does not possess any sugar. Health food shops should be able to supply you with this product. I suggest you spread non-fat cottage cheese on your bread, toasted or not, and, if you cannot stand the blandness, add a dash of salt or an artificial sweetener.

You may prefer to eat cereal in the morning. Again, I urge you to favor whole grain cereals that do not contain any undesirable additives such as sugar, fats, dry fruit, oilseeds, etc. Carefully read the ingredients printed on the package. In any case, you should rule out all rice and corn based products. Choose, instead, those that are rich in fiber, like All-Bran, for example.

Decaffeinated coffee or light tea

I cannot stress enough the importance of abstaining from drinking strong coffee. Light coffee will do. It would be even better if you could get used to drinking decaffeinated coffee with ground chicory. If you drink tea, make sure it is not too strong, since tea also contains caffeine.

Skimmed milk

If you put cream in your coffee or tea, use only skimmed milk. Even partially skimmed milk should be avoided, because it contains lipids. Powdered skimmed milk is your best bet, because you can obtain a highly concentrated mix.

Naturally, no sugar in your coffee or tea (you have already forgotten about it.) Use an artificial sweetener.

Breakfast #2

Breakfast #2 in Phase I is *proteic-lipidic*. There are *no carbohydrates*—good or bad. I suggest you use this one when you are staying in a hotel.

#1 is not always easy to apply when you eat out [13].

Breakfast #2 includes the following choices:
- *eggs,*
- *bacon, sausage and/or ham,*
- *cheese,*
- *decaffeinated coffee, light coffee or light tea,*
- *cream or milk* (preferably cream),
- *artificial sweetener* (if necessary).

This is somewhat of a typically American breakfast without the toast, cereal or jam, of course.

It is crucial that you exclude all carbohydrates in this breakfast.

---

13. If you suffer from hypercholesterolemia, this breakfast choice is not recommended. Those who do not have a cholesterol problem should take care to balance their consumption of lipids (See Chapter VI and Technical Appendix).

As you already know, lipids contain a lot of potential energy. They will be completely burned and disposed of only in the absence of insulin. And, as you also know, insulin is secreted only in the presence of carbohydrates or strong coffee. Be careful not to err.

LUNCH

Since lunch is usually eaten out, it will be *proteic-lipidic* with fibers. This is not to say that you should eat a lot of fats (see chapter on "good" and "bad" lipids). I will give you a few examples so you do not make any mistakes. But I highly recommend that you consult the list of foods that do not contain carbohydrates (see Appendix #1) when you decide what you will be having for lunch. You can even photocopy the list and carry it with you. You will soon have it memorized.

A typical lunch menu:
- *raw vegetables,*
- *fish and/or meat,*
- *authorized vegetables* (see list),
- *salad,*
- *cheese,*
- *beverage: water* (if possible, avoid sparkling water).

Appetizers

Every type of salad is acceptable, as long as none of the ingredients is a carbohydrate. Be sure that what you order does not have potatoes, corn, rice, carrots or beets in it. This is usually the case if you order a "salade niçoise," [14] or any type of exotic salad.

Also avoid (in Phase I) carbohydrate-lipids like nuts. Do not order a salad with walnuts. Bacon bits are authorized, but beware of croutons! Many restaurants have a strange obsession with them.

Be vigilant. Do not let the slightest error slip by you or it can ruin everything. Do you allow any mistakes to occur at work? Are you a push-over for your secretary or employees? Well then, do not be lenient with the restaurant waiter either. If you asked for a salad "without croutons," or "without corn," do not tolerate his error, and say "well, just this once."

If you want the maître d' or the waiter to take you seriously, make sure they understand that you will only accept what you specifically ordered.

Personally, I found that the best excuse is to say you are allergic. It works every time. As long as your salad is served with string beans, leeks, artichokes, cabbage, cauliflower, tomatoes, endives, asparagus, mushrooms, radishes, etc., eat as much as your heart desires. Be sure to avoid beets since they do contain sugar.

You can eat as many eggs as you wish, even if they are served with mayonnaise [15]. Yes! Homemade mayonnaise, like sour cream, is allowed in a lipidic meal. This does not mean you should make a pig of yourself. Eat it in moderation, but if you are prone to high levels of cholesterol, you should abstain from it completely (See chapter VI).

---

14. An authentic "salade nicoise," from the southeast of France, contains lettuce, tuna, tomatoes, olives, hard boiled eggs, anchovies, and olive oil.

15. When you buy mayonnaise, read the label on the jar to make sure there is no sugar, glucose nor flour. This is unlikely in the United States so it would be better to make mayonnaise at home.

Tuna, sardines in oil, crab, prawns, salmon (smoked or marinated) can all be ordered as an hors d'oeuvre. Nevertheless, you should avoid oysters, scallops and "foie gras" [16] while you are still in Phase I. They all contain some carbohydrates and could slow down the weight-loss process without necessarily ruining it. Rest assured you will be able to eat these foods in Phase II.

The Main Course

The main course is essentially made up of meat or fish. There are no restrictions, except with regards to preparation.

You should never order breaded meat or fish. Bread crumbs are bad carbohydrates. Also, beware of fish that is rolled in flour before it is cooked. Always ask for grilled fish.

Be careful of sauces! If you are accustomed to "nouvelle cuisine," you know that the sauces are generally light because they are not made with flour. In these restaurants, the sauces are usually made from the cooking juices and with a light cream.

Keep in mind, from now on, that cream, as long as it is not served with a carbohydrate, is a light food, and I will even go as far as to say dietary. But do not misinterpret what I am saying. This does not mean that the more you eat, the more weight you will lose.

If you eat meat, you can order a bearnaise sauce [17] if

---

16. "Foie gras" is a gourmet paté made with high quality goose and duck liver.

17. Make sure you know what the ingredients are. In top restaurants, a bearnaise sauce is usually made from natural ingredients, and does not contain sugar and additives. Be careful elsewhere.

you wish. *But stay away from mustard in Phase I*. Mustard is made from the flour of the mustard plant. In small quantities, it is a carbohydrate that will not affect your weight. That is why we will reintegrate it in Phase II. As a general rule, you should be suspicious of all sauces available in restaurants as they often contain large amounts of sugar. This is the case particularly with ketchup and all spicy sauces served in seafood restaurants.

Regarding side dishes, select fibrous vegetables if they are an option. You can choose from a never-ending list of tomatoes, squash, string beans, eggplant and cauliflower. Become familiar with the list in the Appendix.

As I said before, if there is nothing else on the menu, order salad. Iceburg lettuce, spinach lettuce, curly lettuce, red-leaf lettuce and endives are all acceptable. You can eat as much as you want, as an appetizer, as an entrée and before or with your cheese.

But, beware of the dressing you choose. Thousand Island, Blue Cheese, French and other dressings common in the United States, usually contain an important amount of sugar. Instead, ask for a "vinaigrette", or you can make your own dressing with olive oil and lemon.

Cheese

In most French restaurants, the menu offers a dessert or cheese option. In Phase I, limit yourself to the cheese. And you should eat the cheese *without bread*. This is not impossible, and you will later see that you will savor it much more this way. Soon enough you will be able to enjoy your cheese with a glass of red wine.

Anyway, if you are familiar with French dining etiquette, you know that cheese is eaten only with a fork and knife. So there is no room for bread as a third utensil. If this bothers you, try eating it with your salad. Another method is to substitute your bread with a hard cheese like Swiss.

In Phase I, just about every cheese is authorized, but you should try to avoid cantal [18] and goat cheese for now, since they contain small amounts of carbohydrates.

Cheese, at the end of the meal, is eaten less in the United States than in France. However, this custom is developing progressively in the U.S. Most of the finer restaurants already list cheese on their menus and, in any event, it is always easy to find them in food stores.

Beverages

In Phase I, as we have already seen, it is important to eliminate all alcoholic beverages, including wine. Drink water or herbal tea if you wish. But avoid sparkling waters that will cause bloating and upset the digestive process.

In any case, I suggest you drink very little during your meals or you may drown your gastric juices and upset the digestion process. If you are really thirsty, start to drink only after you have completed at least half of your meal. Do not drink before you start to eat. It is a bad habit we all have that is responsible for many of our digestive problems. *Drink only between meals.*

If you conduct business meals while you are in Phase I,

---

18. Cantal is a French cheese that is produced in the Massif-Central, the central region of France.

remember that you must skip the alcoholic cocktails. Order tomato juice, and if you absolutely must accept something with alcohol (if, for example a cocktail has been prepared for everyone), be sure not to drink it. Pretend to do so by touching your lips to your drink, but never actually swallow. Then, you can casually forget about your cocktail somewhere where no one will notice. In some places, your drink may be more difficult to "lose." Be creative. Be resourceful. Place your glass in front of one of those heavy drinkers who will always confuse their drink with yours—especially when it is full. If this type of person does not happen to be around, which would surprise me, there is always the flower pot, the champagne bucket, the window (if it is summer time) or the bathroom sink.

If you are at a cocktail party and still in Phase I, here is some advice:

Accept the glass of champagne you have been given, and hold it in your hand for a while. Touch your lips to it occasionally, if you have the will power not to drink, and eventually set it down somewhere.

Food that is served at cocktail parties can often be a problem as well. You may eat the salmon, the salami, the egg or the asparagus in the bite-sized sandwiches. However, you must be subtle and clever enough to separate the bread from the rest. But as the saying goes: where there's a will, there's a way. If this fails, there are often many other foods you can eat at cocktail parties.

Look for the cheese! Cheese is always around in one form or another. Look for the sausage! I would be surprised if it were not available. Little cocktail sausages are always served at these affairs. Dig in and eat as much as you want if you

116

are sure they do not contain flour, but watch out for the mustard!

If you think you cannot resist a bountiful table of food, if you think you will immediately give in because you are hungry, here is a solution. Before you go to the party, nibble on something that you are allowed to eat in order to fill your stomach.

This wise advice comes from my ancestors. Sometime in the mid-1800s my great-great-grandfather, his wife and their six children were invited, once a year, to have lunch with the director of the company where he worked. My great-great-grandmother, I have been told, always fed her children a hearty soup before they went out. These charming *bambinos* never expressed much enthusiasm when they were served elegant and lavishly prepared dishes that they were not used to eating at home. Consequently, my great-great-grandparents acquired the reputation for having very well behaved children.

If you are afraid you will not be able to resist, take my ancestors' advice and eat one or two hard boiled eggs or a piece of cheese before you leave home. Get into the habit of carrying individually wrapped cheeses, wherever you go, "Babybel" or "Laughing Cow."

These should satisfy your hunger pangs and you can eat as many as you want. As a general rule, whenever you get one of these cravings, you can eat anything on the list of "authorized" foods. Just be sure to avoid lipids after a carbohydrate meal. For instance, do not eat a piece of cheese at 9 o'clock in the morning if you just finished breakfast at 8 o'clock.

What if you are invited to a friend's house for lunch or dinner? Your ability to pick and choose is considerably lessened in these circumstances.

Let us look at the situation from every point of view. Maybe these are old friends or even family. In this case, do not be shy and let them know about your new weight-loss method. Ask what is being served, beforehand, and even feel free to make some suggestions.

Now, if you are not on very close terms with your hosts, you will have to wait until the last minute and improvise from there. If this is an exceptional affair, you will probably not be served rice, pasta or potatoes as a main part of your meal.

Eat the foie gras if it is served, but it is not recommended that you eat a lot of it in Phase I. And please do not eat the toast that comes with it. You are not by any means forced to eat it—even Miss Manners would agree.

If you are served a cheese soufflé, eat along with everyone else, even though it contains flour. But do not make matters worse by taking a second or even a third helping. Let your hosts know you are on a diet.

If you are served a "paté en croûte" (a paté in a crust shell) as a starter, eat only the middle, since it is usually a proteic-lipid, and discretely leave the rest on your plate. Don't worry, since you are not among intimate friends, no one will point to your dish and say, "hey, you're leaving the best part!" Even if the host does notice, he/she will probably refrain from asking you why you did not like the crust.

For the entrée you should not have too much trouble, and side dishes are usually optional. You can symbolically help yourself to some rice or pasta, but no one will be offended if you do not eat it.

If you are still hungry after this meal, you can make up for it on the salad and the cheese. If you help yourself to a lot of cheese, your host will appreciate it and certainly excuse you for not liking the paté crust. A plate of cheese usually offers a varied assortment. Other guests may not eat the cheese, because they already stuffed themselves with bread beforehand. So I urge you—honor the cheese plate!

Dessert is probably the most critical time of the meal. It is always hard to say "no thank you, I don't want any." Insist on a very small portion and, like those who are so full that they cannot eat another bite, leave a substantial portion on your plate.

Wait as long as possible before you drink anything. Drink red wine instead of any other type of wine, and try to wait until the cheeses are served.

If the situation is worse than you expected, if you are still in Phase I and you do not know how to escape the bad carbohydrates which abound, just make sure that in the future you are extra careful in following the Phase I guidelines.

Remember that in Phase I, you are still very sensitive to glucose. The whole point of these first few weeks is to raise your tolerance level, and you will remain sensitive as long as a high tolerance level is not attained.

There is no question that if, after denying yourself carbohydrates for quite a while, you suddenly indulge in a large amount, your body will react only too joyously. In one night, you will gain back the fat you lost in the last couple weeks.

The further you are into Phase I the less disastrous the effects.

On the other hand, if you eat an excess amount of bad carbohydrates, only two or three weeks into Phase I, you may very well end up where you started in terms of your weight. This can be very discouraging. So remember—you may lose a battle, but you have not lost the war.

DINNER

Dinner should be either proteic-lipidic or carbohydrate based.

Dinner #1:

A *proteic-lipidic* dinner is identical to the lipidic lunch. The only difference is that your dinners will, more often than not, take place at home. And, at home your choices are generally more limited. But if you have been able to convince your spouse and family to adopt your new eating habits, you will surely encounter fewer problems. The ideal way to start your dinner is with a hearty vegetable soup made from leeks, celery, cabbage, etc. You can use any vegetable as long as it is listed in Appendix #1. Be careful not to add potatoes or carrots. Many soup connoisseurs will tell you that the potato is an essential thickener. This is true, but you can also use celery, an egg yolk or even puréed mushrooms.

For your entrée, you can eat any type of meat your heart desires. You may have been told that older people should refrain from eating meat at night. Both digestion and sleep risk being upset if carbohydrates have been ingested with the meat. It is difficult for the body to eliminate the toxins.

Toxins are more easily dispensed of by a younger person's metabolism, due to a higher rate of physical activity. Here is yet another reason for you, the sedentary being, to avoid eating meat with carbohydrates, even if you only have a few pounds to lose.

Besides meat, there are always eggs. Eggs can be prepared in a wide variety of ways. Eat an omelette with a salad. It is a simply delicious combination!

As for the cheeses, since there are no limitations at home, take advantage of the casual setting to eat a yogurt after your meal. Yogurt is an excellent food because it contains elements that reconstitute the intestinal bacteria that aid the digestion process. Be careful! Stay away from yogurt with artificial flavorings or fruit, and be sure that the lacteal ferment is natural.

If you are eating at home, use that time to enjoy the simple meals you enjoy most—stew for example—or eat what you rarely find in restaurants, like boiled artichokes. They are delicious, full of vitamins and minerals, and they contain a considerable amount of fibers that will help the intestinal flow. Above all, do not forget to eat vegetables: tomatoes, spinach, endives, eggplant, cauliflower, leeks, zucchini, mushrooms, etc.

Dinner #2:

Dinner #2 is *carbohydrate-based*.

Besides the foods that are always forbidden (sugar, potatoes, etc. that is to say, all bad carbohydrates), it is absolutely crucial that you avoid eating lipids with a carbohydrate meal.

No lipids means no meat, no oil, no fish, no butter, no eggs, no cheese except non-fat cheese like the kind you use at breakfast.

So all we have left are green vegetables, brown rice, beans and lentils. But be careful: no butter, margarine or other animal fats. We can also add whole wheat pasta to this list, but this item is relatively difficult to find. If you do happen to find it in a health food or specialty store, read the ingredients carefully to make sure there are no fatty substances in your pasta. Since you will be using neither butter nor cheese, I suggest you use a tomato sauce, also highly recommended for a rice (see rice, chapter VII under starches).

Here is a suggestion for a *#2* dinner:

- *Homemade vegetable soup*,
- *Brown rice/Whole wheat pasta with tomato sauce* (unsweetened or homemade),
- *Non-fat cheese*.

Or:

- *Raw vegetables: celery, cucumbers, cauliflower, etc.*,
- *Lentils*,
- *Low-fat yogurt*.

I have given you these examples of a carbohydrate meal in order to be as thorough as possible. I, for one, prefer dinner #1, because I find the second dinner too limited. I recommend it only to those who are certain they will not make the slightest error. One mistake and everything may fail.

Instead, I would suggest a proteic-lipidic meal, like at lunch, composed of eggs or lean meats such as poultry or fish, served with plenty of authorized vegetables.

122

PICNICS

It often happens that, for a number of reasons, you simply do not have time to eat a full meal. Usually lunch is the meal that is sacrificed, and to save time you either skip the meal completely or you quickly gulp down a sandwich. These are the biggest errors one can make.

Never skip a meal. It is one of the so-called golden rules of proper eating. If you like, eat four or five meals a day, but never forgo one of the three main meals. It is the biggest mistake you could possibly make, and the best way to upset your metabolism. Do not let yourself pursue this foolish habit, and advise others against it. If you do eliminate a meal, your body will act like the hungry dog who stores any bone or scrap of meat he can get his paws on. The body panics and stores the energy from the food consumed in the next meal.

At this point, I am sure you no longer even think about the ham and cheese sandwich from the nearby corner store, or those infamous burgers on the little white buns. In my conclusion, I will discuss the eating habits that are specific to the United States. Although we, the French, love the United States, our respect and admiration are not based on gastronomy nor on nutrition. What can you eat to replace your habitual "picnic" lunch? It simply takes a bit of creativity applied to what you have already learned.

I have listed a few examples of items you can buy for your "picnic" lunch at the office or on a long trip.

- *Ham* (cooked or smoked) is recommended because it always comes in thin slices, so you do not need a fork and knife to eat it.

- *Dry sausage*: You will need a knife, but your letter-opener will do the job.

- *Hard boiled eggs*: They are easy to find in delicatessens and corner stores.

- *Cheese*: Any cheese will do, but since we must stay in the realm of the practical, you should stay away from gooey and smelly cheeses like brie or camembert; they may not be appreciated by your neighbors, especially in a train or in a plane. Choose hard cheeses like Swiss, or individually wrapped cheeses such as "Babybel" and "Laughing Cow."

- *Tomatoes*: Tomatoes are ideal if you are sure to have a supply of paper towels nearby. They can be eaten like a piece of fruit.

(If you have a cholesterol problem, be careful with the first three items of this list.)

If you have not eaten anything all day, you can eat a meal consisting only of fruit. Eat until you are satiated. The only problem is that fruits are rapidly digested. A few hours later, you will probably be hungry again, so just grab an apple.

Even in the most dire situations, never fall back on forbidden carbohydrates like cookies, commercial chocolate, (especially not the pseudo-chocolate bars) and other snacks.

Conclusion

We have now come to the end of Phase I. If you are used to eating a lot of sugar, or are a dessert fanatic, you will be able to lose five or six pounds during your first week in Phase I. But do not stop there, because, in two days, you risk gaining back everything it took you eight days to lose.

124

After this first period, weight-loss will occur more progressively. If you follow the guidelines closely, you should lose weight at a regular pace.

The weight-loss pattern should be steady, yet, as it was previously emphasized, different for every individual.

It is known from experience that men obtain results more quickly than women unless they are anxious or following specific medical treatment, since some medications favor weight gain. A woman is indeed more prone to water retention (during her period, under stress, or for emotional reasons), and calculating weight-loss is, thus, more difficult over a short period of time. But this does not mean the results will be less noticeable. On the contrary...

Some women subjects do have trouble obtaining results at times. Five different causes have been identified:

- anxiety, which stimulates insulin secretion;
- hormonal perturbations during adolescence or menopause;
- thyroid problems, which are rather rare;
- certain female organisms establish a special form of resistance, at least at first, due to previous deprivations suffered following excessive and repeated hypocaloric diets;
- use of medecine (amphetamines, hypertension drugs and anti-depressants).

If you had cholesterol problems beforehand, you no longer need to worry in the least. Once you learn how to intelligently manage your consumption of lipids, you will quickly rid yourself of this concern.

Avoid saturated fats which increase your cholesterol, but most importantly favor fats that will lower bad cholesterol and those that will increase good cholesterol. These ideas are definitely acknowledged by all the specialists in the world and the scientific publications in this field are impressive (See chapter VI and Technical Appendix).

Although it is highly improbable, your doctor may not agree with this new approach, because he or she did not learn about it in medical school. Remember, in this field like others, new ideas take time to develop and evolve, despite the irrefutable scientific proof that contradicts the pre-established ideas.

Today, for example, no one still believes that newborn babies must be wrapped like mummies in order to keep their limbs from becoming deformed. However, for hundreds of years, mothers believed it was their duty to wrap their newborn babies. Only very recently, when respectable members of the medical establishment expressed their disapproval, did this practice cease. Now we shudder just thinking about how many millions of babies were forced to suffer (many did not survive), because their mothers respected these barbarous "pseudo-scientific" beliefs.

How many of you born before or during World War II had to experience the childhood nightmare of swallowing a tablespoon of cod liver oil on a regular basis?

Your well-intentioned mother, following the suggestions of the professional medical corps, would feed you the spoonful of cod liver oil to clear her conscience.

"Here, drink this my dear, it is for your own good," she would say.

"Yuck, yuck, yuck!" you would think as you gulped down the so-called miracle juice.

Today, all doctors agree that this practice was a scientific aberration that led to considerable organic problems, even though the oil contained vitamin D that helped prevent rickets.

If you respect the guidelines given to you for Phase I, you will unquestionably lose weight. If you do not, or if weight-loss is unbearably slow, you are doing something wrong.

In this case, you should, over a period of time, keep a meticulous list of everything you eat from the time you wake up to the time you go to sleep. Under the guidance of this book, you will certainly discover what is wrong.

You may be eating soups on a regular basis and have been assured that only "authorized" vegetables are in it: tomatoes, sorrel, leeks, etc. Be more suspicious and verify what the ingredients actually are. You may realize that your famous soups come in cans or packages. If you read the ingredients on the label you may find that, in addition to the vegetables, the soup also contains bad carbohydrates in the form of starch fillers, sugars, dextrose and other artificial thickeners or additives.

DURATION OF PHASE I

So, be wary! Even if the principles of this method are relatively easy to apply, in the first phase, you are asked to make a little extra effort and, I will be frank, a few sacrifices as well. I beg of you, do not take the risk of foolishly compromising your results. Aside from unburdening ourselves of our excess pounds, our main focus is to give the pancreas a rest in order to enable it to rediscover a high threshold in its tolerance to glucose.

Consequently, if you prematurely leave Phase I, you may

lose pounds without having given the pancreas the necessary time to restore its health.

If you have no weight to lose and you abide by the principles of the method with the sole purpose of rediscovering greater physical and mental vitality, the problem obviously remains the same. It is in your interest to prolong Phase I as long as possible to re-harmonize all your metabolic and digestive faculties for good.

If properly executed, you should not even have to think about managing and calculating the duration period of Phase I. The switch to Phase II will happen progressively and not overnight.

You will see that Phase I is not the least bit constraining and you will not feel to be the victim of deprivation.

You will feel rejuvenated and may even find trouble in getting out of this phase.

NOTE

One of the consequences in implementing the method is to force our system to rediscover its original function of producing its own glucose from the fat reserves. Previously, the body was wrongly satisfied with glucose that was obtained from a large amount of bad carbohydrates.

It is, therefore, not impossible that, at the time you change your eating habits, your system undergoes a sort of resistance by delaying its decision to make its own glucose. This can be interpreted by sudden fatigue, particularly during physical exertion. If this occurs, it is important to know that this problem can continue for only a few days.

Under no circumstances should you immediatlely resume eating bad carbohydrates in order to quickly raise the glycemic level artificially.

During this transition phase, you may, however, ingest dry figs or even dark chocolate with 70% cocoa——both of which are good carbohydrates.

Let us summarize the main principles of phase I

1. *Never mix bad carbohydrates with lipids in the same meal.*

2. *Avoid carbohydrate-lipids:* milk, chocolate, avocados, liver, hazelnuts, etc.

3. *Eliminate sugar completely* from your diet.

4. *Never eat refined flours.*

5. *Only eat whole wheat or bran bread made from unbleached flour (only at breakfast).*

6. *Eliminate potatoes and especially fried potatoes.*

7. *Eliminate white rice.*

8. *Never eat pasta made from refined flours.*

9. *Eat fruit alone, on an empty stomach.* Eat the skin if possible.

10. *Temporarily give up all alcohol:* cocktails, beer, wine, liqueurs.

11. *Avoid strong coffees.* Get into the habit of drinking decaffeinated coffees.

12. *Never skip a meal.* Eat three meals a day at the same time, if possible.

13. *Limit your consumption of "bad" lipids, and favor "good" lipids to prevent cardiovascular diseases.*

14. *Try to drink as little as possible during your meals to*

avoid drowning the gastric juices. Never drink directly before a meal [19].

15. *Take your time to eat. Chew well.*

16. *Avoid tension during meal time.*

17. *Wait three hours after a carbohydrate meal* (like breakfast) *before you consume any lipids.*

18. *Wait five hours after a lipidic meal before consuming any carbohydrates.*

19. *Eat a lot of fibers:* lettuce, leeks, asparagus, artichokes, eggplant, etc. (See chart in Chapter II).

20. *Definitively abandon bad eating habits typical in the United States.*
   - *All sandwiches,* hamburgers, hot dogs, etc.
   - *Candy and sodas.*
   - *Chemically processed sauces* (i.e. ketchup, salad dressing, mayonnaise, etc.)
   - *Pop corn and potato chips.*

21. *Eat three meals a day and avoid snacking.*

WARNING: This list is only a recap of some of the principles evoked in the text. In no case should it be interpreted as a condensed version of the method. Someone who has not assimilated the preceding and following chapters will improperly apply the principles and upset the dietary balance. Such an application can prove dangerous if the lipids are not correctly consumed (Rule #13).

---

19. In American restaurants, it is fairly common for a tall glass of water to be served before the clients order their meal. This tradition dates back to the Old West when cowboys, upon entering saloons, were offered a tall glass of ice water to wash away the dryness and dust in their mouths.

PHASE II: MAINTAINING YOUR WEIGHT

We will now switch gears in order to reach "cruising speed." By now, you understand the basic principles and the philosophy behind this new way of eating. You have forever given up certain "dangerous" foods, and in the last few weeks, you have adopted remarkable new eating habits. You have reached your goal and have lost a number of pounds. So you are ready to move on to Phase II.

Contrary to Phase I, which had to take place over a limited period of time, you will stay in Phase II for the rest of your life. I have been in Phase II for nearly ten years and have not gained a single ounce. Moreover, I never deprive myself of *anything*.

In Phase II, you will learn to really manage your diet, and never gain weight again.

In Phase I, we cut out a number of foods that we labeled "forbidden." In Phase II, hardly anything will be completely eliminated. Certain foods should be avoided, but only under specific conditions. The guiding principles in this Phase will seem more vague and nuanced, but ah!...that is the art of management.

Management does not consist of applying perfectly defined rules in a strict and literal sense. Here, we are more concerned with the art of applying these rules. Any idiot can apply rules. We have learned to put up with rules, every time we deal with any administrative organization, whether public or private. In administration, there are rules, more rules, and nothing but rules. I am not asking you to administer your diet, like you did in Phase I, to the same extent. This would be a useless and fastidious waste of time.

The difference between administrators (in the literal sense of the word) and managers lies in the subtlety of the art. Whereas the administrative clerk blindly applies the principles, the manager is inspired by them.

Here is what I suggest.

We will review the basic criteria to see how they can be interpreted and then applied.

Sugar

Sugar will always be considered a dangerous product. What I told you in Phase I still holds true here. Get into the habit of excluding sugar from your diet. Even if you have forgotten your artificial sweetener, do not knuckle under and say "a little piece of sugar, just this once, can't really upset everything." You can get away with this inadvertence, or

MENU

should I say *faux pas*, only if you are 100% sure you have not eaten, and will not eat, a single bad carbohydrate all day.

Be strict! No more sugar in your coffee! No more sugar in your plain yogurt! Either you will learn to use an artificial sweetener or you will do without.

You should learn to reason through a system of equivalences. Tell yourself that one cube of sugar is equal to two glasses of champagne or half a bottle of Bordeaux wine. You choose!

From now on, in Phase II, the rules will allow you much more freedom than you had in Phase I. But nonetheless, in this "management" phase your discretion should remain scrupulously monitored.

You will be *forced* to eat sugar, since it is found in most desserts. I will teach you to choose among desserts that contain the least amount of sugar. But, if you decide to yield to your cravings to eat a dessert, do not also add sugar to your coffee. In sum, never yield to the temptation of eating sugar when you can avoid it.

Be intolerant towards sugar! It is a poison and you should treat it as such!

We will see that you can be more indulgent with other foods.

And what about honey? This question has probably been on the tip of your tongue since the start. As it is a natural product and therefore unrefined, you may expect me to speak well of it.

I am afraid I will have to disappoint you somewhat. The carbohydrate's glycemic quality is what interests us in regards to honey.

Well, unfortunately, its glycemic index is a very high 90 which categorizes it as a bad carbohydrate.

I also long believed that honey harbored great treasures of health in terms of vitamins, minerals and other trace elements. Deceivingly enough, it does not contain much besides sugars and I have been forever disillusioned since the day an agriculturist informed me that all big honey producers provide their bees with an impressive amount of industrial sugar to make up for the deficiency in the flowers (due to deforestation and the employment of agricultural pesticides), and especially to improve produce substantially.

Bread

One of my brothers, like myself, is a true appreciator of good red wines. He understood the consequences of eating bread during a meal, when I told him: "Each time you swallow a mouthful of bread, you should abstain from one glass of Bordeaux."

To each his own!

During breakfast, if you are eating a carbohydrate-based meal, you should continue to eat *only* whole wheat bread. If, however, after three months, you can no longer stand the mere sight of cottage cheese, you can switch to a light table margarine or a low-fat butter. But do not use astronomical amounts. Use regular butter only if you have no other choice—on a trip, for example.

The same rules apply for milk. Stay in the habit of drinking *only* skimmed milk. If none is available, which often occurs when one is traveling, use a moderate amount of cream or whole milk as a substitute.

The carbohydrate breakfast, as it is described in Phase I, is not very limiting. Do not abandon it in Phase II.

From time to time, I am asked to attend business breakfasts in some of the finest hotels of Paris. It is usually very difficult to bridle my craving to taste the delicious croissants oozing with butter.

In such instances, at the end of the meal, I automatically take into account how my dietary balance has been upset. In other words, I will usually make a mental note of what I had for breakfast, and eat prudently and sensibly the rest of the day. For example, I will probably refrain from eating chocolate at lunch, or I will do without wine, if possible, at dinner.

You should now understand that the secret to a well-managed diet lies in a *healthy and harmonious balance*. If your metabolism can only tolerate the lipid-carbohydrate combination to a certain extent, as long as you do not exceed this limit, you will happily maintain your weight.

I cannot tell you what this limit is, because it varies from one individual to the next. It depends on the degree of your body's sensitivity to glucose and how the pancreas reacts. If you have considerably increased your tolerance to glucose after a serious disintoxication cure in Phase I, your pancreas will be more in control and secrete just enough insulin to flush out the surplus sugar in the blood stream. But rest assured, you will easily find this limit on your own by regularly supervising your scale.

Naturally, like a good manager, you should always keep a sharp eye on your weight and monitor it as you would your bank account. As a professional, you know that you can take care of any discrepancy, as long as you catch it in time.

During lunch, at home, at the cafeteria or in a fine

restaurant, you should always obey the "golden" rule: *no bread with your meal!* If you enjoy oysters, even though they are carbohydrate-lipids, eat three or four more instead of a piece of buttered bread.

I will not reiterate what I said before about the little bite-size rolls that your table companions devour as soon as they sit down for lunch. Those notorious little rolls are to be banned forever!

Also, do not eat the toast that is served with your smoked salmon. Instead, order fresh marinated salmon with dill. Not only is it delicious, but it is served without the little toasts. So—no temptation.

If you order foie gras, the little toasts are officially forbidden. All the more so, since foie gras is somewhat of a carbohydrate-lipid. This is, in fact, one of the reasons why it is not listed as one of the allowed foods in Phase I.

When you get used to eating your meals (not including breakfast) without bread, you will finally be able to savor the delectable tastes of the fine dishes you are served. This is specifically true of foie gras, which I highly recommend you order in a restaurant, especially if it is fresh. You can always eat cooked foie gras at home. This brings up another rule, one that does not have much to do with the point of this book, but with gastronomy in general: *in restaurants, order what you cannot eat at home.*

Many people I have eaten with in restaurants, both Frenchmen and foreigners, surprise me with the unimaginative, conservative selections they make. Whether they are in Paris, New York or Tokyo, their finger inevitably stops at the classic dishes on the menu that are most similar to the foods they are used to eating at home. The maître d' or waiter must then summon his oratory skills to persuade his diners to choose something different instead of the humdrum meat dish they can eat any other day.

If your table companions lack as much creativity and imagination in business, I pity their bosses or their shareholders.

Try to order fish when you are in a restaurant. Our greatest chefs have often proved their talent in the way they cook their fish.

Getting back to our bread, since that is what we were originally discussing, I will grant you one exception concerning cheese. If you are lucky enough to find a restaurant that serves whole wheat bread or something similar, I will allow you, as long as you have not upset your balance with any major discrepancies, the excellent combination of aged goat cheese rolled in ash, warm bread and a glass of your favorite wine.

Starches

Even in Phase II, I remain staunchly opposed to the potato, white rice, white pasta and corn.

You have surely understood in Phase I that these foods are the culprits most often responsible for your excess weight because of their high glycemic consequences. Each time they are mixed with lipids they produce deplorable effects. Like bread, it is better to avoid them at lunch and dinner unless you deliberately decide otherwise. There is nonetheless a way to reduce the negative effects of the bad carbohydrates. When eaten with fibers, the glycemic index is lowered.

For example, if you decide to eat French fries for sheer pleasure, it is best you order an enormous salad to go with your indulgence. The fibers will minimize the dietary imbalance the fries will inevitably create.

However, you may be caught in situations where it is difficult to refuse the discrepancy. But do not give in too quickly. *Program* yourself to instinctively react negatively to the foods you have excluded from your diet. Keep a cool head. Even if you do succeed, there will be many occasions when you will be forced to make exceptions and satisfy your "urge to splurge."

In "nouvelle cuisine" restaurants, each dish is prepared individually. No one will hold it against you if you leave one of the four vegetables on the side.

But say your next door neighbor or your dear old aunt invites you for dinner. If you leave a single noodle or grain of white rice on your plate, you run the risk of destroying some very dear socio-family relations. Suffer through this one discrepancy in your diet, although this one may be more difficult to bear, since you are not compensating your sacrifices with any real gratification.

Remember that when you finish your plateful of carbohydrates, with or without taking pleasure in your meal, you will have to eliminate either your drink or your dessert. If, however, you are not only forced to finish your rice, but also every bite of the rum spongecake that your hosts have prepared especially for you, you will have a considerable amount of re-balancing to do. And maybe, depending on the damages done, you will have to return to Phase I for a few days to readjust your internal equilibrium. Beware of a natural tendency after these binges to consider everything a lost cause. Do not feel desperate and say, "I might as well give up anyway. The damage has already been done." Never succumb to this dangerous temptation that is forever looming over you.

Never abandon your proper eating habits under the pretext that "during the Christmas season it is impossible to apply them anyway."

I know from a long period of experience that even in the most critical situations it is always possible to watch what you eat. You may, of course, upset the balance because of professional or social obligations, but you can maintain the equilibrium by avoiding everything possible to avoid in the next few days.

If you start to apply my method in a roller-coaster fashion you will never get anywhere.

You have by now understood that the key is to raise your tolerance to glucose as high as possible. If you decide to come back to Phase I every time you gain 7 or 8 pounds, you will never endure.

I can tell you that after ten years in Phase II, my glucose tolerance level is extremely high. This proves that the more you are vigilant in the first few months and first few years, the easier it becomes to compensate for any disruption in your dietary balance.

The method presented to you here aims to "decondition" you from or extricate the bad eating habits you have practiced since childhood. One of the keys to achieving your goals rests in a positive "reconditioning." If you are able to recondition yourself well in Phase I, your efforts will be considerably diminished in Phase II. You should, by then, have acquired a number of natural reflexes that will lead you to make the "right" choices in managing your diet.

If you see fresh pasta on the menu, and if you are tempted to order, then do so. But do so knowing what the effect will be. Take advantage of the pleasure you savor, but make a mental note of the negative effects so you can compensate later on.

Let us say that you have decided to order in one sitting, foie gras, oysters, scallops and a Gamay or Beaujolais wine that would go so well with shell fish. If you run into a potato, rice or pasta somewhere near your main course, by all means, avoid it. I know you can do it!

You are probably not convinced from merely reading these sentences that you will have the will power to deliberately leave something you enjoy on your dish.

Well! You will see that it is in fact easier than you think. Once you notice the effectiveness of Phase I and enjoy the superb results, you will automatically continue to limit yourself in your eating. Subconsciously, it will be difficult to yield to temptation.

You will gradually achieve a point of self-regulation, or should I say self-management.

Fruit

As for fruit, the rules in Phase I will continue to be applied here. You should always eat fruit on an empty stomach.

As we saw earlier, it is not the amount of carbohydrates (fructose plus glucose) contained in the fruit that causes the trouble, but whether or not the fruit is mixed with other foods. When you read the chapter on digestion, everything will become much clearer. There are certain fruits, however, whose fructose content is relatively low, and are therefore allowed in Phase II—every day if you wish. They are strawberries, raspberries and blackberries.

From April through October, you can find strawberries in just about every restaurant. If you are allergic to strawberries, keep in mind that there are nine out of ten chances that your allergy is due to side effects from your intoxication to bad carbohydrates. After Phase I, there are many chances your allergies will vanish like magic. You will be surprised to see a number of bothersome problems disappear. I will get back to these strange phenomena in another chapter.

At lunch or dinner, in a restaurant or at home, eat strawberries or raspberries.

If you have finished a 100% proteic-lipidic meal, you can even add fresh cream to your strawberries, but without sugar. You may, however, add an artificial sweetener like "Nutra-sweet."

If you have not created any imbalances in your equilibrium (aside from the wine), or only modestly so, you can even ask for whipped cream on your berries, although it does contain a small dose of sugar. If you are at home, make your own whipped cream with an artificial sweetener.

Cantaloupe is another fruit you can eat without scruples in Phase II—as a starter, of course. If it is eaten as an appetizer, be sure to wait about fifteen minutes before starting the rest of your meal, especially if you will be eating fish or cold cuts. This is often the case in restaurants. Order cantaloupe as an hors d'oeuvre, if it is available, followed by any salad, except for those containing eggs, mayonnaise or meat. But again, this recommendation concerns proper digestion rather than weight-loss. Your risk of gaining weight with melon in Phase II is close to zero.

Many readers of the previous edition have written to

ask me if cooked fruits are considered equal to raw fruits. I am tempted to answer yes, but with a nuanced clarification. Cooked fruit ferments less than raw fruit and the gastric perturbation created is therefore less drastic. Applesauce, stewed pears or a Peach Melba only represent a slight discrepancy.

Nevertheless, it is important to emphasize that the fibers in cooked fruits lose the bulk of their properties, specifically their hypoglycemic quality. As for canned fruit in syrup, they should be completely excluded due to their high sugar concentration. Dry fruits have a medium glycemic index but contain very good fibers. They can be consumed to sustain great physical exertion. Dry figs are certainly the best choice and dry bananas the worst. In any case, I would urge you to avoid breakfast cereals with dry fruit and grain mixtures.

Desserts

This part and the one on wine are very dear to me since I am, by nature, a great appreciator of desserts, and I find them particularly enjoyable at the end of a meal.

Everyone has a few weak spots. You just have to know how to handle them.

Personally, I could do without potatoes for the rest of my life, without fresh pasta for at least a year, but never could I go more than a week without chocolate.

We not only have *nouvelle cuisine*, but *nouvelle pâtisserie* as well. We must recognize the great leaps of progress made in the last ten years, and admire the creativity of our great chefs, who are also our greatest pastry chefs.

The originality, beauty, natural flavors, and especially the lightness of French pastries have gained the pastry chefs of France a world-wide reputation. Gaston Lenôtre [20] is undeniably one of the greatest masters in this culinary field, and he has trained a number of his disciples who are close to being his equal. Similarly, the "Framboisier" chain [21] in Paris make desserts that remain unmatched by any other *pâtissier*. They are famous for their light and original mousses. Within the framework of our eating method, you will be able to indulge in these delicacies throughout Phase II. If you love pastries, try to eat only the lightest ones, which are, by the way, the best ones. Those containing the least amount of sugar and flour are most compatible with our eating principles. Just as *nouvelle cuisine* sauces infrequently contain flour, *nouvelle pâtisserie*, especially mousses, uses very little sugar, and hardly any flour. The bitter chocolate fondant (you will find the recipe in the appendix at the end of the book) requires less than two ounces of flour for a two-pound cake, in other words, about 5%. No sugar is added. The small amount of sugar in the chocolate is enough to make this cake an epicurean delicacy; one that will only cause a slight upset in your dietary balance.

I also suggest the chocolate mousse that possesses few carbohydrates except for those in the bitter chocolate. If you do not find the mousse sweet enough, which would surprise me, add a small dose of powdered artificial sweetener (see recipe in appendix).

I began my exposé on desserts with chocolate, not only because it is one of my greatest passions, but also because, if it is a top quality make (rich in cocoa), it will contain very few carbohydrates.

---

20. Gaston Lenôtre, 44, rue d'Auteuil, 75016 Paris.
21. Framboisier, 11 ave. Colonel Bonnet, 75016 Paris.

But there are other attractive *nouvelle pâtisserie* desserts to choose from. The Bavarois, for example, is a fruit mousse that has the same consistency as a *flan* (i.e. custard pastry). Choose a strawberry or raspberry bavarois if you can. A bavarois does contain sugar and other carbohydrates, but in reasonable amounts. Without getting caught up with fastidious percentage calculations, let us just say that your slice of bavarois has less carbohydrates than a forkful of fries, a piece of toast or a couple of cookies.

There is also the strawberry shortcake. If you are tempted by this cake, eat the strawberries and cream but leave the spongecake that is of no real gastronomic interest and is also a bad carbohydrate.

If you like ice cream and sorbets, do not hold back. There is usually very little sugar in sorbets, and top rate ice creams never contain very much either.

Contrary to the commonly held belief, the cold from the ice cream does not aid the digestion process. Many people believe it does because of the momentary effects of these frozen desserts.

If you are a great ice cream enthusiast, you probably prefer your desserts dripping with a hot chocolate sauce, under a mound of whipped cream, and topped with a paper parasol. Dig in! In terms of upsetting your balance, this treat will not cause as much damage as one horrible potato can. Ice cream's glycemic index is only 35.

As for pies, homemade, upside-down, or prepared any other way, you should stop and think before you order because of the amount of bad carbohydrates contained in the flour. But again, everything is a matter of choice. Your slice of pie is no worse than one baked potato or two spoonfuls of white rice.

If you have not upset your diet all day, then you are free to decide. As in any other case, only indulge if you are sure your gratification is worth the sacrifice you are making.

Alcohol

Alcoholic beverages should be managed in the same way. In Phase II, as I have said before, you are allowed to reintroduce alcohol into your daily diet in a limited way. Again you will have to make choices. Do not begin by reintegrating the aperitif, white wine, red wine and the after dinner liqueur all at once (I hope this is not how you used to drink.) Even during an exceptional meal (which will also force you to make other sacrifices in your diet), it is hardly possible to drink to that extent. We will manage our drinking habits as we do our eating habits.

Aperitifs

For the aperitif, choose a glass of quality champagne instead of a high proof alcohol such as whisky or gin, even if you do add water or a tonic [22]. The imbalance is less serious. A glass of whisky is equal in alcohol to about half a liter of red wine. This is why, in restaurants, I never order an aperitif. To trick my table companions, I usually order a glass of wine in the guise of an aperitif. Most of the time, however, I simply ask the maître d' to bring us the bottle of wine we will be enjoying with our meal. A young Bordeaux

22. Tonic, alone or with alcohol, contains sugar. Avoid it.

146

or a superior Gamay or Beaujolais goes well with just about anything. So, it is not necessary to wait until everyone has ordered before selecting a wine. And, you can always order more wine during the meal, even a half-bottle, if so desired.

Ironically enough, wine as an aperitif is a habit we, the French, have picked up abroad. In New York, Berlin or Singapore, you can order a glass of wine as a cocktail and, unlike in France, the maître d' will not raise an eyebrow and take you for a very gauche tourist or a Chevrolet factory worker.

I do not think I need to tell you not to order a second aperitif, especially if it is whisky or anything similar. If you are really obligated to, which would surprise me, order a second glass of champagne.

Cocktails are the hardest part of a meal to get through when you are concerned about what you are eating. They can drag on for over an hour, especially when dining at a friend's home and the hosts wait until the last guests have arrived.

If you have the decency to arrive on time, it will be unbearably difficult to spend hours over the aperitif when there are only bad carbohydrates to nibble on; especially if you have decided to save your sacrifices for the excellent wines your host has lovingly let age in his private cellar, or for the house specialty, a raspberry gratin.

British cocktail parties are some of the most tedious to endure. You are told to come at 6:30 p.m., and even if you arrive a half hour to an hour late, do not count on being served dinner before 9:30 or 10 o'clock.

I can remember one sad evening at the home of some British friends who had just moved to Paris. At 11:45, a French couple got up to leave.

"Why, you are leaving just when dinner is about to be served," the hostess exclaimed.

The couple, believing that the British ate early, arrived punctually at 7 o'clock. Four hours later, after only one drink (on the verge of hypoglycemia, no doubt) they were nearly desperate.

At cocktail parties, I am always astonished at the amount of alcohol the hosts and guests are able to drink on an empty stomach. You may also have met the well-intentioned host who perpetually checks to make sure that his guest's glass is always full. Consequently, you can never keep track of how much you are drinking, and it is the least of their worries. I am often amused when my American friends bring their cocktail glass to the dinner table with them. They take extreme caution not to forget their glass in the living room or at the bar, especially if it is full.

One last warning about aperitifs:

When you enter a restaurant, to get from the door to your table, you must always pass by the notorious bar. Depending on the will power of your friends, your pit stop here can drag on for hours until it seems like purgatory. But do not think you are home free when you finally reach your table. You will be served yet another drink—the last one, of course.

I was rather lengthy in discussing the aperitif in order to make clear what kind of trap you can be cornered into when you are trying to manage your diet. But experience tells me that you can always avoid this trap. Where there's a will there's a way.

At any rate, remember this essential rule: eat proteiclipids (cheeses, cold cuts, etc.) beforehand. Drinking on an empty stomach is not only a heresy, it is also a metabolic catastrophe.

Wine

I often referred to wine in the previous chapters, and you probably know by now that I am particularly fond of red wines, and more specifically, Bordeaux.

It is true, and I will tell you why, but this is not to say that I exclude all white wines or red wines other than Bordeaux from my diet. I generally enjoy many of the American wines that have, in this last decade, reached high levels of excellence. Once again, everything is a matter of choice within the framework of your eating principles.

For example, I will not deny that Sauterne is the best wine to accompany an excellent foie gras.

Good management is also the art of compromises!

Liver, as you now know, is a carbohydrate-lipid. Even though the dietary imbalance it creates is insignificant it nonetheless exists. Sauterne is fairly sweet and can potentially be slightly more dangerous to your equilibrium. If you use all your "wild cards" at the beginning of the meal, how will you "manage" the rest?

Feel free to decide whether or not to drink your Sauterne, as long as you limit yourself to a strict minimum; in other words, the amount necessary to enjoy your foie gras. But please note that one glass of Sauterne is approximately equal to two glasses of Cabernet.

Since we can drink more than one glass of wine at dinner without disrupting the carbohydrate-lipid balance, we might as well choose one that will create the least amount of damage. Red wines and dry whites are advantageous in this respect.

However, I must distinguish the nuances among the different red wines. At the top of the hierarchy, we will find young red wines (of about 9 to 12 degrees proof). These include Beaujolais, Gamays, Zinfandels and a number of other California wines you can drink young. The further south you go, the higher the degree of alcohol in the wine. But these wines should not be excluded for that mere reason. Many people believe that a Bordeaux is only good after it has aged a number of years. This is false! And I would like to thank all the wine specialists and editors of gastronomical reviews who have promoted the idea that many Bordeaux can be enjoyed young. For this reason, many fine restaurants have now included excellent young Bordeaux on their wine list. Many food critics have made a note of this, and are always satisfied with the quality/price relation.

This is not to say that we should neglect the fine vintages sleeping away in the cellars. On the contrary... But remember, you never drink an aged wine, a Bordeaux or a Burgundy, you savor it. As a cultured individual and as a professional, you should never forget this.

Many times, I have sadly noted that Frenchmen are shamelessly uncultured compared to a number of foreigners who have proved themselves impressively adept in what concerns wines. I, for one, have found my knowledge of wines quite helpful in the context of public relations and especially during business meals. Just as a conversation starter or to introduce foreigners to your region's specialty, this topic is far more interesting than the weather or the stock market.

I once had an American boss who was the president of

a wine-tasting club in Chicago. I can assure you that, whereas everyone else perceived him as an impossible and unapproachable boss, I held privileged relations with him, simply because I was always able to complement his erudition in the field of wines—a true passion of his. I owe him for a lot of what I know today about wines because he persistently encouraged me to update my knowledge.

But getting back to my wine suggestions for you in Phase II, you can enjoy three to four glasses of any red or dry white wine with your meal without upsetting your dietary equilibrium. Here is an example of a perfectly well-balanced meal:

- *Fresh marinated salmon*
- *Grilled trout with fennel and ratatouille*
- *Salad*
- *Raspberries and cream*
- *Decaffeinated coffee*

Three glasses of wine during this meal will not cause you to gain a single ounce, as long as you refrain from drinking until after the first course; in other words, after having consciously ingested a sufficient amount of food to neutralize the alcohol's effects. The wine will not even make you sleepy, as many have a tendency to believe.

Next time you have a meeting after lunch, pay attention to who dozes off. It will more than likely be those who have eaten an excess amount of bad carbohydrates, especially white bread, and ironically enough refused to drink wine. Take advantage of times like these to conduct negotiations. You will come out ahead twice.

It is more than obvious that you would be even better off if you abstained from wine as well. But the point of this book is to show you how, by following a few basic rules, you can continue to fulfill your professional obligations and eat according to your fancy.

I will encourage you, however, to refrain from drinking on an empty stomach. It is a wise habit I urge you to adopt.

If you drink on an empty stomach, the alcohol will flow directly into your blood stream, and cause the effects we are, by now familiar with: insulin secretion, creation of fat reserves, and sometimes giddiness, if you have not had much experience with alcohol.

If the alcohol is mixed with other foods in the stomach, the metabolic process will slow down, and the effects will be less portentous.

We can thus conclude that it is better to start drinking as *late* in the meal as possible, even if you will be forced to catch up to your fellow diners at the end.

I will also recommend that you *never* drink water and wine during the same meal. This may seem contradictory, but let me explain myself.

When you drink wine with your meal, it is metabolized at a slower rate since the alcohol is absorbed by the other foods. The metabolic process will be even slower if the foods ingested are proteins or lipids (meat, fish). We saw earlier that they always undergo a slow digestion process. And, we also know that the slower the digestion process, the less "fattening" the results.

However, if you alternate drinking water and wine, you will dilute the alcohol and facilitate its permeation into the blood stream through the stomach's lining. The diluted wine will overflow into the blood stream (because of saturation), and metabolize right away.

You have probably been told that water will eliminate

the toxins from your body. Even though this is true, water is bad for digestion; it dilutes the gastric juices, and speeds up the metabolism of alcohol.

So, drink as little as possible while you are eating, and never mix water with wine.

After Dinner Drinks (Digestifs)

Since I told you that alcohol is more efficiently digested at the end of a meal, you may expect me to say that an after dinner drink will do less harm than a glass of non-sparkling mineral water.

The "little digestif" at the end of your meal, you may think, will aid the digestion process, since alcohol helps dissolve fats. If your meal has been rich in fats, then by all means, a little digestif can only help, you are likely to believe.

My grandmother (originally from Bordeaux), who quietly passed away at the beautiful age of 102, religiously ended each meal with a glass of a famous liqueur and during her meal, she only drank Bordeaux. I had never seen her drink a glass of water while she ate.

My other grandmother, from the region of Armagnac [23], died much younger at the age of 99. She also drank a quick little "pick-me-up" at the end of every meal, although not always regularly.

We can conclude that these dear women found the solution to longevity in their little after dinner drinks. However, I will not go so far as to attribute their long life to

---

23. Armagnac is a type of brandy, almost as famous as Cognac in France, produced in the department of Gers.

their drinking habits. We always run into a few phenomenal individuals every now and then.

Technically, I would say that, if the meal is not accompanied by wine, the small amount of alcohol cannot have any catastrophic effects.

Now if you decide to drink a glass of cognac that rivals the size of your swimming pool, I do not want to be held responsible for the results—especially if you have imbibed four or five glasses of wine during your meal already.

Take into account that a generous glass of alcohol represents about three or four glasses of wine; tally it up and "here comes trouble..."

I will let you come to your own conclusions.

Coffee

In Phase II, I recommend you stick to the habits you adopted in Phase I—only drink decaffeinated coffee. You will by now have gotten rid of mid-day exhaustion, due to hypoglycemia or bad digestion, and your caffeine cravings, by now, will have disappeared. I will let you know that giving up caffeine is as healthy as giving up nicotine.

As you succeed in raising your tolerance level, which controls insulin secretion, consuming a little bit of caffeine will not dramatically harm your rediscovered equilibrium.

Other beverages

All other beverages, sodas, milk and fruit juices, have been covered in Phase I. I have nothing more to add. Respect these same rules in Phase II.

Conclusion

Phase II is both easier and more difficult than the previous phase. Easier, because there are very few restrictions, and nothing is absolutely forbidden. But it is more difficult because you must assume a knowledgeable and subtle management of your diet. Permanence and rigor are two key characteristics of this phase. You must always be on your guard to avoid a number of dangers.

The first danger you should avoid is bad management. One of the greatest mistakes you can make is to take into account only one item at a time. For example, say you drink a glass of whisky before your meal, and then wait for your main course before starting to drink the first of four glasses of wine that you have allowed yourself. Even if you remembered that alcohol's effects are lessened when your stomach is full, do not expect any spectacular results after you have imbibed an aperitif on an empty stomach.

At the end of this chapter I have summarized some of the rules of Phase II. Learn them well in order to apply them harmoniously and efficiently.

The greatest danger is to manage your diet like a yo-yo; alternating "letting everything go" with a stringent return to Phase I to "save everything." If you start applying this roller-coaster method, I can assure you that in less than three months you will completely give up and end up where you started in what concerns pounds and fatigue.

The objective you set for yourself, and the purpose of this book, is to reach a stabilized weight. You will achieve this goal only through proper management in Phase II that should last the rest of your life. Even if Phase II seems restrictive at first, you will see that every day it becomes easier to apply. You will see that eventually and gradually your dietary principles will become one with your natural habits and reflexes. And, you will have successfully conditioned yourself to a new eating philosophy and way of life.

If you have 20 to 30 pounds to lose, Phase I can last anywhere between a few weeks to a few months. Do not let yourself be influenced or discouraged by those around you who may try to interfere.

But, do not try to change the ways of those who do not want to change their habits. I made the big mistake of wanting to "convert" everyone to my new found "religion" after I discovered it. Dedicate yourself only to yourself. Manage your diet without informing your table companions of your new found weight-loss method. Even if they make abhorrent mistakes in front of you and almost by reflex you want to comment, do not say anything if they have not asked for your advice. You run the risk of making them defensive and giving them a bad conscience. Many of them know they are not eating properly. They also know they do not have the willpower to get out of their rut.

I already said that although you have a lot more freedom in Phase II, you should watch yourself more closely. Never be a slave to your weight, but be on guard by keeping a watchful eye on your scale. Your scale should be sensitive enough to reveal if and by how much you have upset your dietary balance. Little by little, through trial and error, you will get used to knowing how to maintain your ideal weight. If, one unfortunate day, you find you have strayed from your course, make the necessary corrections in your diet, and you will happily be back on track.

Soon, you will have switched to an "automatic-pilot program" without even realizing it.

20 important rules to maintaining your weight phase II

1. *Continue to avoid mixing bad carbohydrates with lipids.* If you are forced to do so, try to consume only a minimum and with as many fibers as possible (a salad, for example).

2. *Never eat sugar cubes, powdered sugar, honey, jams or candy. Persist in using an artificial sweetener if you find it necessary.*

3. *Do not eat starches unless you do so only rarely* (except for brown rice, whole wheat pasta and dry vegetables such as lentils and beans).

4. *Carry on eating bread at breakfast.* Eat only whole wheat bread.

5. *Beware of sauces.* Make sure they do not contain flour or sugar.

6. *Whenever possible,* use sunflower margarine instead of butter, especially at breakfast.

7. *Only drink skimmed milk.*

8. *Try to order fish and favor "good" lipids to prevent cardiovascular diseases.*

9. *Be careful of desserts made with flour.*
Only eat strawberries, raspberries and blackberries.
In moderation, you can eat chocolate, sorbets, ice cream and whipped cream.
Avoid pastries made from flour and sugar, unless you have eaten no other carbohydrates during your meal.
Try to order mousses made only from fruit and eggs, or artificially sugared puddings.

10. *Try to drink as little as possible while you eat.*

11. *Never drink alcoholic beverages on an empty stomach.*

12. *Avoid aperitifs and after dinner drinks.* Drink them only rarely.

13. *Drink champagne or wine as an aperitif,* but first eat hors d'oeuvres, preferably cheese, cold cuts or crabs' legs.

14. *During your meal, drink either water* (non-sparkling) *or wine* (no more than a half-liter a day).

15. *Do not drink water if you are drinking wine.*

16. *Avoid drinking water before your meal.*

17. *Wait until your stomach is partially full before you start drinking your wine.*

18. *Never drink any type of soft drink, except diet sodas.*

19. *Only drink decaffeinated coffee, or light coffees and teas.*

20. *Distribute your dietary "imbalances" evenly over the course of many meals.*

CHAPTER VIII

HYPOGLYCEMIA
THE DISEASE OF THE CENTURY

We have already learned that the body's metabolism processes the ingested foods and transforms them into vital elements. When we speak of the metabolism of lipids, we are referring to the transformation of fats. The true purpose of this book is to discuss the metabolism of carbohydrates and its consequences.

We have seen in previous chapters how insulin (a hormone secreted by the pancreas) affects the metabolism of carbohydrates. The basic function of this hormone is to act on the glucose in the blood so it will permeate into the cells to create muscular (and hepatic) glycogen and sometimes produce stored fats.

Insulin chases the glucose (sugar) out of the blood stream, and, thus, reduces the sugar level in the blood.

If the pancreas secretes insulin too frequently and in excess amounts, the insulin:glucose ratio will be disrupted. Consequently, the sugar level in the blood will continue to drop to an abnormally low level. The body is then in a state of hypoglycemia.

Contrary to popular belief, hypoglycemia stems not from a deficiency of sugar, but rather from an excessive secretion of insulin (hyperinsulinism) that is subordinate to a previous sugar binge.

Not only is insulin responsible for stored fats, but this hormone also hampers the ability of the body's organs (especially the liver) to replenish the amount of sugar in the blood, when there is a deficiency. For example, if at around 11 o'clock in the morning you are feeling tired, it is highly possible that your sugar level is below average and you are in a state of hypoglycemia.

If you consume a carbohydrate—a cookie or any other sweet snack—it will rapidly be broken down into glucose. The presence of glucose in your blood will raise the sugar level, and you will feel invigorated. However, the presence of the glucose in your blood will trigger the secretion of more insulin that will in turn lower your sugar level even more than before. Once again, you will be in a state of hypoglycemia. It is a vicious circle that leads to somewhat of an addictive behavior.

Many scientists have proven that alcoholism is a consequence of chronic hypoglycemia. As soon as the alcoholic feels his sugar level dropping, he feels depressed and needs a drink. Alcohol metabolizes very quickly into glucose, thereby raising the sugar level and the alcoholic is suddenly overcome with elation. Unfortunately, this euphoric feeling will only last a short while. The newly secreted insulin will lower the sugar level even more.

And, a few minutes after his first drink, the alcoholic feels a greater urge for another. And so the cycle continues...

The symptoms of hypoglycemia are as follows:
- fatigue, sudden exhaustion

HER MAJESTY'S DINNER,
THURSDAY, 13TH MARCH, 1879.

POTAGES.
A la Reine   A la Tortue   A la Royale.

POISSONS.
Le Turbot sauce Homard   Les Filets de Soles frits.

ENTRÉES.
Les Croquettes de Volaille à la D'Artois
Les Côtelettes de Mouton à la Soubise
La Cailles farcies à la Bohemienne

RELEVÉS.
Les Poulets à la Jardinière
Roast Beef   Haunch of Venison.

RÔTS.
Les Cannetons   Les Poulets

ENTREMÊTS.
Les Artichauts à la Lyonnaise
Les Biscuits glacés au Chocolat.
Les Gelées garnies de Fruit.

RELEVÉ.
Les Croutes de Brioche aux Abricots.

Queen Victoria's Dinner
on March 13, 1879
at Buckingham Palace in London

- irritability, crankiness
- nervousness
- aggressiveness
- impatience
- anxiety
- yawning, loss of concentration
- headaches
- sweaty palms, excessive perspiration
- digestive problems
- frigidity
- impotence
- predisposition to ulcers
- insomnia
- neuropsychiatric disorders, depression, etc.
- nausea
- difficulty of expression

The list is not very long but it is quite impressive. If one suffers from hypoglycemia, all these symptoms will not necessarily manifest themselves, nor are they permanent. In fact, the symptoms are only temporarily apparent and can very well disappear as soon as food is consumed. You may have noticed that many people become progressively nervous, unstable, aggressive and even cranky as their regular meal time comes around.

One symptom is more common than others, and you may have already guessed which one it is: fatigue.

In our era, fatigue is fairly widespread.

The most tired people are, you may have noticed, those who sleep the most, those who have the most free time, those who take the most vacations. In the morning when they get up, they are already zonked. By the end of the morning they can barely stand. And, by early afternoon, you will find them snoozing away at their desk. Then comes the after-lunch slump, and by the end of the afternoon they gather all their remaining strength to pick up their things and go home. In the evening, they doze in front of the television set, and when it is time to go to bed, they cannot get to sleep. Before they know it, the alarm goes off, and another day begins. So, they blame their perpetual exhaustion on the stress, the noise and the pollution of modern times, and a number of other alibis. To fight against this incessant fatigue, they drink a lot of coffee, swallow boxes full of vitamin pills, or take up yoga. But in most cases, fatigue is due to hypoglycemia and an unbalanced diet.

The average person's blood sugar level, in this day and age, is abnormally low. And, this situation is a direct result of a disproportionate amount of bad carbohydrates in the average diet. Too much sugar, soft drinks, white bread, potatoes, pasta and rice will inevitably result in an overabundant secretion of insulin.

For a long time, it was believed that the only potential candidates for hypoglycemia were obese people. Recent studies, particularly in the United States, have shown that many thin people are also victims of a low blood sugar level, given the excessive amounts of bad carbohydrates they consume. Some people tend to gain weight while others do not because of a difference in their metabolism, but the consequences of a low sugar level are the same.

These studies have also shown that women are particularly sensitive to glycemic variations, and many believe this explains the all too frequent mood shifts. Whether or not this is true, it has been proven that the "post-baby blues" are a direct result of the tremendously low sugar level in the mother's blood after she has given birth.

If you seriously apply the method presented to you here, you will find that besides a slimmer body, you will also rediscover a certain optimism, vitality and *joie de vivre*. If you are prone to fits of insomnia, you will sleep well at night. Your mid-day fatigue will disappear. In sum, you will rediscover a physical and mental rejuvenation.

When you eliminate all the sugar from your diet and limit your consumption of bad carbohydrates, your pancreas will stop secreting excess amounts of insulin and the sugar in your blood will stabilize itself at a normal level. When sugar is no longer ingested and only a moderate amount of glucose is metabolized, the body will eventually turn to its natural instincts and produce the glucose it needs from the stored fats. An optimum blood sugar level will be attained only under these conditions.

According to the scientists and doctors I interviewed, hypoglycemia is very difficult to diagnose since the symptoms are so numerous and varied. Maybe this is because, in most medical schools, only a few classroom hours are devoted to hypoglycemia. Moreover, it has always been officially admitted that hypoglycemia is diagnosed when the blood sugar level falls below 0.45 g/l, whereas the normal level is about 0.90 to 1.0 g/l. However, specialists in the field have confirmed that hypoglycemia occurs even if the sugar level is only slightly below average.

If you follow the guidelines explained in the previous chapter, you will know if you are hypoglycemic or not. You will notice a phenomenal difference in your physical and mental condition in less than one week. You will discover a well-being you never experienced before, despite the years of scrupulously drinking 8 glasses of mineral water each day.

CHAPTER IX

DIGESTION

Do not be tempted to skip this chapter, assuming that you have already covered the essentials in the previous pages. Let me tell you now that you would be depriving yourself of extremely interesting information.

Not only will you learn to understand the reasons behind certain gastro-intestinal problems you may have encountered, but you will also learn to avoid them in the future.

It is true that digestion is a technical topic that you may be tempted to rebuff. Trust me. I will stick to a simple presentation that emphasizes the vital mechanisms of digestion in order for you to perfectly understand how it all works.

TECHNICAL ASPECTS OF DIGESTION

Digestion is a physiological process that leads to the metabolism of food. There are physical or mechanical aspects as well as chemical aspects, which is what concerns us here. The four main stages of the digestion process are:

1. the mouth
2. the stomach
3. the small intestine
4. the large intestine (colon)

The mouth

- *Mechanical role*

- mastication
- swallowing

- *Chemical role*

- saliva secretion

Saliva contains an important enzyme,[1] called ptyalin, whose function is to transform starch into maltose—a complex sugar that will undergo the digestion process up into the intestine.

Nothing much happens in the mouth besides the formation of the alimentary bolus, the mass of food that is swallowed. Only starch, affected by the ptyalin, begins to be metabolized in the mouth; hence thorough mastication and a healthy dentition is essential.

---

1. An enzyme is a catalyst. Many substances cannot be combined without the help of a third substance that creates a chemical reaction. This third substance is what we call the catalyst.

Menu from the Elysée Palace, 1903.

The stomach

● *The mechanical role* is purely peristaltic, like in the intestine. In other words, a series of muscular contractions in the stomach pushes the foodstuff out of the stomach and into the intestine.

● *The chemical role*

The stomach will secrete gastric juices (hydrochloric acid, mucin) in order for the pepsin to take effect (the diastasis enzyme of the stomach).

Pepsin will then start the metabolic transformation of the proteins (meats), and the fats will begin to undergo hydrolysis which continues into the intestine.

The small intestine

● *Mechanical action:* peristaltic

● *Chemical action*

The starch, now maltose, is broken down into glucose (simple sugars) by the pancreatic juices.

The milk sugar, lactose, is broken down into glucose and galactose.

Lipids are converted into fatty acids.

Proteins are changed into amino acids.

If everything goes well in the small intestine, it is at this stage that the nutritional substances—glucose (former carbohydrates), amino acids (former proteins) and fatty acids (former lipids)—will be altered, released into the blood, and then, from there, assimilated by the organism.

The large intestine (ascending, descending, right, left and transverse colons)

- *Mechanical action:* peristaltic

- *Chemical action*

Through fermentation, the bacteria in the large intestine acts on the starch and cellulose remnants, and, through putrefaction, on the protein residues. At this level, elements are absorbed into the system, inassimilable matter is transformed into fecal matter, and, eventually, gas is produced.

FOOD COMBINATIONS

When the cave man went hunting during the day he would eat the wild fruit he picked on the way. Back at the cave, he ate the meat he had killed. When food was scarce, when he lacked game, he would live on different kinds of roots. Untamed animals also have the habit of never mixing different kinds of food. Birds, for instance, eat worms and insects at a certain time of day, and they will eat grains at another. Man is the only living animal that eats combined foods, which is why he suffers from so many intestinal problems.

Intestinal complications are caused by a perpetually upset digestive system, which is also often responsible for a number of other illnesses, even though the link is never very clear.

I will not go into a lengthy and detailed analysis of the different possible food combinations and their consequences.

Since this is not the purpose of my book, I will leave that to specialists in physiology.

I simply want to give you a general idea of how the process works in order for you to understand the *positive* side effects of your new eating habits.

Surely you remember my advice (chapter VII) that *fruit should never be combined with other foods*.

When consumed with other foods, not only does fruit upset the digestion process, but it also loses its beneficial properties (vitamins, etc.).

Since you now understand the basics of the digestion process, let me explain the reasons behind this statement so you do not interpret it as a gratuitous remark.

Fruit-starch combination

Fructose (monosaccharide or simple sugar) contained in the fruit spends little time in the stomach and is digested almost completely in the intestine.

Starch, on the other hand, begins its metabolic process in the mouth. In the presence of ptyalin, the enzyme secreted in the saliva, it is transformed into maltose. The maltose spends some time in the stomach before it is completely digested in the small intestine. Maltase, an enzyme secreted by the pancreas, acts on the maltose to transform it into glucose before it is absorbed into the blood stream.

If fruit is consumed with a starch, the effects are the following:

The acidity from the fruit will destroy the ptyalin, which will, thus, not be able to assume its catalyzing effects on the starch. Furthermore, instead of passing directly into the small intestine, the fruit will spend time in the stomach with the starch. Because of the heat and humidity in the stomach, the simple sugar in the fruit will undergo fermentation. The fruit will continue to ferment into the intestine, carrying the starch with it. Despite the presence of amylase (another enzyme secreted by the pancreas), the starch will only be partially transformed into glucose. The rest will continue to ferment into the colon.

Consequences:

- bloating
- flatulence
- intestinal irritation
- deterioration of the vitamins in the fruit
- constipation, etc.

Fruit-protein (meat) combination

The first phase of protein digestion takes place in the stomach in the presence of a diastasis enzyme called pepsin [2]. Pepsin develops in an acidic medium created by the gastric juices.

You may conclude that since pepsin develops in an acidic medium, proteins will be harmoniously digested in the presence of acidic fruit. Well, this is incorrect. From the moment acidity develops in the mouth, the conditions for pepsin secretion are upset and the enzyme cannot be produced.

---

2. For adults, drinking milk during the meal is a dangerous mistake from a digestive point of view. Milk penetrates into the stomach and coagulates. The milk curds will then coat the food particles already in the stomach and form a protective shield against the gastric juices, thereby compromising the digestive process. Milk with a meal is a sure way to digestive troubles, even for children over the age of 10.

Consequently, when fruit and proteins are consumed together, the fruit (like in the previous example) becomes stuck in the stomach where it will ferment. In the absence of pepsin, the proteins will not be able to undergo the normal digestion process. In the large intestine they will putrefy and emit residual toxins that will have to be eliminated by the body.

One of the basic principles of this book is to avoid eating bad carbohydrates (starches) with meat (protein-lipids) in order to lose or maintain weight. Therefore, you should not be surprised to learn that the starch-protein combination creates digestive problems as well as weight problems.

Starch-protein combination

When starch is consumed with proteins (in a ham sandwich, for instance), the following chemical reactions take place:

Ptyalin, necessary for starch digestion, is neutralized by the acidic medium produced to allow for pepsin secretion, essential in protein digestion. And, reciprocally, pepsin production is upset by the acidic medium created by the ptyalin.

The digestive consequences are similar to those explained above:

- Starch is fermented in the stomach and in the intestine, thereby causing ballooning.
- Proteins are only partially metabolized, which leaves undigested residues.
- These wastes putrefy in the large intestine.
- Toxins are emitted into the blood stream.

The symptoms of an upset digestion system are more or less obvious. Whereas metabolic troubles and gastro-intestinal problems generally develop during childhood or adolescence, the physical symptoms are rarely revealed before adulthood.

Once again, although this is not the purpose of the book, keep in mind that many indigestion problems stem from bad food combinations.

Do not look any further to understand the reasons for:

- allergies
- bad breath
- coated tongue
- stomach aches
- ulcers
- colitis
- constipation
- colon cancer
- nausea
- heartburn
- cellulite
- bloated stomachs (frequent among women)
- chronic angina
- loss of hair
- sebhorrea
- abnormal or excessive perspiration
- hemorrhoids
- migraines, etc.

I, myself, suffered a number of gastro-intestinal problems for many years. I visited several of the best specialists in France, and the impressive lists of medication I collected brought no improvement to my condition. The prescriptions often produced negative side effects that were usually worse than my original problems.

These specialists, with whom I had to book appointments months in advance, never knew how to respond when I told them that I had been losing my hair since the age of 18, and that my head perspired excessively whenever I drank or ate.

I finally gave up looking for the solution to this obscure and enigmatic problem that always baffled these eminent gentlemen. You can get used to anything if you really try.

Strangely enough, a few years later, these symptoms miraculously disappeared. You now know why.

It was only once I had decided to look into nutrition more in depth that, much to my surprise, I discovered a direct link between the new eating habits I had adopted and the disappearance of all my ailments.

Since my youth, I have always suffered from chronic angina. The slightest draft or change in temperature inevitably affected me.

Because I was allergic to penicillin, I had to resort to more inefficient methods or obscure old wives' remedies.

I must have been ten or eleven years old when, one bright summer day, a country doctor told me as he stuck his chubby finger down my little mouth, "the best cure for angina is to eat good camembert and gargle well with an old Bordeaux wine."

I was all ears and hung on to his every word. My former classmates still recall that I never went anywhere without my cheese and wine. It was actually a very efficient remedy [3]. And even though Social Security did not compensate for my

---

3. See Chapter XI on the benefits of wine.

"medical treatment," the pleasures I savored were enough of a reward.

Very soon after I started to seriously apply the principles compiled in this book. My family and friends noticed that my angina had apparently disappeared. I felt it was still too early to draw a direct link between the two circumstances.

But ten years later, it was obvious. My angina had completely disappeared. However, this is not to say that my camembert and old Bordeaux have been forever stored away in the medicine cabinet.

Slave cutting sugar cane in the West Indes
18th century etching

CHAPTER X

SUGAR IS POISON

Sugar is poison! The damage it has done to 20th century man is as serious as the effects of alcohol and tobacco put together. The dangers of this substance are emphasized and repeated at every colloquium or seminar for pediatricians, cardiologists, psychiatrists and dentists. The ever increasing rate of sugar consumption today is particularly frightening.

Sugar did not exist in the times of the Ancient Greeks. They did not even have a word for it.

Around 325 B.C., Alexander the Great, who had pushed his world conquest to the plains of Indus described sugar as "a type of honey that is found in canes and reeds and grows by the water."

Pliny the Elder, in the first century A.D., also refers to sugar as the "honey of the cane."

It was not until the time of Nero that the word "saccharum" was invented to refer to this exotic product.

In the seventh century A.D., cane sugar appeared in Persia and Sicily, and the Arab countries eventually acquired a taste for it.

Doctor Rauwolf, a German scholar, noted the following in his diary in 1573:

"The Turks and the Moors are no longer the intrepid soldiers they were in the times before they discovered sugar."

The Western countries discovered sugar during the great Crusades. Soon thereafter, the Spanish tried to cultivate it in the southern regions of their country.

The conquest of the New World and the triangular trade that ensued led sugar to become an important economic stake. Spain, Portugal and England made fortunes trading raw materials for slaves in order to cultivate sugar for importation to Europe. By 1700, France had already built a number of refineries.

The defeat of Trafalgar in 1805 and the continental blockade that resulted, led Napoleon, against scientists' recommendations, to develop a way to produce sugar from beets. This became truly possible only after Benjamin Delessert discovered the extraction procedure in 1812.

By the middle of the 19th century, there was a surplus of sugar in France, even though the level of sugar expenditure was very far from what it is today.

In 1880, the average consumption of sugar in Europe per capita was approximately 17 pounds a year [1], which is about equal to ten sugar cubes per day. Twenty years later, in 1900, the rate more than doubled and reached 37 pounds. In 1960, Europeans consumed 66 pounds, and in 1972, 83 pounds.

In two centuries Europeans multiplied their average yearly rate of sugar usage from 2 to over 80 pounds per capita.

---

1. In 1789, about 100 years earlier, the consumption rate was significantly less: 2 pounds per capita.

Over 3 million years, mankind has never so abruptly and brutally altered its eating habits.

And Europeans are far from being the worst off. The situation is much more abominable in the United States where the average person consumes over 130 pounds of sugar a year, in spite of the numerous "dietetic," "low-cal," and "health food" campaigns.

It is even more distressing to note that the amount of "hidden sugar"[2] represented in these statistics continues to rise. In 1977, the amount of sugar indirectly absorbed (in drinks, desserts, preserves, etc.) was 58% of total sugar consumption. In 1985, it jumped to 63%.

This leads to a sticky situation. The rate of direct sugar intake is stagnating or even dropping because of the availability of artificial sweeteners and the medical establishment's warnings.

On the other hand, the indirect amount of sugar consumed per capita is alarming. The increase of "hidden sugars" particularly affects children and adolescents. A 150 ml glass of soda is equal to five sugar cubes. Moreover, the coldness of the drink conceals the sweet taste.

Soft drinks are now part of the majority of the population's diet. Soda companies are powerful multinational trusts and the impact of their advertising campaigns is simply phenomenal. It is frightening to think that they have established themselves in Third World countries where the populations' primary nutritional requirements are not even satisfied.

Eskimo pies and other frozen desserts are no longer a "treat" we buy on special occasions, but a permanent item

2. "Hidden sugar" is sugar added in commercial foods and beverages.

in our freezers. We can thank modern technology for that one. Vending machines, selling candy bars and soft drinks, have been set up in all public places and are a constant appeal. Obtaining these goodies is easy since they are relatively cheap. In a supermarket, a pound of candy costs less than a dollar. The potential consumer is perpetually solicited and enticed by large-scale advertising slogans. To turn away from these temptations can be considered a heroic act.

It is stating the obvious to say that sugar is responsible for a great number of ailments. Everyone is aware of this fact, but this is not to say we have changed our eating habits or, even less, those of our children.

Sugar is the principle cause of cardiovascular illnesses. Doctor Yudkin notes that the East African tribes, Mascar and Samburee, eat a diet rich in fats that was practically free of sugar. The amount of coronary illnesses in these tribes is close to zero. But the natives of the Island of Saint-Helena who eat a lot of sugar and not many fats, have suffered from a significant amount of coronary illnesses.

The cavity, due to too much sugar, is so widespread in Western countries that the World Health Organization ranks dental and oral diseases third, after cardiovascular diseases and cancer, among the top health problems afflicting industrialized countries.

When we associate sugar with disease, we immediately think of diabetes. Not all diabetics are obese, but this is generally the case. Unfortunately, the United States has one of the greatest problems with obesity which is a direct result of a diet rich in bad carbohydrates, especially sugar.

Studies have shown that an excessive consumption of sugar is also responsible for a number of mental illnesses.

From the previous chapters you now understand that

sugar, a purely chemical product, responsible for hypoglycemia, upsets the body's metabolism and creates digestive disorders.

It is also important to know that sugar can also lead to a vitamin B deficiency. Large amounts of vitamin B are necessary to absorb the glucose in the blood. Since sugar, like refined starches (flour, rice, etc.), contains no vitamin B, the body is forced to draw on its reserves. The consequences of a vitamin B deficiency generally include: neurasthenia (nervous exhaustion), fatigue, depression, and loss of concentration, memory and perception. This is an area that should be studied more in depth for children having trouble in school.

ARTIFICIAL SWEETENERS

I advise you to completely eliminate sugar from your diet. Of course, this is impossible to do when it is hidden, such as in desserts. But you are already taking a giant step in the right direction if you stop using castor sugar and sugar cubes.

You can either do without or use an artificial sweetener.

There are three major types of artificial sweeteners. None of them contains any potential energy and therefore has no nutritional value.

Saccharine

Saccharine, discovered in 1879, is the oldest sugar substitute. It is not assimilated by the human system and is 350 times as sweet as the saccharose in natural sugar. It sometimes has the advantage of being very stable in an acidic medium, and can tolerate an average temperature. Saccharine was the most commercialized sweetener until the discovery of aspartame.

Cyclamates

Although their discovery dates back to 1937, cyclamates are less well known. They are made from benzene, are not as sweet as saccharine, and are sometimes said to leave an unpleasant aftertaste.

The advantage of cyclamates is that they are completely thermostable; in other words, resistant to high temperatures. The most commonly used cyclamate is made from sodium cyclamate. Other kinds include calcium cyclamate and cyclamate acid.

Aspartame

Aspartame was discovered in 1965 in Chicago by James Schlatter, a researcher for Searle Laboratories.

This sugar substitute is the product of two natural amino acids: aspartic acid and phenylalanine.

It has a sweetening potential 180 to 200 times greater than saccharose. It does not possess any bitter aftertastes and taste tests have proven that it does not have an artificial quality.

Over 60 different countries use it in manufacturing foods and beverages. A French law recently passed to allow aspartame to be used as an additive.

Artificial sweeteners have always been the topic of many debates.

Saccharine was, for many years, suspected of being a carcinogenic. However, it does not present the least danger if consumed under 2.5 mg/k, which would correspond to 130 to 165 pounds of sugar for an adult of average weight. Other countries, such as Canada, have outlawed the use of saccharine.

Cyclamates have also been suspected of being carcinogenic, and were outlawed in the United States in 1969.

Aspartame, ever since it was discovered, has been the object of numerous controversies, but every study has proven that it is free of toxins, even when it is consumed in high doses. This has been officially recognized by the Food and Drug Administration in the United States.

After undergoing tests for 15 years in the United States, aspartame was finally commercialized under the name of "Nutrasweet."

"Nutrasweet" is available in two forms:

- in tablets that rapidly dissolve in hot and cold drinks,
- in powder form, particularly recommended for desserts and other homemade recipes.

One "Nutrasweet" tablet is as sweet as 0.2 ounces of sugar and contains 0.004 ounces of absorbable carbohydrates. In powdered form, one teaspoon of "Nutrasweet" is as sweet as one teaspoon of sugar and contains 0.14 ounces of assimilable carbohydrates.

In 1980, the accepted daily dose recommended by the World Health Organization was of 1 tablet per pound. In other words, a person weighing 120 pounds could consume up to 120 tablets in one day without noting any toxic long term effects. This dose was confirmed in 1984 and 1987 by the Scientific Committee on Human Diet, the European Economic Community equivalent of the Food and Drug Administration in the United States.

In any case, artificial sweeteners should only be used transitorily. Ideally, you should progressively decondition yourself from the taste of sugar.

CHAPTER XI

THE BENEFITS OF WINE
or
THE BLESSING OF WINE

> "Wine is a professor of taste.
> By teaching us inner awareness,
> wine liberates the mind and
> enlightens the spirit."
>
> Paul Claudel

Wine is not an ordinary beverage. It is more than a mere thirst quencher.

Since the beginning of civilization wine has been endowed with mystical qualities. The spirit of wine and its physiological and organoleptic traits led Huysmanns to call wine "a sacramental substance."

Wine has always held a number of symbolic meanings. The moment Noah and his "companions" set foot on earth after the Great Flood, they planted a vineyard to celebrate rebirth and the start of a new life. In Greek mythology,

Dionysus [1] associates wine with joy, happiness and high spirits. It is not surprising that Jesus chose wine to symbolize his blood in Christian liturgy, so strong was its spiritual imprint.

Even today, wine, graced with a noble quality, is still a sign of celebration and cheerful gatherings among family and friends. Nevertheless many destroyers of the myth perceive wine as nothing more than an alcoholic beverage.

Recent findings have shed light on different therapeutic characteristics of wine that had already been discovered by our ancestors. Let us hope that the doctors of tomorrow will learn about them in medical school, because, as Baudelaire said, "if the human race abandoned the production of wine, a void in human health and spirit would ensue; an absence more horrible than the excesses of wine could ever provoke."

THERAPY OF THE ANCIENTS

Plato recommended wine, which he called "milk of gray-beards," for good health. To the Greeks, wine represented human identity and assured Wisdom.

The ancient Egyptian medicine men used wine as a healer as early as 6000 B.C.

But it was Hippocrates, the father of medicine, who revealed the nobility and efficiency of wine as a therapeutic agent. When modern doctors take their oath they should always remember Hippocrates' words:

---

1. Dionysus, or Bacchus, the son of Zeus and Semele, is the Greek god of wine associated to the Liber Pater of the Romans.

ST VINCENT, PATRON OF THE VINE

19th century icon

"Wine is highly suitable for man if, in sickness and in health, he takes care to drink it with purpose and in proper measure according to his individual condition."

Hippocrates, a humorous fellow, claimed that sadness and somberness were the cause of illness. In these instances, he recommended a glass of wine to "have a good laugh and to inspire a good mood."

Saint Paul, Apostle of the Gentiles, is said to have told one of his disciples who suffered from digestive problems,

"They tell me you only drink water. Have a glass of wine for your stomach and your feebleness."

In 79 A.C., Pliny the Elder generalized that "wine, by itself, is a remedy: it nourishes the blood of man and appeases his chagrin."

The Benedictine monasteries in the Middle Ages perpetrated the tradition of the vineyard. Certain famous vestiges still exist in the region of Burgundy. One of the Fathers Superior, better known today as Saint Benoit, told his Benedictine brothers to drink a couple of glasses of wine at every meal, to stay alert and to avoid digestive troubles.

Wine, during the Renaissance, ranked among the medicines of choice.

Rabelais [2] a doctor from the region of Chinon and Bourgueil, wrote that "the juice of the vine clears the spirit, heightens understanding, appeases anger, makes sadness flee and brings joy and jubilation."

According to Montaigne, a noble from Bordeaux and a famous 16th century philosopher, nothing is better than a dry white wine to cure bladder stones. He regularly imbibed

---

2. Francois Rabelais: a 16th century French author who wrote the tales of Gargantua.

his precious liquid endowed with diuretic virtues for his personal health.

It is said that the Dutch philosopher, Erasmus, put an end to his stomach pains by drinking wine from the region of Burgundy.

Ambroise Pare, royal doctor and surgeon, healed his patients' war wounds with bandages soaked in red wine.

And lastly, it is interesting to know that when our dear and famous Louis the XIV suffered from gout, his doctor replaced his bottle of Burgundy with a bottle of Champagne.

THE PHYSIOLOGICAL EFFECTS AND PROPERTIES OF WINE

The nutritional and therapeutic properties of wine are now recognized by modern science. It goes without saying that excellent results will be ensured only with an excellent wine.

Wine as sustenance

Wine has an important nutritional value and contains essential elements that the body can easily assimilate.

Wine as a tonic

The tonicity of wine comes principally from tannin. The richer the wine is in tannin, the more invigorating it is. The analeptic quality of wine manifests itself physically and psychologically.

So wine is a natural means of recuperation after heavy physical exertion.

Red wine, especially if it is old, is recommended during periods of convalescence, or for infectious diseases and serious viruses.

Wine as a nerve suppressor

Professor Fiessinger once said "wine maintains a perfect balance between the views of the mind and the play of emotions."

Wine helps cure depression in that it provokes a certain feeling of euphoria. It is recommended, for example, to patients who must follow a restrictive diet for therapeutic reasons. Without doubt, a fine vintage is less toxic than any synthetic product sold at your local drugstore.

Wine helps digestion

In the words of Paul and Saint-Benoit, a quality wine, in moderate amounts, enjoyed during a meal facilitates the digestion process. Wine is rich in vitamin B [3] which regenerates

---

3. As we saw in the last chapter, sugar and other carbohydrates can provoke a vitamin B deficiency.

the liver and allows for the elimination of toxins. These vitamins play an important role in the metabolism of protein and carbohydrates.

Furthermore, wine also secretes gastric juices and particularly facilitates the digestion of proteins (meats and fish). Red wine, rich in tannin, acts on the intestinal muscle fibers. It heightens the peristaltic action and relieves constipation. A fine vintage is usually an efficient means to treat spasmodic colitis (inflammation of the colon).

According to Doctor Maury [4], Cardinal Richelieu, a personal and influential advisor to the French king, Louis XIII, suffered from "intestinal languor." He cured himself by regularly drinking a Bordeaux wine, now known as "the Richelieu infusion."

Wine as a diuretic

Wine, particularly white wine, is a diuretic. Hippocrates had already discovered this and recommended it to his patients. We already saw how Montaigne scrupulously imbibed his white wine to cleanse his kidneys. Acidic white wines (Chardonnay, Pinot Blanc, Zinfandel, Amador and champagnes) are rich in tartrate and potassium sulfates. These elements, which ensure a proper elimination of toxins, are beneficial to the kidneys.

---

4. *La médecine par le vin*, by Dr. Maury; Editions Artulen.

Wine renews body minerals

Wine contains a high concentration of minerals that are perfectly assimilable by the body, including calcium, potassium, magnesium, silicium, zinc, fluoride, copper, manganese, chrome and sulfuric mineral anion.

Wine as a bactericide

Since Antiquity, wine was said to have anti-bacteria effects. This has been proven true on many occasions and especially during great epidemics. In 1886, Rambuteau, a reputable figure in 19th century French history, noted that the wine drinkers were less prone to cholera than the water drinkers. In 1892, polluted water was not considered dangerous if it was mixed with one third of wine. A few years later, doctors began to prescribe wine to help cure typhoid fever. More recently, Professor Masquelier, of the University of Bordeaux, demonstrated the bactericidal effects of red Bordeaux on colibacillosis, and on polluted water and vegetables. At the same time, two Canadian researchers discovered that red wine attacked certain viruses, particularly polio and herpes [5].

Finally, it is important to note that the antiseptic effects of wine are relative to its age. A young wine that is drunk soon after fermentation (such as a Beaujolais Nouveau) is not a very effective bactericide.

---

5. Herpes: a viral disease characterized by the formation of blisters on the skin or on mucous membranes.

Wine fights allergies

In the 19th century, those with sensitive skin were advised to dip strawberries in their wine to avoid skin rashes.

Professor Masquelier proved that wine worked as an antihistamine and, thus, prevented allergies. He also noted that the rich manganese and vitamin P content in certain wines, Côtes de Ventoux, Corbières and Minervois, also prevented allergies.

Wine's beneficial effects on the cardiovascular system

Wine has been proven to be most efficient for cardiovascular troubles.

As early as 1786, the British doctor Heberden discovered that wine relieved his patients' angina pains. More recently, Professor Masquelier found that the elements contained in wine were capable of preventing a myocardial infarct.

In 1979, a serious medical investigation conducted in England revealed that, among 18 Western countries, the number of deaths due to myocardial arrests was lowest among populations who habitually consumed wine (3 to 5 times lower in France and Italy).

It was thus concluded that wine worked as a protective agent against arteriosclerosis.

In 1982, after years of research, Professor Masquelier, discovered which elements constituted this preventive effect.

According to Masquelier, the procyanidines in wine control three factors:

1. By strengthening the effects of vitamin C, they accelerate the purification of cholesterol in the blood stream, and

thus reject the fatty deposits in the atheromatous shields (vitamin C is necessary to the purifying of cholesterol).

2. They stabilize the collagen fibers that act as a support for certain arterial membranes.

3. They work against the local production of histamines that are suspected of causing atherogenesis.

The tannin in the wine contains the procyanidines.

The beneficial effects of this beverage are quite well-known, and I fear that the pharmaceutical industry will discover in this molecule the remedy for cardiovascular illnesses. That would be a shame, since the remedy already exists in such a pleasurable form.

As I reread this chapter, I cannot help thinking of my grandmother from Bordeaux who lived until the age of 102. She hated water and only drank red wine.

To end this chapter on wine, it is important to remember that wine constitutes a dietary discrepancy and it should not be consumed in Phase I. The beverage will be reintroduced sparingly in Phase II under the following conditions:

- never drink wine on an empty stomach;
- wait as long as possible into the meal before drinking;
- drink moderately; no more than a half-liter a day.

HOW TO CURE YOURSELF WITH WINES*

Again, you should take care to drink no more than a half-liter a day. Remember that one glass of wine at the end of the meal is enough to benefit from the beverage's therapeutic properties.

CLINICAL INDICATION	TREATMENT
Acidosis	Pouilly-Fuissé - Sancerre
	Fumé Blanc, Napa
Allergies	Corbières - Médoc - Minervois - Ventoux
	Grey Riesling, Monterey - Barbera, Santa Clara - Cabernet, Napa

---

* This chart is from Dr Maury's book *Soignez-vous par le vin*, Editions Universitaires, (*Wine is the Best Medicine*, Sheed, Andrews and McMeel, 1974) and from *La Medicine par le Vin*, Editions Artulen.

Beneath the French wines, you will find a list of suggested American counterpart wines.

The information contained in the chart above should not be interpreted as nor substituted for an actual medical prescription. Instead, it provides general recommendations that should only be used as a complement to regular treatment. The results obtained from these indications are essentially dependent on the individual's sensitivity. In any case, no more than a quart of wine should be consumed per day.

Anemia	Cahors - Côtes-de-nuit - Côtes-de-Beaune - Côtes-de-Graves - Corsican wines - Pomerol - Madiran *Pinot Noir, Napa - Pinot Noir, Sonoma - Cabernet, Napa - Merlot, Napa*
Angina	Médoc - Julienas - Moulin-à-vent *Cabernet, Napa - Gamay, Beaujolais, Monterey*
Antibiotics (side effects)	Médoc - Mercurey *Cabernet, Napa - Pinot Blanc, Sonoma*
Arteriosclerosis	Dry champagne - Corsican wines (Ajaccio) Graves - Muscadet - wines from Provence - Sancerre - Saint-Emilion *Champagne, Napa, Sonoma, Mendocino - Zinfandel, Amador - French Colombard, Mendocino - Fumé Blanc, Napa - Cabernet, Sonoma*
Arthritis	Alsace - Chablis - Crépy - Minervois - Pouilly - Saint-Veran - Seyssel *Gewurztraminer, Sonoma - Muscat of Alexandria - Pinot Blanc, Monterey - Emerald Riesling, Santa Clara - Johannisberg Riesling, Monterey - Sylvaner, Monterey - Pinot Noir Rosé, Sonoma*
Arthrosis	Rosé wines from Provence (Bandol - Cassis)
Asthma	Corbières - Minervois *Grey Riesling, Monterey - Barbera, Santa Clara*
Bile insufficiency	Anjou - Vouvray *California Grenache Rosé - Chenin Blanc, Napa - California Chenin Blanc*
Bloating	Dry Champagne - Gaillac-perlé *Champagne, Napa, Sonoma, Mendocino - California Sparkling Muskat*
Breast feeding	Graves reds - Beaujolais - Blanquette de Limoux *Zinfandel, Amador - California Zinfandel- California Gamay Beaujolais Nouveau*
Bronchitis	Julienas - Médoc - Moulin-à-vent - Muscat de Rivesaltes *Cabernet, Napa - Gamay, Beaujolais, Monterey*
Cholelithiasis	Touraine dry white wines

Cholesterol	Alsace - Muscadet - Provence rosé
	Gewurztraminer, Sonoma - Muscat of Alexandria - Pinot Blanc, Monterey - Emerald Riesling, Monterey - Sylvaner, Monterey - Pinot Noir Rosé, Sonoma
Colibacillosis	Champagne brut - Médoc
	Cabernet, Napa
Colitis	White Gaillac - Gaillac perlé
Constipation	White Anjou - Bandol - White Bergerac - Cassis - Jurançon - Montravel doux - Morgon - Pécharmant
	Chenin Blanc, Napa - California Chenin Blanc
Convalescence	Médoc - Corsican wines - Frontignan - Red Graves - Mercurey - Monbazillac - Vouvray
	Cabernet, Napa - Zinfandel, Amador - Pinot Blanc, Sonoma - Chenin Blanc Napa - California Chenin Blanc
Convulsions	Red Côtes-de-Provence - Red Côtes-du-Rhône
	California Zinfandel (red)
Coronary Diseases	Champagne brut - Morgon - Saint-Emilion
	Cabernet, Sonoma
Cysts	White Anjous
Decalcification	Arbois - Champigny - Corbières - Côtes-de-Beaune - Côtes-de-Nuit - Côtes-du-Rhône - Madiran - Maury - Premiers Côtes-de-Bordeaux - Saint-Emilion - Saumurois
	Grey Riesling, Monterey - Barbera, Santa Clara - Pinot Noir, Napa - Pinot Noir, Sonoma - California Zinfandel - Cabernet, Sonoma
Demineralization	Premiers Côtes-de-Bordeaux - Châteauneuf-du-Pape - Gevrey-Chambertin - Clos-Vougeot
	Petite Sirah, Napa and Sonoma - California Sauvignon Blanc
Diabetes	Champagne brut - White Gaillac - Muscadet - wines of Provence - Sancerre
	Fumé Blanc Napa
Diarrhea	Beaujolais - Madiran - Médoc
	California Zinfandel, California Gamay Superior - Gamay, Napa - Gamay Beaujolais, Monterey

197

Dyspepsia	White Anjou - Champagne brut - Iroulegy - Monbazillac - Montlouis - Vouvray
	Champagne, Napa, Sonoma, Mendocino - Chenin Blanc, Napa - California Chenin Blanc
Eczema	Sylvaner - Gros-Plant - Muscadet - Dry Jurançon
	Sylvaner, Monterey - French Colombard, Mendocino
Edema	Chablis - Crépy - Muscadet - Sylvaner
	Chardonnay, Sonoma - Chardonnay, Napa - Pinot Blanc, Napa - Pinot Blanc, Sonoma - French Colombard, Mendocino - Sylvaner, Monterey
Emaciation	Muscat-du-Cap-Corse - Muscat-Banyuls
Fatigue (see stimulants)	Médoc - Pouilly-Fuissé - Puligny-Montrachet
	Cabernet, Napa - Chardonnay, Napa
Fever	Champagne - Julienas - Médoc - Moulin-à-Vent
	Champagne, Napa, Sonoma, Mendocino - California Sparling Muscat
Flu	Champagne brut - Côtes-Rotie - Morgon - Saint-Emilion
	Champagne, Napa, Sonoma, Mendocino - California Petite Sirah - Cabernet, Sonoma
Gallstones	Anjou - Vouvray
	California Grenache Rosé - Chenin Blanc, Napa - California Chenin Blanc
Gout	Province rosé - White Savoie - Sancerre - Champagne
	Fumé Blanc, Napa
Hemorrhages (tendency to)	Côtes-de-Beaune - Cahors - Pécharmant - Saint-Emilion
	Pinot Noir, Sonoma - Cabernet, Sonoma
High sodium diet	Chablis - Dry champagne
	Chardonnay, Sonoma - Chardonnay, Napa - Pinot Blanc, Napa - Pinot Blanc, Sonoma
Hyperchlorydria	Sauternes - Barsac
	Johannisberg Riesling (white), Monterey

198

Hypertension
(High blood pressure)

Alsace - Chablis - White graves - Pouilly-Fuissé - Sancerre

Gewurztraminer, Sonoma - Muscat of Alexandria - Pinot Blanc, Monterey - Emerald Riesling, Santa Clara - Johannisberg Riesling, Monterey - Sylvaner, Monterey - Pinot Noir Rosé, Sonoma - Chardonnay, Sonoma - Chardonnay, Napa - Pinot Blanc, Napa - Pinot Blanc, Sonoma - Zinfandel, Amador (white) - Fumé Blanc, Napa

Hypoglycemia

Muscat-de-Banyuls - Muscat-de-Corse - Muscat-de-Frontignan

Hypotension
(Low blood pressure)

Côtes-de-Beaune (red) - Beaulolais - Château-Chalon - Roussillon wines

Pinot Noir, Sonoma - California Zinfandel - California Gamay Beaujolais Nouveau - Gamay, Napa - Gamay Beaujolais - Chilled California Dry Sherry

Infarcts
(tendency to)

Dry champagne - Blanc de blanc - aged Bordeaux

Champagne, Napa, Sonoma, Mendocino

Kidney stones

Pouilly-Fuissé - Sancerre - Seyssel

Lithemia

Gros-Plan - Muscadet - White Saumur - Savoie wines - Sylvaner

California Champagne - French Colombard, Mendocino - Sylvaner, Monterey

Loss of appetite

Banyuls - Jurançon - Frontignan - Monbazillac - Sauternes

Johannisberg Riesling (white), Monterey

Menopause

Red Burgundy - Cahors - Saint-Emilion - Pécharmant

Pinot Noir, Napa - Pinot Noir, Sonoma - Cabernet, Sonoma

Nervous depression

Chablis - Médoc-Listrac

Chardonnay, Sonoma - Chardonnay, Napa - Pinot Blanc, Napa - Pinot Blanc, Sonoma - Cabernet, Napa

Neurosis

Blanquette-de-Limoux - Red Irougely

199

Obesity	Alsace - White Bergerac - White Gaillac - Dry Montravel - Pouilly
	Gewurztraminer, Sonoma - Muscat of Alexandria - Pinot Blanc, Monterey - Emerald Riesling, Santa Clara - Johannisberg Riesling, Monterey - Sylvaner, Monterey - Pinot Noir Rosé, Sonoma
Osteoporosis	Côtes-de-Nuit - Côtes-du-Rhône - Médoc
	Pinot Noir, Napa - California Zinfandel - Cabernet, Sonoma
Phosphate loss	Dry or semi-dry champagne - Clairette-de-Die
	Champagne, Napa, Sonoma, Mendocino
Polio (prevention of)	Médoc - Mercurey
	Cabernet, Napa - Pinot Blanc, Sonoma
Prevention (of viral and infectious diseases)	Red Bordeaux - Red Burgundy - Côtes-du-Ventoux
	Ruby Cabernet, Santa Clara - California French Colombard - Zinfandel, Amador - Cabernet, Napa - Merlot, Napa - Cabernet, Sonoma - Pinot Noir, Napa - Pinot Noir, Sonoma
Rheumatism (chronic)	Dry champagne - Corbières - White Galliac - Minervois
	Champagne, Napa, Sonoma, Mendocino
Rickets	Saint-Emilion
	Cabernet, Sonoma
Senescence (old age)	Aloxe-Corton - Natural champagne
	Champagne, Napa, Sonoma, Mendocino
Sports (diets for)	Chablis - Côtes-de-Nuit
	Chardonnay, Sonoma - Chardonnay, Napa - Pinot Blanc, Napa - Pinot Blanc, Sonoma
Stimulants	Champagne brut - Pouilly-Fuissé - Médoc
	Champagne, Napa, Sonoma, Mendocino - Cabernet, Napa
Stomach prolapse	Dry Champagne or Brut
	Champagne, Napa, Sonoma, Mendocino - California Sparkling Muscat
Stomach (sluggishness)	Médoc
	Cabernet, Napa

Suppurations	Bourgueil - Chinon - Corsican wines - Lirac - Premiers Côtes-de-Bordeaux - Tavel - Madiran
	California Zinfandel - California Grenache
Tonics	Côtes-de-Nuit - Côtes-de-Beaune - Cahors - Corbières - Jurançon - Iroulegy - Roussillon wines
Tuberculosis	Champagne, dry or brut - Médoc - Mercurey
	Champagne, Napa, Sonoma, Mendocino - California Sparkling Muscat
Ulcers (skin)	Red Bordeaux - Red Burgundy
	Ruby Cabernet, Santa Clara - California French Colombard - Zinfandel, Amador - Cabernet, Napa - Merlot, Napa - Cabernet, Sonoma - Pinot Noir, Napa - Pinot Noir, Sonoma
Urine (retention)	Chablis - Gros-Plan - Muscadet - Pouilly-Fuissé - Sancerre - Savoie wines
	Chardonnay, Sonoma - Chardonnay, Napa - Pinot Blanc, Napa - Pinot Blanc, Sonoma
Urticaria	Corbières - Côtes-de-Ventoux - Médoc - Minervois
	Cabernet, Napa
Vegetarian (diet)	Médoc - Red Beaujolais
	Cabernet, Napa - California Zinfandel - California Gamay Beaujolais Nouveau - Gamay, Napa - Gamay Beaujolais, Monterey
Vitamin deficiency	All red wines
Weight-loss	Beaune red - Corsican wines
	Pinot Noir, Sonoma

CHAPTER XII

THE MARVELS OF CHOCOLATE

Christopher Columbus discovered chocolate in the Caribbean during his fourth voyage to the Indes in 1502.

The strange drink was first offered to him by the Aztec chief of an island where he had docked his boat. Columbus and his crew found the brew quite repulsive, and never tried it again. One might add that the natives' recipe was rather bitter and spicy.

So, it was not until Cortes discovered Mexico in 1519 that the Europeans really acquired a taste for chocolate. However, at first the crusaders of the Old World were more interested in its economic value.

Cocoa beans constituted the wealth of Mexico and were the only means of trade and barter in the land. Therefore, the Spaniards needed to obtain the beans in order to gain access to the local riches, particularly the gold. Moreover, since wine was not available, the Spanish soldiers eventually took to this "chocolaté," and noticed that "when you drink it, you can travel all day without being tired and without needing food."

They soon discovered they could lessen the bitterness with sugar, and add vanilla, cinnamon or aniseed to the cocoa. Thanks to the priestesses of Oaxaca [1], who came up with the first recipes, chocolate became delicious.

Hoping to make a fortune, the European colonists, who had understood the financial interest of their discovery, decided to take this product to the New World.

Chocolate quickly became part of Spanish mores. The colonists, upon their return to the motherland, could not do without this exotic product and introduced it to their fellow countrymen. The import market grew, and chocolate trade routes were established.

But it took many years for chocolate to cross the frontiers of Spain. It was not until the 17th century that it began to appear throughout the rest of Europe.

In France, chocolate made its debut in the court of Louis the XIII in 1615 when the king married Anne of Austria, daughter of Phillip the II, king of Spain. The child queen loved chocolate and introduced her "passion" to the rest of France. The Cardinal of Lyon, brother of Richelieu, often drank chocolate "to arouse high spirits and appease (his) rage and foul temper." As for Cardinal Mazarin [2], he would never travel without his personal Italian chocolate-maker. Every morning when he awoke, the Regent Phillip of Orléans, during the reign of Louis XIV, organized what would have been called a "chocolate party" if he had not been one to drink alone. To attend the Regent's parties was considered a high honor and privilege.

---

1. A town in Southern Mexico at the foot of the Sierra Madre mountains, founded in 1486 by the Aztecs and occupied by the Spaniards until 1522.
2. He succeeded Richelieu and was also a personal advisor to the king.

"Napoleon offering chocolate to Marshal Lefebvre after the fall of Danzig", May 1807
Bibliotheque Nationale

THE VIRTUES OF CHOCOLATE

Without a doubt, more has been written about chocolate than any other food. Who can remain indifferent to chocolate?

Besides its delicious taste, 17th and 18th century contemporaries exalted the therapeutic properties of this exotic beverage.

Chocolate was prescribed as an antidote to exhaustion and weakness. Today we can attribute its invigorating effects to a high magnesium content. Also rich in phosphorous, chocolate was used by "scholars" to give them intellectual sustenance.

Ecclesiastics found that chocolate helped them endure the fasts they regularly undertook, especially during Lent.

Most of our ancestors recognized the digestive wonders of chocolate. Brillat-Savarin, father of all food critics, wrote in his *Treatise on the Physiology of Taste*,

> "If one swallows a cup of chocolate only three hours after a copious lunch, everything will be perfectly digested and there will still be room for dinner."

He claims to have tested his hypothesis on a number of women who were always amazed and, ever since, never ceased to glorify him.

In her remarkable book on chocolate, Martine Jolly [3] quotes a certain Doctor Blegny, who described the merits of chocolate as an antidote to a broken heart.

---

3. Martine Jolly, *Chocolat : une passion dévorante*, R. Laffont.

"Those who love, and are unfortunate enough to suffer from the most universal of all gallant illnesses, will find (in chocolate) the most enlightening consolation."

Other 18th century contemporaries claimed that chocolate cured tuberculosis.

In a nutshell, those are the virtues of chocolate. If you love it, you will surely find others to add to the list.

If you are a chocolate aficionado, you may indulge in it, but certainly not in excessive amounts. If I were to claim you could eat it without scruples at every meal, you would find my method somewhat contradictory.

As delicious as chocolate may be, it is still a carbohydrate-lipid.

In order for it to represent only a slight imbalance in your diet, it must contain the least amount of carbohydrates possible. In other words, a lipid with a low carbohydrate content, is, in every way, compatible with our method.

First, we must select a high quality chocolate with at least 60% cocoa. The percentage of cocoa is always written on the chocolate wrapping. Chocolate with around 70% cocoa exists and is a far better alternative. Not only does a high cocoa content lessen the percentage of carbohydrates, but it also tastes much better.

The second strategy is to choose chocolate desserts with no flour or sugar (or very little). The chocolate mousse or the bitter chocolate cake (the recipes are in the appendix) are perfect examples. For the past ten years, these two recipes have been my specialties, and I can assure you that my family and friends are mad about them.

We must, nonetheless, emphasize the fact that chocolate remains a discrepancy, and should be treated as such.

It is, therefore, not allowed in Phase I.

During Phase II, it can be consumed under the conditions we have just specified; for dessert.

One of the best moments in the day to indulge in chocolate is in the middle of the afternoon on an empty stomach. Two or three squares of chocolate only create a slight dietary imbalance in relation to our standards. It has been proven [4] that chocolate is an anti-depressant and therefore should be preferably eaten when you are feeling low to raise your spirits or just to make yourself happy.

In any case, you should eat it in reasonable quantities and favor only high quality. The ideal chocolate should be dark, bitter and contain around 70% cocoa.

One last piece of advice to end this chapter, I suggest that if you decide to snack on a tablet of dark chocolate, be sure to limit yourself since chocolate is of an addicting nature. To stop your "chocoholism," drink a tall glass of fresh water.

---

4. See *Les Vertus thérapeutiques du chocolat*, Dr. H. Robert; Editions Artulen.

CHAPTER XIII

EXERCISE DOES NOT CAUSE WEIGHT-LOSS

In his song, "Tu t'laisses aller" ("You're lettin' yourself go"), the French singer Charles Aznavour advises his homely girlfriend to "Exercise a little to lose some weight!"

Yet another preconceived idea. Our dear Aznavour certainly did not have a weight problem, or he would have realized that, contrary to what everyone believes, *exercise has never caused anyone to lose weight.* When you became concerned with your excess weight, I suppose, like everyone else, you decided to take up a sport; either jogging or biking, or sometimes both at once.

Having tried both, I can guarantee you that the results are not positive.

Exercise is wonderful to unwind, to let off steam, to invigorate oneself, to get together with friends or to get out of the house. But, do not think it is the answer to losing weight if you continue to eat unhealthily like most of our contemporaries.

Exercising to lose weight is similar to the calorie myth.

When you take up a sport with the intention of shedding some pounds, you may have a tendency to measure your efforts according to how much you perspire.

What you are actually losing is water. Do not think you are "burning calories," because you are only spending energy from your temporary reserves (glycogen) which are fueled by your consumption of carbohydrates.

The first time you get back into exercising you may indeed notice (only with a very precise scale) about one-fourth of a pound difference in your weight.

If you have gotten into the habit of exercising regularly, every Saturday for example, your body will gradually readjust its "supply" with your new demands. And if your demands increase, well...! your body will quickly start stocking enough glycogen to satisfy your energy requirements.

You will very rapidly notice that not only are you not losing pounds, but you may be back at your initial weight. You may even have gained a little more. Remember the hungry dog who buries his bone? If your physical exertion increases, not only will your body produce more energy, as cautious as it is, it will also stock up its fat reserves. And so the vicious circle begins.

You decide to add 3 miles to your cycling route to outwit your body. But your little internal computer, understanding the laws of the market, will readjust its supply to meet your demands.

This is how, for a couple of ounces lost, you not only gain a couple more, but your health is put in serious jeopardy. In exercise, there is one rule we must never forget: "never push your body beyond its limits." You would never drive across the country in an old, dilapidated Volkswagen Bug,

Velocipede race in the Luxemburg gardens in Paris, 1818
Etching by Jules Duavaux
Bibliotheque Nationale

Bicycle and tricycle velocipede race in the Bois de Boulogne, close to Paris, 1886
Drawing by H. de Montant

so do not set goals for yourself that are too ambitious for your age, your physical condition or your level of training.

You should exercise for the reasons commonly stated or only for pleasure, but do not count on finding the solution to your weight problem if you have not decided to change your eating habits.

Adopting the eating method presented in this book when you take up exercise will enable you to accelerate the weight-loss process in Phase I, but even more importantly, your physical efforts will contribute to reharmonize your metabolic functions.

Physical exertion is particularly beneficial to the obese whose fat cells do not always acknowledge the insulin, thus leading the pancreas to produce a surplus amount (hyper-insulinism).

Moreover, obesity upsets thermogenesis so, paradoxically, the fatter the individual, the less energy is spent on a physical effort.

The alimentary principles of this method and a reasonable amount of physical exertion are entirely compatible and will contribute to the successful rediscovery of a normal weight.

CHAPTER XIV

A PRACTICE RUN IN ONE
OF THE FINER RESTAURANTS OF PARIS

Usually when one of my friends or colleagues asks me for advice with the serious intent of losing weight, I always suggest a practice run.

We go to a restaurant and I begin my explanations. The theory is important, but you will agree that practice is indispensable.

This is why, when I decided to write this book, I immediately planned to demonstrate, in a concrete way, how my method could be applied in some of the restaurants where I frequently ate.

First, I thought we could practice on a dozen Parisian restaurant menus. But I soon realized this would be tedious and boring for my reader, given the similarity of the drills.

Furthermore, I was in a quandary over what restaurants to select.

How could I avoid playing the role of restaurant critic or following the recommendations of others word for word?

How should I select the best Parisian restaurants, when many of them are outside the capital?

I, therefore, decided to elect only one. But which one? What would I base my choice on? Three stars in the Michelin Guide? The "Super four chef's hats" in the Gault-Millau guide? Or the one closest to my home or office?

As luck would have it, the decision was easier than I anticipated.

One Sunday afternoon on the Bordeaux-Paris train, I was rereading one of the first chapters of my book. At Tours, a fellow traveler, his charming wife and their lovely daughter took a seat in my compartment. He looked familiar despite the absence of his famous chef's hat. It was Joel Robuchon [1].

So, together, we will scrupulously study his February 1986 menu and apply the method that I hope you are firmly resolved to try.

---

1. Joel Robuchon's restaurant Jamin - 32, rue de Longchamp, 75016 Paris, Tel: (1) 47.27.12.27 - is the only restaurant in the history of the Michelin Guide to obtain a new star, consecutively, every year. It is one of the most exceptional restaurants in Paris, and Robuchon, in the words of a notable French critic, remains "the greatest of great chefs."

A restaurant in the Palais Royal in Paris in the 19th century
Carnavalet Museum

JAMIN

JOEL ROBUCHON
Meilleur Ouvrier de France 1976

JOEL ROBUCHON

Recipient of the Prize "Meilleur Ouvrier de France," 1976

MENU

Saucisson au foie gras *
Duck sausage with foie gras

Frivolité de saumon fumé au caviar
Smoked salmon and caviar

Lapereau mitonné en gelée aux légumes
Simmered baby rabbit in a vegetable aspic

Gelée de caviar à la crème de choux-fleur
Caviar gelée with a cauliflower purée

Salade de homard breton au Bolero
Breton lobster salad "au Bolero"

Ravioli de langoustine aux choux **
Prawn ravioli with cabbage

Foie gras chaud à la crème de lentilles **
Warm foie gras with cream of lentils

Galette de truffes aux oignons et lard fumé
Truffle crepes with onions and smoked bacon

Fricassé de langoustines aux champignons de courgettes
Prawn fricassee with mushrooms and zucchini

Medley d'huitres et de noix de Saint-Jacques au caviar *
Oysters and scallops with walnuts and caviar

Rouelles de homard à la vapeur aux herbes en civet
Steamed lobster with stewed herbs

Soupe crèmeuse au potiron
Cream of pumpkin soup

Entrée (Fish)

Merlan aux épices et aux encornets
Spiced whitefish and calamary

Etuvée de homard et de noix de Saint-Jacques aux truffes **
Baked lobster and scallops with truffles
- Served with fresh pasta -

Blanc de bar cuit en peau, sauce verjutée
White bass served with a verjuice sauce

Homard meunière aux fins aromates
Longtailed lobster with aromatic herbs

Entrée (Meats)

Ris de veau truffé aux asperges
Truffled calf sweetbreads with asparagus

Agneau pastoral aux herbes en salade
Pastoral lamb with herb salad

La fameuse tête de cochon mijotée "Ile de France"
Famous stewed pig's head "Ile de France"

Volaille truffée en Vessie, sauce fleurette
Truffled turkey in a cream sauce
- Served with fresh pasta -

Rôti d'agneau aux herbes, en croûte de sel **
Roast lamb with herbs in a salt crust

Mignonnettes de chevreuil poêlées à l'Aigre doux *
Filet of young goat stir-fried in a sweet and sour sauce

218

Cheese plate

Desserts

Chaud-froid de pommes à la pistache ou à la canelle *
Hot and cold apple pie with pistachio or cinnamon

Crème caramélisée à la cassonade *
Creme caramel with brown sugar

Gratin de Fruits *
Clafoutis de poires au miel **
Pears baked in batter with honey

Soupe de fruits au vin rouge *
Fruit soup with red wine

Mousse au chocolat *
Chocolate mousse

Tarte a l'orange **
Orange tart

Tarte au citron **
Lemon tart

Sorbets *
Nougat glacé au coulis de framboise
Frozen nougat draped in raspberry sauce

---

* Dishes containing carbohydrates, but in small quantities
** Dishes containing carbohydrates, enough to create an "imbalance"
In Phase I avoid all dishes with asterisks
In Phase II avoid all dishes with two asterisks.

We will study the menu in the same way we approached our method. We will look at both cases: weight-loss (Phase I) and weight maintenance (Phase II).

If you are in Phase I

Here is what you should select:

● *Aperitif*: Tomato juice or sparkling water with a slice of lemon.

● *Appetizer*: You may opt for any of the appetizers except those that contain even the slightest amount of carbohydrates.

You should avoid:

- "saucisson de canard au foie gras" *
  Duck sausage with foie gras,
- "ravioli de langoustines aux choux" **
  Prawn ravioli with cabbage,
- "foie gras chaud à la crème de lentilles," **
  Warm foie gras with cream of lentils,
- "Medley d'huîtres et de noix de Saint-Jacques au caviar" *
  Oysters and scallops with caviar.

● *Main Dish*: Again, you can pick any dish except those that contain carbohydrates, or are served with carbohydrates.

In Phase I, you should avoid choosing:

- "étuvée de homard et de noix de Saint-Jacques aux truffes" **
  Baked lobster and scallops with truffles,

220

- "le rôti d'agneau aux herbes en croûte de sel" **
  Roast lamb with herbs in a salty crust,
- "mignonnette de chevreuil poêlée à l'aigre doux" *
  Filet of young goat stir-fried in sweet and sour sauce.

These three dishes should be avoided because the first two are accompanied by fresh pasta and the third is served with a quince and huckleberry sauce.

● *Dessert*: Cheese only.

● *Beverage*: Water or a small glass of wine that can be enjoyed with the cheese at the end of the meal.

If you are in Phase II

As you have learned, in this phase you can order anything as long as you intelligently administer a proper balance.

First, try to identify what would upset your balance—in other words, anything that contains carbohydrates.

The following items are included in this category:
- "foie gras chaud à la crème de lentilles" **
  Warm foie gras with cream of lentils (because of the lentils),
- "ravioli aux langoustines aux choux" **
  Prawn ravioli with cabbage,
- the two dishes served with fresh pasta (the baked lobster and the roast lamb), **
- desserts **.

If you wish to order a dessert—which is what I would recommend since they are excellent—in your entrée selection, avoid one of the two dishes served with fresh pasta. If, on the other hand, you decide you cannot resist the fresh pasta, avoid one of the appetizers we already mentioned, and if you really want a dessert, choose a sorbet*, a "gratin de fruit"* or a "crème caramel"* which contain only a small amount of carbohydrates.

As always, avoid the bread (homemade at Robuchon's), but you may drink whatever you wish (always in reasonable amounts), starting with a glass of champagne as an aperitif.

CONCLUSION

I hope that in reading this book you have found the answers to your questions. In any case, I hope you have enjoyed it.

I, for one, took great pleasure in writing this book, because the research I did enabled me to organize information in my mind that I have haphazardly learned over the years.

The greatest conclusion I have come to, supported by my research and synthesizing, has become my conviction:

We are what we eat!

In other words, our physical condition is a result of what we have consumed in the past. And since I am speaking to a large audience of "managers," I can freely say, as I am sure you have already understood: *your energy, dynamism, competitiveness, ambition and strength all rely on your diet.*

If you learn to manage what you eat, you will, in sum, be able to manage your life.

Modern Man is unfortunately no longer a very sensible being. He has lost most of his wisdom. Today he is able to walk on the moon, but does not know how to manage his diet.

223

Zoologists take great interest in studying animals' eating habits. Herein lies the key to survival.

When the female monkey is no longer fertile, when a bear's hide has lost its fur, when the lion becomes docile or when the elephant loses its memory, the zoologist verifies and adjusts the animal's diet.

When, at the dawn of the 21st century, the average man wakes up to a frightening rash on his face, a splitting headache, or breath more fetid than an open sewer, it is highly probable that his doctor will not even ask about his diet. Animals and machines often get better attention than humans.

If the gas station attendant mistakenly puts diesel fuel in your BMW, you will probably raise havoc. You know what kind of fuel your car requires.

If you offer a T-Bone steak to a giraffe, he probably will not touch it even if he has not eaten in over a week. Animals instinctively know what does not agree with their metabolism. But man, this superior mammal, graced with intelligence and language, is, in fact, the only animal who can be fed just about anything and he will blindly accept it without instinctively expressing reticence or disapproval.

Governments of industrialized countries should be more concerned with their populations' eating habits, and give priority to this atrocious problem.

Some time ago I visited Disney World in Florida and, as I stood among a typically American crowd, I was truly scandalized by the obesity I saw. Approximately 18% of all Americans are obese or will be obese (i.e. about one out of every five Americans).

Obesity, in the United States, has become a social phenomenon, accepted and integrated into everyday life. There are fashion lines created especially for the hefty woman, and business suits available in sizes Extra-Extra Large.

This situation, and the all too scarce experts have agreed, results from a collective intoxication from bad carbohydrates. The most distressing fact is that the greatest percentage of obese people are among today's youth. This proves that the phenomenon is directly linked to eating habits developed after the last war. In France, I believe we will be able to resist because of our culinary traditions. This occurrence, however, is in an embryonic stage in France, and is growing. A number of hamburger joints are establishing themselves in all our major cities. Moreover, statistics show that the national consumption rate of soft drinks here is booming, and we can thereby conclude that the collective poisoning from bad carbohydrates is well on its way in Europe.

Yielding to publicity and practicality, we are involuntarily encouraging our children to develop eating habits we would not necessarily accept ourselves. In a few years, it may be too late to do anything.

Many people could explain to you in detail how to get a car to drive 100,000 miles, but they do not know how to prolong the lives of their children. Tragically enough, it is not a generally widespread concern.

The human body is a remarkable "machine," capable of enduring so much, to the point that it no longer knows when it has reached "the danger zone."

Women are generally a bit more resistant than men, since they are endowed with greater sensitivity (and I am only referring to physical sensitivity). Women, therefore, are more easily able to adopt a reasonable mode of conduct, when they must, and can therefore take greater care of their bodies.

A man, because of his "virility," by nature does not know his limits. He will push himself too far, until his body resists. Like a rock, he will endure all the excessive physical effort he takes upon himself, and one day "the idol with feet of clay" will crumble.

Your body has recorded all the nutritional mistakes you have made since childhood, and has undertaken a number of procedures to handle them. You probably have felt the side effects of these reactions (headaches, stomach pains, digestive troubles, liver problems). Your body has expressed signs of saturation or weakness by becoming more sensitive.

The symptoms vary from one individual to another, but the underlying reason is always the same—an unhealthy diet.

Consider yourself lucky, because, by looking for a means to weight-loss, you have found the solution to a number of other ailments from which you have been suffering—particularly a lack of vitality.

This is exactly what happened to me a few of years ago.

When I was in college, I was studying at an institute that prepared students for high administrative jobs and politics, although I chose a completely different course.

The first day of classes, the Director gathered the students to give us the following message:

"As Director of this establishment, my only goal is *to teach you to read, write and speak.*"

As the author of this book, my only goal has been *to teach you how to eat.*

APPENDICES

APPENDIX #1

CLASSIFICATION OF ALLOWED FOODS
PHASE I: WEIGHT-LOSS

APPETIZERS	ENTREES	VEGETABLES	DESSERTS
EGGS	MEATS	TOMATOES	YOGURT
COLD CUTS	(except liver)	SPINACH	COTTAGE CHEESE
SALADS:	COLD CUTS	ENDIVES	CHEESES
- TOMATOES	FISH (all)	SPINACH LETTUCE	
- STRING BEANS	POULTRY	WATERCRESS	
- ENDIVES	RABBIT	ICEBURG LETTUCE	
- CUCUMBERS	LOBSTER	RED LEAF LETTUCE	
- CAULIFLOWER	CRAYFISH	EGGPLANT	
RADISHES	EGGS	CELERY	
LEEKS		CABBAGE	
MUSHROOMS	*SEASONING:*	CAULIFLOWER	
ASPARAGUS		SAUERKRAUT	
CELERY	BUTTER	STRING BEANS	
TUNA	OLIVE OIL	TURNIPS	
FRESH SALMON	PEANUT OIL	LEEKS	
SMOKED SALMON	MARGARINE	BELL PEPPERS	
SARDINES	BEARNAISE SAUCE	SQUASH	
MUSSELS	SALT	BROCCOLI	
CRAB	PEPPER	SORREL	
LOBSTER	ONIONS	FENNEL	
CRAYFISH	GARLIC	MUSHROOMS	
	SHALLOTS		
	HERBS		

Note: Be careful of prohibited "parasites" often found in salads (rice, corn, croutons, carrots, etc.). Keep in mind that this chart does not contain *all* the allowed foods but only a sample of some common ones. You should be able to determine others after reading this book.

229

APPENDIX #2

CLASSIFICATION OF ALLOWED FOODS
PHASE II: WEIGHT MAINTENANCE

ENTREES	ENTREES	VEGETABLES	DESSERTS
FOIE GRAS*	MEATS (all)	TOMATOES	RASPBERRIES*
EGGS	COLD CUTS	SPINACH	STRAWBERRIES*
COLD CUTS	FISH (all)	ENDIVES	BLACKBERRIES*
SALADS:	POULTRY	SPINACH LETTUCE	YOGURT
- TOMATOES	RABBIT	WATERCRESS	COTTAGE CHEESE
- STRING BEANS	LOBSTER	RED LEAF LETTUCE	CHEESES
- ENDIVES	CRAYFISH	ICEBURG LETTUCE	"BAVAROIS"*
- WALNUTS*	EGGS	EGGPLANT	STRAWBERRY
- CUCUMBERS		CELERY	SHORTCAKE
- CAULIFLOWER		CABBAGE	CHOCOLATE
- MUSHROOMS	*SEASONING:*	CAULIFLOWER	MOUSSE*
RADISHES		SAUERKRAUT	SORBET*
LEEKS	BUTTER	STRING BEANS	- RASPBERRY
LETTUCE	OLIVE OIL	TURNIPS	GRATIN*
CELERY	PEANUT OIL	LEEKS	- STRAWBERRY
HEARTS OL PALM*	MARGARINE	BELL PEPPERS	
AVOCADOS*	MAYONNAISE	SQUASH	
TUNA	BEARNAISE SAUCE	BROCCOLI	
FRESH SALMON	SALT	FENNEL	
SMOKED SALMON	PEPPER	SORREL	
SARDINES	MUSTARD*	MUSHROOMS	
MUSSELS	ONIONS	SALSIFY*	
CRAB	GARLIC		
SHRIMP	SHALLOTS		
PRAWNS	HERBS		
LOBSTER			
CRAYFISH			
OYSTERS*			
SCALLOPS*			

Note: The foods marked with an asterisk are allowed if they are in eaten in moderate amounts. Refrain from eating more than two per meal. According to the method, anything not listed should be avoided, but certain "discrepancies" are possible. Refer to the chapter on Phase II to learn how to manage and master your dietary discrepancies.

230

APPENDIX #3

CHOCOLATE RECIPES

CHOCOLATE MOUSSE

Makes 6 to 8 servings

Ingredients

- 14 oz. quality dark chocolate (2 tablets) with at least 60% cocoa
- 8 eggs
- 3 tbs. rum
- 1 orange
- 4 tsps. ground coffee
- a pinch of salt

Equipment

- 1 electric beater
- 1 large double boiler
- 1 grater
- 2 large bowls
- 1 spatula

Break the chocolate in pieces and put into double boiler. Make a half cup of strong coffee or espresso and add to chocolate with the rum. Melt the chocolate over low heat and smooth mixture with the spatula. If it is too thick, add water.

While the chocolate is melting, grate the orange peel (only use the top part of the skin, the white pith is bitter) and add half to the chocolate mixture. Break the eggs and separate the whites from the yolks. Put in two separate bowls. Beat the egg whites with a pinch of salt until they are very stiff. Lightly whisk the yolks, then add to chocolate mixture. Mix to obtain a smooth and homogenous mixture. Add to whites. Make sure there are no unmixed pieces of chocolate or egg whites at the bottom of the bowl.

Put the mousse in the refrigerator (you can pour it into another bowl if you prefer), but first sprinkle the remaining orange zest on top.

Make the mousse at least five hours prior to serving. Ideally, make it a day before.

BITTER CHOCOLATE CAKE

Ingredients

- 14 oz. quality dark chocolate (2 tablets) with at least 60% cocoa
- 2 1/2 sticks of butter (10 oz.)
- 2 tbs. cognac
- 7 eggs
- 1 orange
- 4 tsps. ground coffee
- 1/4 cup of flour

Equipment

- 1 electric beater
- 1 large double boiler
- 1 cake mold
- 1 grater
- 1 spatula
- 1 large bowl

Break the chocolate in pieces and put into double boiler. Make a half cup of strong coffee or espresso and add to chocolate with cognac. Cut the butter in cubes and put it together with the chocolate. Melt chocolate to obtain a smooth and creamy mixture.

Beat the eggs in a bowl while gradually adding the flour. Make sure there are no lumps.

Grate orange peel and add half to chocolate mixture. The orange is optional. If you do not like orange-flavored chocolate, a superb combination nonetheless, do not add it. If you do, be sure to grate only the top part of the orange since the white pith is bitter. If possible, use a Teflon mold. Be sure it is big enough since the cake rises 20% during baking. If you do not have an appropriately sized Teflon mold, use aluminum foil greased with butter. Make sure the foil rises above the mold.

Add the warm chocolate mixture to the well-beaten eggs and mix until smooth and even. Fill the mold and sprinkle the remaining orange zest on top. Bake at 250° to 350° for 35 minutes.

Let cool at room temperature for 45 minutes before serving.

Cut thin slices (approx. 1/2 inch) that you can serve with two or three tablespoons of custard.

If you make a homemade custard, substitute artificial sweetener for the sugar.

One last piece of advice: if you keep the cake in the refrigerator, take it out at least four hours prior to serving, or the cold may cause it to lose its moistness.

Dr. Hervé Robert

Nutritionist

with the collaboration of
Professor Attilio Giacosa,
Head of Nutrition at the
National Cancer Institute (Genoa, Italy)

TECHNICAL APPENDIX
for
Dine Out and Lose Weight

This document is especially intended for doctors and dietary specialists. Its primary aim is to clarify the concepts of the Montignac Method.

TECHNICAL APPENDIX I

by Doctor Hervé Robert

BIOGRAPHY

Doctor Hervé Robert was born in Paris in 1946. A graduate of the Paris School of Medicine in 1974, he practiced for more than ten years in the rheumatology ward in a local hospital where he also participated in the operation of an analgesic center.

In order to broaden his therapeutic range, he consequently studied acupuncture, homeopathy, mesotherapy and trace elements. Today he teaches these alternative medical disciplines to his colleagues.

He is the president of the Medical Association of Neuro-Acupuncture and Biostimulation. Acutely aware of the importance of a well-balanced diet in the prevention of certain diseases, he has devoted the last several years to personal research on nutrition.

He is the director of the Institut Vitalité et Nutrition, a non-profit organization that unites all French doctors and scientists who practice the Montignac method.

In addition to public conferences and personal seminars for various companies, he helped with the distribution of the Montignac Method, in collaboration with doctors from France and other countries in the nutritional field.

The former editor of a medical review, he is also the author of a number of articles and several books (Ed. Artulen).

DIETARY BALANCE IN THE MONTIGNAC METHOD DIET

- should be rich in protein;
- should only include 5.25 ounces of meat per day;
- should select poultry rather than meat;
- should include fish (10.5 ounces per week minimum);
- should contain a daily consumption of dairy products (for calcium), preferably non-fat.

FATS

- Choose lipids that limit the risks of cardiovascular diseases;
- Limit your consumption of saturated fats (meat, cold cuts, eggs, full fat dairy products);
- Increase your consumption of mono and polyunsaturated vegetable fats (olives, safflower oil);
- Augment your intake of polyunsaturated animal fats (fish).

CARBOHYDRATES

- Elect carbohydrates that prevent hyperglycemic and hyperinsulinic peaks;
- For breakfast, eat breads rich in fiber (whole wheat bread) and cereal;
- Eat fruits;
- Eliminate sugar and refined carbohydrates;
- Use an artificial sweetener if necessary (i.e. Nutrasweet).

FIBER

- Considerably increase the fiber content in your diet: fruits and vegetables (raw or cooked) can be eaten at breakfast and during other meals to provide a healthy daily fiber intake;
- Bring legumes back into your diet.

BEVERAGES

- In the weight-loss phase, it is preferable to drink only water, especially between meals;
- Eliminate chemically sweetened beverages (sodas);

- Avoid distilled alcohols;
- Do not drink too much coffee. Coffee increases the cholesterol levels and stimulates insulin secretion;

FOOD COMPOSITION

Because the Montignac method does not ask you to count calories or weigh your foods, food choices should be made according to their biochemical composition. The foods we eat are made up of the following components:
- proteins
- carbohydrates or sugars
- lipids or fats
- fibers
- water
- mineral salts
- trace elements
- vitamins

In terms of weight-loss, the first four elements are of the most interest to us. However, the others also deserve a few words.

Despite the rich and varied types of food that exist in our countries, we are facing deficiencies in trace elements (selenium, iron, germanium), in mineral salts (magnesium) and in vitamins (folic acid). This is particularly due to the deterioration of the soil.

Although they do not result in major diseases, these minor disequilibria can favor metabolic troubles which explain certain cases of chronic fatigue.

Losing weight means losing fatty mass and not just urinating to eliminate a few pounds of water! Nevertheless, many doctors still prescribe diuretics that only eliminate water. This type of treatment is useless, illusory and even dangerous since it also causes the elimination of useful minerals. In addition, the organism reacts like a sponge, recovering lost water as soon as it can.

It is also important to realize that thyroid extracts rarely affect fatty mass. Instead, they attack the lean muscular mass. They weaken the muscles (causing cramps and fatigue) and can lead to serious troubles in the cardiac muscle. They also disrupt the metabolic function of the thyroid gland. The thyroid is seldom responsible for obesity).

PROTEINS

A) GENERALITIES

Foods containing nitrogen are called proteins and are vital to nutrition. Proteins are large molecules composed of thousands of amino acids. Amino acids are the building blocks of proteins. There are approximately 20 amino acids required by the

240

human body. Among these, eight must be obtained through food sources since the body is unable to synthesize them independently. These amino acids are isoleucine, leucine, lysine, methionine, phenylalanine, theonine, tryptophane and valine.

These proteins are indispensable to the human body because they:
- build cellular structures,
- are an energy source in the citric acid cycle,
- combine RNA and DNA, which are essential to cellular reproduction,
- synthesize certain hormones and neurotransmitters (e.g. thyroxin and adrenalin),
- blend together bile acids, melanin and respiratory pigments.

Daily protein intake for children and teen-agers should be approximately 60 grams and 90 grams respectively. For adults, the protein intake should represent 15% of the daily energy intake, which is approximately 1 gram per kilo per day. Women should get a minimum of 55 grams and men a minimum of 70 grams.

In 1985, the major sources of protein in the American diet were meat, poultry, and fish (43.4%); dairy products (20.6%); and grain products (19%). On the average, protein intake in the United States is 20-30 percent above the RDA. (Nutrition Monitoring in the United States, pg. 51).

B) PROTEIN SOURCES

1) Animals as a Source of Protein

Proteins are found in meat, cold cuts, poultry, fish, seafood, eggs, milk and dairy products.

The concentration of proteins in 3.5 oz (100 grams) of food is:

* MEAT			* EGGS		
- veal	.70	oz (20.0 g)	- per egg	.45	oz (13.0 g)
- mutton	.56	oz (17.0 g)	* FISH		
- beef	.56	oz (17.0 g)	- tuna	.95	oz (27.0 g)
- pork	.56	oz (17.0 g)	- spotted dogfish	.90	oz (25.0 g)
- lamb	.53	oz (16.0 g)	- mullet	.77	oz (22.0 g)
- salami	.90	oz (25.0 g)	- sardines, ray fish, trout.	.70	oz (19.0 g)
* COLD CUTS			- mackerel	.65	oz (19.0 g)
- baked ham	.75	oz (20.0 g)	- hake, gilt-head, sole	.60	oz (17.0 g)
- smoked ham	.50	oz (15.0 g)	* SEAFOOD		
- hot dogs	.50	oz (15.0 g)	- shrimp	.90	oz (25.0 g)
* POULTRY			- crayfish	.80	oz (23.0 g)
- game animals	.77	oz (22.0 g)	- lobster	.55	oz (16.0 g)
- duck	.77	oz (22.0 g)	- squid	.60	oz (17.0 g)
- chicken	.75	oz (21.0 g)	- scallops	.60	oz (17.0 g)
- turkey	.70	oz (20.0 g)	- mussels	.40	oz (11.0 g)
			- oysters	.30	oz (8.0 g)

* DAIRY PRODUCTS

- cow's milk	.10	oz	(3.5 g)	- yogurt	.20 oz (5.2 g)	
- sweetened condensed milk	.32	oz	(9.0 g)	- cheeses	.10 to .55 oz (3-6 g)	
- unsweetened condensed milk	.25	oz	(7.0 g)			

2) Plant and protein sources

- soy	1.25	oz	(35.0 g)	- beans (red cooked)	.30	oz	(8.0 g)
- wheat germ	.93	oz	(26.0 g)	- chestnuts	.30	oz	(8.0 g)
- spirulin (algae)	.90	oz	(25.0 g)	- rice (cooked)	.30	oz	(8.0 g)
- grilled salted peanuts	.90	oz	(25.0 g)	- bread (white)	.25	oz	(7.0 g)
- almonds	.65	oz	(19.0 g)	- lentils (cooked)	.85	oz	(24.0 g)
- oats	.50	oz	(14.0 g)	- white beans (cooked)	.75	oz	(21.0 g)
- rye bread	.45	oz	(13.0 g)	- chick peas	.20	oz	(6.0 g)
- wheat bread	.42	oz	(12.0 g)	- cocoa (powder)	.60	oz	(17.0 g)
- barley	.40	oz	(11.5 g)	- whole wheat noodles	.30	oz	(8.0 g)
- walnuts	.36	oz	(10.2 g)	- white flour noodles	.10	oz	(3.0 g)
- corn	.32	oz	(9.0 g)	- potatoes (cooked)	.07	oz	(2.0 g)
				- chocolate	.30	oz	(8.0 g)

C) PROTEINS' FOOD VALUES

Except for the egg, the different animal and vegetable proteins do not contain the necessary balance of amino acids. If one amino acid is missing, it can constitute a limiting factor which can impede the assimilation of other amino acids. Therefore, animal and vegetable proteins must be combined in the diet to create this needed balance.

A diet made up exclusively of vegetable amino acids is not considered a balanced diet as it lacks cysteine. This deficiency can cause hair and nail problems.

Similarly, a protein intake based solely on meat and fish will lead to a lack of lysine which can block the absorption of acids.

In order to obtain a proper protein intake, a balance must be struck:
- among essential amino acids,
- between the required amino acids and others,
- between vegetable and animal proteins,
- among proteins, vitamins A & C and trace elements.

D) TO LOSE WEIGHT

It is important to remember that proteins are crucial dietary elements. They do not cause weight gain and are even sometimes used in hospital weight-loss programs. They are even included in high-protein diets used to treat paradoxal obesity. What is important is the type of fats as well as the foods they are associated with in the diet.

BIBLIOGRAPHY

APFELBAUM M., FORRAT C., NILLUS P.	*Diététique et nutrition* Ed. Masson 1989
BRINGER J., RICHARD J.L., MIROUZE J.	*Evaluation de l'état nutritionnel protéique* Rev. Prat. 1985, 35, 3, 17-22
RUASSE J.P.	*Les composants de la matière vivante* Ed. L'indispensable en nutrition 1988
RUASSE J.P.	*Des protides, pourquoi, combien ?* Ed. L'indispensable en nutrition 1987

CARBOHYDRATES

A) INTRODUCTION

Carbohydrates are ternary compounds (made up of carbon, hydrogen and oxygen). They are so called because their general formula is $Cn(H_2O)n$. This category covers monosaccharides (ie. simple sugars) that cannot be decomposed by hydrolysis, and polysaccharides, which on hydrolysis yield one or more monosaccharides.

B) GLYCEMIA

Glucose is the body's principle fuel. It is stored in the form of glycogen in the muscles and the liver. Glycemia is the amount of glucose in the blood; on an empty stomach the usual glycemic level is 5.5 mmol/l or 1 g/l.

After a carbohydrate has been absorbed on an empty stomach, the blood sugar levels vary as follows:
- first, glycemia increases (according to the type of carbohydrate consumed);
- second, insulin is secreted by the pancreas; this causes the glycemic level to decrease once the glucose has entered the cells;
- third, glycemia reverts back to its normal level of 5.5 mmol/l.

243

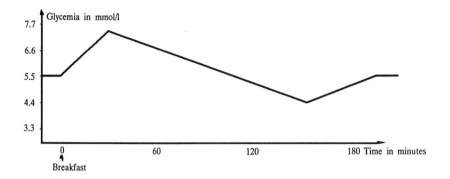

C) CARBOHYDRATES AND THEIR CHEMICAL FORMULAE

1) Simple sugars (or oligosaccharides)

These are composed of one molecule. They include:
- glucose (in fruits, honey, corn, wheat)
- fructose (in fruits, honey)
- galactose (in milk)

2) Disaccharides

These are composed of two simple sugar molecules. They include:
- saccharose (glucose + fructose) is extracted from beets or sugar cane. Saccharose is also found in carrots and fruits.
- lactose (glucose + galactose), the sugar in mammal's milk.
- maltose (glucose + glucose), a malt extract, which is the sugar in beer.

3) Polysaccharides

- glycogen from liver
- starch, in which the molecule contains about 200 glucose molecules. It is found in all starchy foods:

Cereals	wheat (flour, bread, semolina, pasta)	Grains	peas
	corn (popcorn, cornflakes)		chick peas
	rice		white beans
Tubers	potatoes		lentils
Roots	rutabaga		peanuts

The above classification was long the basis for the theory that since oligosaccharides and disaccharides have a simple molecular structure, they demanded only limited intestinal processing, and were thus, rapidly absorbed in the small intestine. They were consequently named "quick sugars".

244

Conversely, polysaccharides, made up of starches with more than 200 glucose molecules, were thought to require a long hydrolysis due to their complex molecular structure. Their absorption was believed to take longer. They were named "slow sugars".

In fact, this categorization was purely theoretical. The glycemic peak for all carbohydrates, both "quick" and "slow", taken individually on an empty stomach, occur at almost the same time, 20 to 25 minutes after initial ingestion.

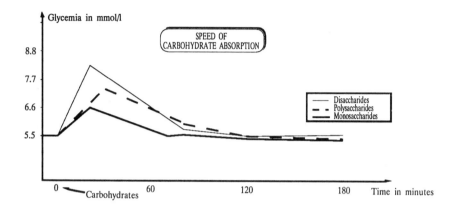

However, when several types are eaten together, for example in a meal, the absorption rate depends on:
- the type of food
- how it was prepared
- the caloric value of the meal

- the meal composition: the presence of fiber or proteins slows down starch digestion
- how quickly the gastro-intestinal tract is emptied (this process is faster for liquids).

D) GLYCEMIC INDEX

Rather than being concerned with absorption speed, it is more germane to study carbohydrates in terms of the glycemic increase they can induce.

The level of blood sugar increase caused by ingesting a given carbohydrate is defined by the glycemic index established by Dr. P.A. Crapo in 1976. The glycemic level corresponds to the triangular surface area under the blood sugar curve induced by the food tested. Glucose is arbitrarily given a rating of 100. The index of other foods is calculated using the formula:

$$\frac{\text{triangle surface area for the food tested}}{\text{triangle surface area for glucose}} \times 100$$

245

The higher the blood sugar increase induced by the tested carbohydrate, the higher the glycemic index.

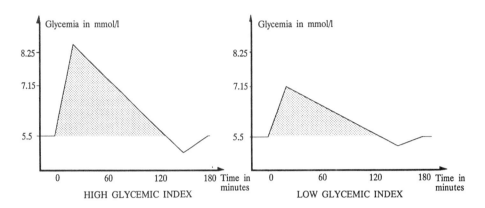

Glycemic index for different carbohydrates:

Maltose	110	Whole wheat bread	50
Glucose	100	Oatmeal	50
White bread	95	Whole wheat pasta	45
Instant mashed potatoes	95	Fresh white beans	40
Highly refined sugar	95	Whole rye bread	40
Honey, jam	90	Green peas	40
Cornflakes	85	Whole grain cereal	35
Carrots	85	Multi-grain bread	35
White sugar	75	Milk products	35
Corn	70	Fresh fruits	35
French bread	70	Wild rice	35
White rice	70	Lentils	30
Beets	70	Chick peas	30
Cookies	70	Milk	30
Boiled potatoes	70	Dried beans	30
Pasta	65	Dark chocolate	22
Sherbet	65	Fructose	20
Banana	60	Soy	15
Grapes	60	Peanuts	15
Bran cereal	50	Green vegetables	< 15
Brown rice	50		

It is imperative to keep in mind that chemical processing of foods increases their glycemic index (cornflakes = 85 whereas corn = 70; instant mashed potatoes = 95 whereas boiled potatoes = 70).

246

When the glycemic index is equal to or greater than 60, the initial glycemic peak favors hyperinsulinism. In order to simplify matters, carbohydrates in this category are called "bad carbohydrates." On the other hand, the other carbohydrates, whose glycemic indices are inferior to 50, are due to "good carbohydrates."

Just as chemical processing increases a food's glycemic index, foods consumed in their natural state have a low glycemic index. Whole grain cereals and whole wheat breads containing fiber, vitamins and trace elements, are quite effective in lowering the body's blood sugar peaks.

Composition of 100 g or 3.5 ounces of wheat flour:

	whole wheat flour Ounces Grams	refined white flour Ounces Grams
proteins	.49 oz (14.0 g)	.330 oz (9.6 g)
fats	.07 oz (2.0 g)	.035 oz (1.0 g)
carbohydrates	2.54 oz (72.0 g)	2.680 oz (76.0 g)
fibers	.40 oz (11.9 g)	.010 oz (0.3 g)
	Milligrams	
calcium	41.0 mg	16.0 mg
phosphorous	370.0 mg	87.0 mg
magnesium	90.0 mg	25.0 mg
iron	3.3 mg	0.8 mg
Vitamin B1	550.0 mg	63.0 mg
Vitamin B2	116.0 mg	
	43.0 mg	

A comparative study of the glycemic effect and insulin levels after absorption by healthy subjects and non-insulino-dependant diabetics of whole wheat or refined flour gave the following results:

	whole wheat flour	refined white flour
Healthy subjects - Glycemia triangle - surface area (mmol/l/mn)	93	141
- Insulinemia triangle - surface area (mU/l/mn)	3,095	3,992
Diabetic subjects - Glycemia triangle - surface area (mmol/l/mn)	553	683
- Insulinemia triangle - surface area (mmol/l/mn)	3,397	4,157

The presence of fibers in whole wheat flour helps diminish blood sugar and insulin peaks.

The following graph shows that the glycemic peak is lower for brown rice than it is for white rice. As the degree of processing of a carbohydrate increases, so does the glycemic peak it causes.

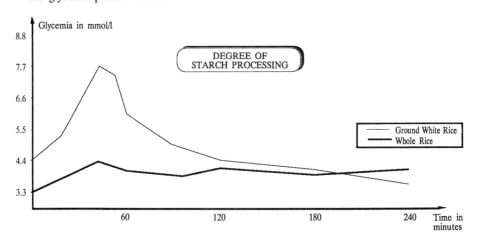

Moreover:
- the glycemic index rises when foods are cooked.
- the glycemic index lowers during a balanced meal. For example, the glycemic index is 65 for spaghetti alone, but drops to 30 if the pasta is absorbed as part of a balanced meal. The speed with which the gastro-intestinal tract empties is slower because of the presence of proteins and fats.

248

In fact, when a carbohydrate is absorbed, it produces an insulin peak that is even stronger than the glycemic peak. An index of blood insulin levels should be established to help obese persons determine which carbohydrates they can most safely consume.

E) GLYCONEOGENESIS

Glucose is produced from carbohydrates. However, glucose from carbohydrates is not the body's only source of glycogen. The Krebs cycle is the key of the metabolism: the organism is capable of manufacturing glucose from amino acids or from fatty acids (a process called glyconeogenesis).

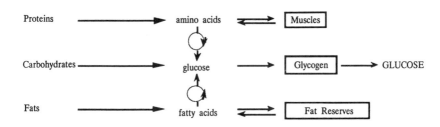

Taken to extremes, it could be assumed that the organism could survive without carbohydrates since it is capable of glyconeogenesis. Atkins took this extreme position by completely eliminating carbohydrates from his weight-loss method. However, the absence of carbohydrates, resulted in ketosis, causing metabolic disorders. In addition, Atkins made no distinction among the type of fat prescribed, so that his diet, too rich in fats, created an increased risk of cardiovascular disease.

The Montignac method avoids Atkins' error by preserving all carbohydrates with a low glycemic index in Phase I (weight-loss), and reintroducing carbohydrates with a medium glycemic index in Phase II (weight stabilization). Moreover, the method gives exact advice on the choice of fats.

From this explanation of the body's ability to produce sugar using carbohydrates, many parents will perhaps be better able to understand the error they may be committing when they give their children white sugar. Perhaps they believe it is important for their growth and development. They therefore ply their children with candy, cakes, and sugary soft drinks, and fail to realize that the ingestion of glucose is not necessary because the need for glucose can be fully satisfied through the ingestion of (good) carbohydrates which help ensure healthy growth and development.

BANTLE J.P., LAINE D.C.	*Post prandial glucose and insulin responses to meals containing different carbohydrates in normal and diabetic subjects* New Engl. J. Med. 1983, 309, 7-12
BORNET F.	*Place des glucides simples et des produits amylacés dans l'alimentation des diabétiques en 1985.* Fondation RONAC. Paris
CRAPO P.A.	*Plasma, glucose and insulin responses to orally administered simple and complex carbohydrates* Diabetes 1976, 25, 741-747
CRAPO P.A.	*Post prandial plasma, glucose and insulin response to different complex carbohydrates* Diabetes 1977, 26, 1178-1183
CRAPO P.A.	*Comparison of serum glucose-insulin and glucagon responses to different types of carbohydrates in non-insulin dependent diabetic patients* Am. J. Clin. Nutr. 1981, 34, 84-90
CHEW L.	*Applications of glycemic index to mixed meals* Am. J. Clin. Nutr. 1988, 47, 53-56
DANQUECHIN-DORVAL E.	*Rôle de la phase gastrique de la digestion sur la biodisponibilité des hydrates de carbone et leurs effets métaboliques* Journées de diabétologie de l'Hôtel-Dieu 1975
DESJEUX J.F.	*Glycémie, insuline et acides gras dans le plasma d'adolescents sains après ingestion de bananes* Med. et Nutr. 1982, 18, 2, 127-130
FEWKES D.W.	*Sucrose* Science Progres 1971, 59, 25, 39
GABREAU T., LEBLANC H.	*Les modifications de la vitesse d'absorption des glucides* Med. et Nutr. 1983, XIX, 6, 447-449
GUILLAUSSEAU P.J., GUILLAUSSEAU-SCHOLER C.	*Effet hyperglycémiant des aliments* Gaz. Med. Fr. 1989, 96, 30, 61-63
HEATON K.W.	*Particule size of wheat, maïze and oat test meals : effects on plasma, glucose and insulin responses and on the rate of starch digestion in vitro* Am. J. Clin. Nutr. 1988, 47, 675-682
HERAUD G.	*Glucides simples, glucides complexes*
HODORA D.	*Glucides simples, glucides complexes et glucides indigestibles* Gaz. Med. Fr. 1981, 88, 37, 5, 255-259
JENKINS D.J.A.	*Glycemic index of foods : a physiological basis for carbohydrates exchange* Am. J. Clin. Nutr. 1981, 34, 362-366
JENKINS D.J.A.	*Dietary carbohydrates and their glycemic responses* J.A.M.A. 1984, 2, 388-391
JENKINS D.J.A.	*Wholemeal versus wholegrain breads : proportion of whole or cracked grains and the glycemic response* Br. Med. J. 1988, 297, 958-960
JIAN R.	*La vidange d'un repas ordinaire chez l'homme : étude par la méthode radio-isotopique* Nouv. Presse Med. 1979, 8, 667-671
KERIN O'DEA	*Physical factor influencing post prandial glucose and insulin responses to starch* Am. J. Clin. Nutr. 1980, 33, 760-765
NOUROT J.	*Relationship between the rate of gastric emptying and glucose insulin responses to starchy food in young healthy adults* Am. J. Clin. Nutr. 1988, 48, 1035-1040

250

NATHAN D.	*Ice-cream in the diet of insulin-dependent diabetic patients* J.A.M.A. 1984, 251, 21, 2825-2827
NICOLAIDIS S.	*Mode d'action des substances de goût sucré sur le métabolisme et sur la prise alimentaire. Les sucres dans l'alimentation* Cool. Sc. Fond. Fr. Nutr. 1981
O'DONNELL L.J.D.	*Size of flour particles and its relation to glycemia, insulinoemia and calonic disease.* Br. Med. J. 17 June 1984, 298, 115-116
REAVEN C.	*Effects of source of dietary carbohydrates on plasma, glucose and insulin to test meals in normal subjects* Am. J. Clin. Nutr. 1980, 33, 1279-1283
ROUX E.	*Index glycémique* Gaz. Med. Fr. 1988, 95, 18, 77-78
RUASSE J.P.	*Des glucides, pourquoi, comment ?* Collection « L'indispensable en nutrition » 1987
SCHLIENGER J.L.	*Signification d'une courbe d'hyperglycémie orale plate ; comparaison avec un repas d'épreuve* Nouv. Pr. Med. 1982, 52, 3856-3857
SLAMA G.	*Correlation between the nature of amount of carbohydrates in intake and insulin delivery by the artificial pancreas in 24 insulin-dependent diabetics* Diabetes 1981, 30, 101-105
SLAMA G.	*Sucrose taken during mixed meal has no additional hyperglycemic action over isocaloric amounts of starch in well-controlled diabetics* Lancet, 1984, 122-124
STACH J.K.	*Contribution à l'étude d'une diététique rationnelle du diabétique : rythme circadien de la tolérance au glucose, intérêt du pain complet, intérêt du sorbitol.* Thèse pour le doctorat en Médecine, Caen 1974
THORBURN A.W.	*The glycemic index of food* Med. J. Austr. May 26 th 198 ? 144, 580-582
VAGUE P.	*Influence comparée des différents glucides alimentaires sur la sécrétion hormonale. Les sucres dans l'alimentation.* Collection Scientifique de la Fondation Française pour la Nutrition

FATS

A) INTRODUCTION

Lipids or fats are indispensable to our diet because they:
- supply energy
- allow the constitution of fat reserves
- are required to build cellular membranes
- are part of the tissue and nervous system composition
- facilitate the synthesis of hormones, prostacyclins, thromboxanes and leukotrienes
- are the basis of the synthesis of biliary salts
- constitute the only source of so-called vital fatty acids, linoleic acid and alpha-linolenic acids
- contain the liposoluble vitamins, A, D, E, and K
- play a key role in cardiovascular pathology

Per capita, fat consumption in the American diet has increased between 1909 and 1985, reaching 169 grams or 6 oz per day in 1985. In the United States, the proportion of total fats from meat, poultry, and fish has changed only slightly, reaching 31.4 percent in 1985. The relative amount of fat from whole milk has declined steadily from a high of 10.4 percent in 1947-49 to 3 percent in 1985, while the ratio from fats and oils has increased from 38 percent to 47 percent in the same period. (Nutrition Monitoring in the United States: An Update Report on Nutrition Monitoring, pg. 52).

B) LIPID BIOCHEMISTRY

Fat compounds are composed of 98% triglycerides. Triglycerides are produced by linking three fatty acid molecules (hence the prefix "tri") onto a glycerol molecule, which is, in fact, an alcohol. The remaining two percent of fat are phospholipids (especially lecithin), sterols (including cholesterol and ergosterol) and liposoluble vitamins.

A fatty acid is made of a long chain of carbon atoms, to which hydrogen atoms are attached. There are three types of fatty acids: saturated fatty acids and mono and polyunsaturated fatty acids. Sometimes the carbon atoms are connected by a double bond.

- If there is no double bond, the fatty acids are saturated. The saturated fatty acids most commonly found in foods are lauric, myristic, palmitic and stearic acids.
- If there is only one double bond, the fatty acid is mono-unsaturated; the most common type is oleic acid.
- If there is more than one double bond, the fatty acids are polyunsaturated; linoleic acid and alpha-linolenic acid are the most important types. They must be obtained through food because the body is not capable of synthesizing them independently.

C) INDISPENSABLE FATTY ACIDS

These are polyunsaturated fatty acids:

1) Linoleic acid (C 18 : 2n-6 or omega 6):

Linoleic acid is found in sunflower oil, corn oil and grape seed oil. It is part of the cellular membrane, and the messages transmitted through the nervous system are dependent upon its availability. It neutralizes free carcinogenic radicles, preventing the development of skin cancer in mice, for example.

- It is a precursor of prostaglandines and prostacyclines.
- It limits the ability of platelet aggregation and helps reduce blood pressure.

252

- A deficiency in linoleic acid causes:
  . growth problems
  . cellular modifications in the skin, mucous membranes, endocrine glands and genitals
  . mitochondria dysfunctions
  . anomalies in the transportation of blood lipids
- The recommended intake is .90 ounces (25 g) per day. This quantity can be obtained by consuming:
  . 1.2 oz of sunflower oil (35 g)
  . 1.3 oz of walnut oil (37 g)
  . 1.5 oz of corn oil (45 g)
  . 1.8 oz of soy oil (50 g)
  . 1.9 oz of safflower margarine (55 g)
  . 2.9 oz of peanut oil (83 g)

2) Alpha-linolenic acid (C 18 : 3n-3 or omega 3).

- This acid is especially found in walnut oil, soy oil, wheat germ, lecithin and algae.
Little is found in peanut oil, sunflower oil, corn oil or grape seed oil.
- A deficiency in alpha-linolenic acid causes:
  . structural anomalies of cellular membranes
  . a malfunctioning of the retina when stimulated by light
  . learning difficulties
  . lowered alcohol tolerance
  . anomalies of the nervous transmission due to a loss of ionic equilibrium. (It diminishes the Na-K ATPase's activity by half).
- The body requires .07 to .11 ounces (2 to 3 g) per day.
- Amount of alpha-linolenic acid in 3.5 ounces (100 g) of oil:
  . soy oil: .21 ounces (6.0 g)
  . corn oil: .032 ounces (0.9 g)
  . peanut oil: .028 ounces (0.8 g)
  . olive oil: .018 ounces (0.5 g)
  . safflower oil: .018 ounces (0.5 g)
  . grape seed oil: .018 ounces (0.5 g)

3) Arachidonic acid (C 20 : 4n-6)

Arachidonic acid is also considered indispensable because the body sometimes has difficulties in synthesizing it from linoleic acid.

It is present in animal fats. It is necessary in the formation of type 2 icosanoids which play a major role in preventing inflammations.

D) FAT SOURCES

Fats are found in animal tissues and in plants.

1) Animal fats:

Quantity of lipids in 3.5 ounces (100 g) of food:

Meats

. Beef: .14 - .90 oz (4 - 25 g)   - steak or roast: .14 oz   (4.0 g)
                                       - neck: .24 oz   (7.0 g)
                                       - ribs: .45 oz (13.0 g)
                                       - shin: .70 oz (20.0 g)
                                       - hamburger: .90 oz (25.0 g)

. Veal: .07 - .50 oz (2 - 15 g)   - brains: .31 oz   (9.0 g)
                                       - filet: .35 oz (10.0 g)
                                       - ribs: .50 oz (15.0 g)

. Pork: .07 - .50 oz (2 - 15 g)   - shoulder: .24 oz   (7.0 g)
                                       - chops: .90 oz (25.0 g)
                                       - roast: .90 oz (25.0 g)

. Lamb: .17 - 1.0 oz (5 - 30 g)   - leg: .56 oz (16.0 g)
                                       - neck: .60 oz (17.0 g)
                                       - shoulder: .90 oz (25.0 g)
                                       - chops: .90 oz (25.0 g)

Cold Cuts   - lean ham, sweetbreads,
                                         bacon, roast pork   .32 oz   (9.0 g)
                                       - dry ham, tripe sausages,
                                         headcheese   .35 - .70 oz (10 - 20 g)
                                       - sausages   .70 - 1.00 oz (20 - 30 g)
                                       - dry sausages   1.00 - 1.40 oz (30 - 40 g)
                                       - bacon bits   2.500 oz (70.0 g)

Eggs   - whole eggs   .350 oz (10.0 g)
                                       - albumen (white)   0 oz (0.0 g)
                                       - yolk   1.200 oz (33.0 g)

Poultry   - chicken without skin   .240 oz (7.0 g)
                                       - chicken with skin   .420 oz (12.0 g)
                                       - duck   .350 oz (10.0 g)
                                       - rabbit   .350 oz (10.0 g)
                                       - chicken   1.000 oz (30.0 g)

Dairy Products   - skim milk   .003 oz (0.1 g)
                                       - low-fat milk   .060 oz (1.7 g)
                                       - whole milk   .120 oz (3.5 g)
                                       - sweetened condensed milk .350 oz (10.0 g)

Cheese	- non-fat cottage cheese	0 oz	(0.0 g)
	- cottage cheese (40% fat)	.350 oz	(10.0 g)
	- cottage cheese (60% fat)	.450 oz	(18.0 g)
	- plain yogurt	.050 oz	(1.5 g)
	- low-fat yogurt	.003 oz	(0.1 g)
	- cheese spread	.770 oz	(22.0 g)
	- Swiss	1.100 oz	(32.0 g)
	- blue, roquefort	1.200 oz	(34.0 g)
Fish	- lean fish: sole, coal fish, ray fish	.070 oz	(2.0 g)
	- semi-fat fish: sardines, herring, salmon	.14 - .30 oz	(4 - 8 g)
	- fatty fish: mackerel, tuna	.35 - .50 oz	(10 - 15 g)
Shellfish	- crab	.070 oz	(2.0 g)
	- shrimp	.100 oz	(3.0 g)
	- oysters	.070 oz	(2.0 g)
	- mussels	.070 oz	(2.0 g)
	- scallops	.035 oz	(1.0 g)

2) Vegetable fats:

- Peanuts
- Corn
- Sunflower
- Grape seeds
- Walnuts
- Soy
- Copra
- Palm

E) FATS AS COMPONENTS OF FOODS

1) Virtually pure fats

- Oils: 3.5 oz of lipids for 3.5 oz of food
  100 g of lipids for 100 g of food
- Lard: 3.60 oz (94.0 g)
- Butter: 2.85 oz (81.0 g)
- Margarine: 2.90 oz (82.5 g)
- Light butter: 1.48 oz (42.0 g)
- Cream (30% fat):   1.00 oz (30.0 g)

2) Fat-Protein Associations

- Meat
- Cold cuts
- Eggs
- Fish
- Shellfish
- Milk, dairy products
- Cheese

3) Fat-Carbohydrate Associations

	Carbohydrates	Fats		Carbohydrates	Fats
- Liver	.14 oz (4.0 g)	.17 oz (5.0 g)	- Black olives	.95 oz (27.0 g)	1.30 oz (36.0 g)
- Breaded fish	.25 oz (7.0 g)	.32 oz (9.0 g)	- Avocados	.17 oz (5.0 g)	.60 oz (17.0 g)
- Oysters	.14 oz (4.0 g)	.07 oz (2.0 g)	- Soy	1.10 oz (32.0 g)	.60 oz (17.0 g)
- Scallops	.10 oz (3.0 g)	.03 oz (1.0 g)	- Pasta with eggs	.85 oz (2.4 g)	.07 oz (2.0 g)
- Milk	.17 oz (3.0 g)	.12 oz (3.5 g)	- Fries, chips	1.80 oz (50.0 g)	1.40 oz (40.0 g)
- Condensed milk	1.20 oz (34.0 g)	.35 oz (10.0 g)	- Coconut	2.00 oz (60.0 g)	.25 oz (7.0 g)
- Powdered soup	1.90 oz (55.0 g)	.40 oz (11.0 g)	- Chestnuts pureed	.30 oz (1.0 g)	1.40 oz (40.0 g)
- Sauces with flour	1.80 oz (50.0 g)	.42 oz (12.0 g)	- Dark chocolate	1.90 oz (55.0 g)	.95 oz (27.0 g)
- Walnuts	1.70 oz (5.0 g)	1.80 oz (50.0 g)	- Crackers	2.40 oz (75.0 g)	.14 oz (4.0 g)
- Almonds	.50 oz (15.0 g)	1.90 oz (55.0 g)	- Ice cream	.90 oz (25.0 g)	.25 oz (7.0 g)
- Roasted salted peanuts	.70 oz (20.0 g)	1.80 oz (50.0 g)	- Apple pie	.93 oz (28.0 g)	.30 oz (8.0 g)
			- Waffles	2.30 oz (73.0 g)	.70 oz (20.0 g)

F) FATS AND THEIR IMPACT ON CHOLESTEROL

1) Saturated fatty acids

These acids increase the cholesterol level, particularly those found in meats, cold cuts, milk, dairy products and cheese.

So, to a lesser extent, do the acids found in eggs, poultry without skin and shellfish.

2) Mono and polyunsaturated fatty acids help lower the cholesterol level

a) Monounsaturated fatty acids are found in olive oil.

b) Polyunsaturated fatty acids of vegetable origin are found in sunflower oil, corn oil, grape seed oil, and peanut oil.

c) Polyunsaturated fatty acids from animal sources are found in fish oils.

G) FAT CONSUMPTION

The recommended daily averages are:
- 2.45 to 2.80 oz. for men (70 to 80 g)
- 2.1 to 2.8 oz. for women (60 to 80 g)

Today, the average daily consumption comprises approximately:
- 60% saturated fatty acids
- 33% monounsaturated fatty acids
- 7% polyunsaturated fatty acids

To prevent cardiovascular disease, the World Health Organization recommends the following distribution:
- 25% saturated fatty acids

256

- 25% monounsaturated fatty acids
- 50% polyunsaturated fatty acids.

It is therefore imperative to implement this consumption pattern by eating more fish, decreasing meat consumption, and by broadening the range of vegetable oils we eat.

BIBLIOGRAPHY

BOURRE J.M.-	*The importance of dietary linoeic acid in composition of nervous membranes.*
DURAND G.	Diet and life style, new technology De M.F. Mayol 1988 John Libbey Eurotext Ldt p. 477-481
DYERBERG J.	*Linolenic acid and eicospentaenoic acid* The Lancet 26 Janvier 1980, p. 199
JACOTOT B.	*Olive oil and the lipoprotein metabolism.* Rev. Fr. des Corps Gras 1988, 2, 51-55
MAILLARD C.	*Graisses grises* Gazette Med. de Fr. 1989, 96, n° 22
RUASSE J.P.	*Des lipides, pourquoi, comment ?* Coll. L'Indispensable en Nutrition.
VLES R.O.	*Connaissances récentes sur les effets physiologiques des margarines riches en acide linoléique.* Rev. Fr. des Corps Gras 1980, 3, 115-120

Documentation Astra-Calvé :
L'essentiel sur les acides gras polyinsaturés
Lipides et santé. Quelles vérités ?
Connaissance des corps gras.
Mémento des corps gras.

DIETARY FIBERS

A) WHAT IS FIBER?

Dietary fiber is sometimes classified as indigestible carbohydrates. However, it can actually be defined as plant cell residues, resistant to the enzyme action of the small intestine, but which is, nonetheless, partially hydrolyzed by colic bacterial flora.

B) THE MAIN FIBER TYPES

They include:
- cellulose
- hemicellulose
- lignin
- pectin
- gums

C) WHERE FIBER IS FOUND

Fibers are found in cereals, fresh vegetables and legumes, fruits and algae.

Cereals contain:	- cellulose	- some pectin
	- hemicellulose	- bran cereal has a fiber content of 50% while white flour contains 3% fiber
	- lignin	
Fresh vegetables contain:	- cellulose	- some lignin
	- hemicellulose	
	- pectin	
Dried legumes contain:	- cellulose	- gums
	- hemicellulose	- some lignin
	- pectin	
Fruits contain:	- cellulose	- lignin
	- hemicellulose	- pectin
Algae contains:	- agar	- alginates
	- carraghenates	- gums

D) DAILY RATION OF FIBERS

The recommended daily fiber intake is 1.4 oz in the United States, however, the average person is far below this daily recommended allowance (RDA). Estimates of mean daily dietary fiber intake over a four-day period from the CSFII 1985-86 are .39 oz for women aged 20-49 years and .35 oz for children aged 1-5 years. This survey showed that only five percent of the women surveyed had intakes of .7 oz or more of dietary fiber per day. One-day data from the CSFII 1985 indicated that on average the dietary fiber intake of men is higher than that of women (approximately .6 oz per day). (Nutrition Monitoring in the United States: An Update Report on Nutrition Monitoring, 1989, pg. 54)

It is worth noting that .60 oz of bran contain as much fiber as 24.5 oz of carrots or 52.5 oz of apples.

E) FIBER SOURCES AND FIBER CONTENT PER 3.5 oz (100 g) OF FOOD

		Ounces	Grams		Ounces	Grams
Cereal products:	- bran	1.40 oz	(40.0 g)	- brown rice	.17 oz	(5.0 g)
	- whole wheat flour	.35 oz	(10.0 g)	- white bread	.035 oz	(1.0 g)
	- whole wheat bread	.31 oz	(9.0 g)	- white rice	.035 oz	(1.0 g)
	- whole grain bread	.17 oz	(5.0 g)			

258

Dried legumes:	- beans	.90	oz	(25.0 g)	- lentils	.42	oz	(12.0 g)
	- split peas	.80	oz	(23.0 g)	- chick peas	.07	oz	(2.0 g)
Dried fruits and nuts	- dry coconut	.85	oz	(24.0 g)	- prunes	.25	oz	(7.0 g)
(Oil-rich vegetable	- dry figs	.63	oz	(18.0 g)	- raisins	.25	oz	(7.0 g)
products)	- almonds	.48	oz	(14.0 g)	- cocoa	.20	oz	(6.0 g)
	- dates	.32	oz	(9.0 g)	- walnuts	.17	oz	(5.0 g)
	- peanuts	.30	oz	(8.0 g)	- olives	.17	oz	(5.0 g)
Fresh fruits:	- raspberries	.30	oz	(8.0 g)	- strawberries	.07	oz	(2.0 g)
	- currants	.25	oz	(7.0 g)	- oranges	.07	oz	(2.0 g)
	- pears with skin	.10	oz	(3.0 g)	- cantaloupe	.07	oz	(2.0 g)
	- apples with skin	.10	oz	(3.0 g)	- grapes	.035	oz	(1.0 g)
	- peaches	.07	oz	(2.0 g)				
Fresh vegetables:	- cooked peas	.42	oz	(12.0 g)	- cabbage	.14	oz	(4.0 g)
	- parsley	.32	oz	(9.0 g)	- green beans	.07	oz	(2.0 g)
	- cooked spinach	.25	oz	(7.0 g)	- eggplant	.07	oz	(2.0 g)
	- canned peas	.20	oz	(6.0 g)	- zucchini	.07	oz	(2.0 g)
	- dandelion greens	.17	oz	(5.0 g)	- carrots	.07	oz	(2.0 g)
	- artichokes	.14	oz	(4.0 g)	- lettuce	.07	oz	(2.0 g)

F) PHYSIOLOGICAL EFFECTS OF FIBERS

- They stimulate salivary and gastric secretions.

- They fill the stomach, creating the sensation of having eaten enough.

- They delay the emptying of the gastrointestinal tract.

- They foster bile salt secretion which is necessary to digest fats.

- They ensure regularity in the colon.

- They increase the volume and moisture content of the feces, which helps prevent constipation.

G) ACTION OF FIBERS IN PATHOLOGICAL CASES

1) Obesity

Some fibers, especially when consumed raw, form a thick hydrophilic gel which coats the walls of the gastrointestinal tract. This gel slows down the emptying of the gastrointestinal tract, thereby creating a type of filter that limits carbohydrate absorption.

259

The energy absorbed from sugars is then reduced and post-prandial hyperglycemic peaks are avoided. This effect is especially apparent with pectin and gum.

One of the greatest problems of obese individuals is hyperinsulinism and insulin resistance. These disorders are caused by hyperglycemic peaks induced by the consumption of certain carbohydrates. Pectin and gums are fibers that counteract these effects.

- Pectin is found in fruits (especially apples), peas and dried beans.
- An apple contains .44 oz of usable carbohydrates and .087 oz of fiber (pectin and cellulose).

Holt's experiments show that .48 oz of pectin considerably reduce the glycemic reaction after the ingestion of 1.75 oz of glucose.

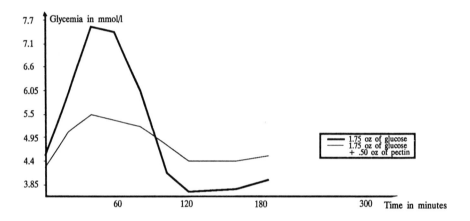

- Gums:

The most widely used gum is guar gum, an industrial derivative of an Indian bean. There is also some gum content in vegetables and oats.

Tagliafero clearly demonstrates the effect of .30 oz (8 g) of gum per day, taken in two doses, on glycemic and insulinemic levels following injections of glucose.

	Without Gums	With Gums
Glycemia	7.25 ± 0.05	6.75 ± 0.03
Insulinemia	13 ± 3	10 ± 1,5

Guar gum improves peripheral sensitivity to insulin and reduces insulin resistance. By smoothing out post-prandial glycemic peaks, it reduces stimulation of the pancreatic B-cells.

260

Jenkins shows that a daily intake of .51 oz of guar gum eliminates any glycemic peak after meals and reduces insulin secretion by more than 50%.

Monnier's experiments demonstrate that the addition of fiber in the diet diminishes the post-prandial hyperglycemic reaction·

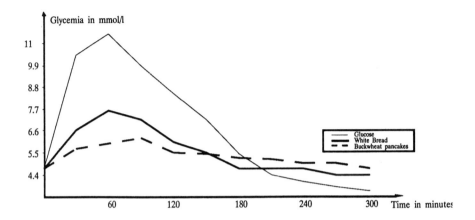

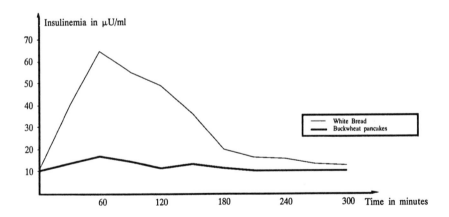

The insulinic response is in part induced and stimulated by the entero-hormonal system (gastric inhibitory polypeptides GIP) and entero-glucagon.

Increased dietary fiber consumption contributes to a reduction of the GIP and entero-glucagon responses. Moreover, fibers are accountable for the disappearance of reactionary hypoglycemia due to either a decrease in the insulinic effect or the reactivation of pancreatic glucagon secretion three hours following the beginning of the alimentary intake.

261

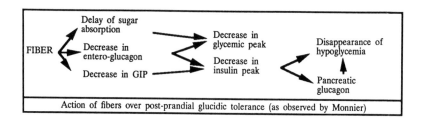

Action of fibers over post-prandial glucidic tolerance (as observed by Monnier)

2) In Diabetic Cases

The same beneficial effects for diabetics are found in terms of glucidic tolerance. Miranda proved that .70 oz of fiber can decrease a diabetic's glycemia from 57% to 13%.

3) Hypercholesterolemia

As we will see later, fiber also improves cholesterol levels. Anderson has given a number of hypotheses on this subject:

Soluble fibers bind to bile acids and interfere with the formation of micelles in the proximal ileum. This binding process diminishes the quantity of cholesterol and fatty acids absorbed and/or modifies the size of lipoproteinic molecules formed by the intestinal mucosa.

Soluble fibers increase fecal excretion of bile acids and block the hepatic synthesis of lipoproteins.

Soluble fibers undergo colic fermentation by bacteria, producing gases and short-chain fatty acids which enter the portal circulation. This modifies hepatic synthesis of cholesterol.

4) Digestive Problems

Fibers
- treat constipation
- relieve spasmodic colitis
- prevent cholesterolic vesicular lithiases, colic diverticulosis, and colon and rectal cancers.

BIBLIOGRAPHY

« Council Scientific Affairs ». *Fibres alimentaires et santé* JAMA 1984, 14, 190, 1037-1046

ANDERSON J.W. *Dietary fiber: diabetes and obesity* Am. J. Gastroenterology 1986, 81, 898-906

BERNIER J.J. *Fibres alimentaires, motricité et absorption intestinale. Effets sur l'hyperglycémie post-prandiale* Journée de Diabétologie Hôtel-Dieu 1979, 269-273

HABER G.B. *Depletion and disruption of dietary fiber. Effects on satiety, plasma, glucose and serum insulin.* Lancet 1977, 2, 679-682

HEATON K.W.   *Food fiber as an obstacle to energy intake* Lancet 1973, 2, 1418-1421

HEATON K.W.   *Dietary fiber in perspective* Humon Clin. Nutr. 1983, 37c, 151-170

HOLT S.   *Effect of gel fiber on gastric emptying and absorption of glucose and paracetamol* Lancet 1979, March 24, 636-639

JENKINS D.J.A.   *Decrease in post-prandial insulin and glucose concentration by guar and pectin* Ann. Int. Med. 1977, 86, 20-33

JENKINS D.J.A.   *Dietary fiber, fiber analogues and glucose tolerance : importance of viscosity* Br Med. J. 1978, 1, 1392-1394

LAURENT B.   *Etudes récentes concernant les fibres alimentaires* Med. et Nutr. 1983, XIX, 2, 95-122

MONNIER L.   *Effets des fibres sur le métabolisme glucidique* Cah. Nutr. Diet. 1983, XVIII, 89-93

NAUSS K.M.   *Dietary fat and fiber : relationship to caloric intake body growth, and colon carcinogenesis* Am. J. Clin. Nutr. 1987, 45, 243-251

SAUTIER C.   *Valeur alimentaire des algues spirulines chez l'homme* Ann. Nutr. Alim. 1975, 29, 517

SAUTIER C.   *Les algues en alimentation humaine* Cah. Nutr. Diet, 1987, 6, 469-472

HYPERCHOLESTEROLEMIA
CARDIOVASCULAR DISEASE AND DIET

A) CARDIOVASCULAR DISEASE

In the United States, between 1950 and 1985, heart disease continued to be the leading cause of death, and cerebrovascular disease was the third most important cause; together, the two accounted for approximately one half of all deaths. Thus, despite the drop in mortality from these cardiovascular diseases in recent years, they remain major public health concerns. (Vital Statistics data NCHS, 1988).

Coronary heart disease and cerebrovascular disease have many causes: obesity, nicotinism, arterial high blood pressure, diabetes and hypercholesterolemia.

Complications generally appear after the risk factors have accumulated, approximately 20 to 30 years later. However, to prevent diseases, early detection is important since a number of hereditary diseases can cause premature death: four percent of the deaths caused by cardiovascular disease occur between the ages of 15 and 24!

B) CHOLESTEROL

Cholesterol is not an intruder in the body: the organism contains approximately 3.5 oz (100 g) of cholesterol to be found in the central nervous system, in the myelin surrounding nerves, in cellular membranes and in circulating molecules.

It is indispensable to hormonal synthesis in the adrenal glands, ovaries and testicles.

263

The cholesterol found in the blood (blood cholesterol) can, of course, come from food, but most circulating cholesterol is made by the organism itself. For example, 12 to 800 to 1000 mg per day is released with bile in the small intestine.

Cholesterol is found not only in the blood, but also bound to proteins. There are two types of proteins found in the blood: Low-Density Lipoproteins (LDL) and High-Density Lipoproteins (HDL). Low-Density Lipoproteins (LDL) distribute the cholesterol to the cells, and in particular, to the arterial walls which are the victims of fat deposits. Hence the name "bad cholesterol" is responsible for coating and clogging the vessel walls.

The resulting obstruction of the arteries can cause:
- arteritis in the lower limbs
- angina pectoris or coronary thrombosis
- cerebrovascular incidents which can possibly result in paralysis

High-Density Lipoproteins (HDL) carry the cholesterol to the liver, where it is eliminated. No vascular deposits are formed. Hence the name "good cholesterol" attributed to HDL-cholesterol since it removes atheromatous deposits from the arteries. When HDL levels are high, the danger of a cardiovascular incident is reduced.

C) BLOOD CHOLESTEROL LEVELS

The current standards for blood cholesterol levels are far more stringent than those applied a few years ago.

Usually, the total cholesterol level should be less than or equal to 5.16 mmol/l.
- the LDL-cholesterol level should be less than 3.35 mmol/l.
- the HDL-cholesterol level should be greater than 1.16 mmol/l for men, and greater than 1.41 mmol/l for women.

In borderline cases, the purely protein part of the lipoproteins is also measured:
- the apolipoprotein A1 level (related to HDL-cholesterol) should be greater than .04 oz per quart (1.30 g/l).
- the apolipoprotein B level (related to LDL-cholesterol) level should be greater than .015 oz per quart for men, and greater than .019 oz per quart for women.

The triglyceride level is affected by consumption of carbohydrates and alcohol, instead of fats. It should also be carefully watched. This level should be less than or equal to 1.72 mmol/l.

D) CARDIOVASCULAR RISKS

Cardiovascular risks increase twofold if the cholesterol level increases from 4.64 to 5.67 mmol/l, and become four times as great if the cholesterol level is higher than 6.7 mmol/l.

The average serum cholesterol level in the United States observed in 1980 and 1982 was the following:

264

Serum Cholesterol

	Ethnic Origin 50 years	Men Women 50 years
Mexican American	5.68 mmol/l	5.81 mmol/l
Cuban	5.65 mmol/l	5.98 mmol/l
Puerto Rican	5.82 mmol/l	5.96 mmol/l
White	5.92 mmol/l	6.30 mmol/l
Black	5.96 mmol/l	6.28 mmol/l

(Nutrition Monitoring in the United States: An Update Report on Nutrition Monitoring, 1989).

Lowering the total cholesterol level by 12.5% allows for a 19% decrease in the myocardial infarction rate and in the frequency of lethal myocardial ischemia.

However, measuring the total cholesterol level is not sufficient, as Ginsburg proved by showing that 15% of all myocardial infarction occurs in individuals whose total cholesterol level is between 3.87 and 5.16 mmol/l. Instead, it is important to measure the HDL-cholesterol level and calculate the total cholesterol level/HDL-cholesterol level quotient. This quotient should be lower than 4.5 mmol/l.

E) IMPROVED DIET

Alimentary precautions are sufficient for treating ordinary hypercholesterolemia (Fredericksen's type "IIA").

Medication is not always needed and should only be used as a second resort.

1) Weight-loss

Losing weight improves biological parameters in all cases.

To treat obesity, it is necessary to follow an adapted diet in order to bring weight back to normal.

2) Limit alimentary intake of cholesterol

Foods have varying cholesterol levels. For example, organ meats are very rich in cholesterol.

Cholesterol Milligrams

- 2 1.75 oz eggs	600 mg	- beer yeast	700 mg
- 3.5 oz egg yolk	1,500 mg	- shrimp	280 mg
- butter	250 mg	- fish	50-90 mg
- cheese (30% butter fat)	100 mg	- meat, cold cuts, poultry	70 mg
- whole fat dairy products	80-100 mg		

265

- organ meats:

. beef kidney	430 mg	. beef heart	175 mg
. veal kidney	400 mg	. veal tongue	90 mg
. beef liver	250 mg	. beef tongue	50 mg

The World Health Organization recommends a daily cholesterol intake of no more than 300 mg in order to avoid an increased cholesterol level.

However, recent studies have shown that this dietary aspect is only secondary. For example, a daily cholesterol intake of 1000 mg only increases the cholesterol level by approximately five percent.

Therefore, the cholesterol quantity in food can be ignored so long as the level of saturation of fatty acids is taken into consideration.

3) Therefore, fatty acids must be selected properly. More mono and polyunsaturated fatty acids should be consumed, and fewer saturated fats.

a) Saturated fatty acids

Saturated fatty acids are not recommended. They are found in meats, poultry, eggs, milk, dairy products and cheeses.

They increase the total cholesterol level, especially the LDL-cholesterol level. It is the LDL-cholesterol, as seen earlier, that is responsible for deposits on the arterial walls and cardiovascular disease.

However, a number of recent publications (Nutritional Reviews 1983, 41, #9 pp. 272-274) question these seemingly well-established facts. For example, although eggs are rich in saturated fatty acids, they do not seem to have the negative effects that they were accused of having. If three eggs are added to the daily diet of a group of 21 to 35 year old individuals, corresponding to a total daily ingestion (diet + eggs) of 975 mg of cholesterol (compared to 412 mg for the control group), no increase in the blood cholesterol level is observed!

The effect of poultry eaten without the skin, in terms of increasing the cholesterol level is low due to the corresponding low lipid level. This is also true for peanut oil. In this case, the effects of the saturated fatty acids are largely counterbalanced by the presence of polyunsaturated fatty acids.

b) Vegetable polyunsaturated fatty acids

Vegetable polyunsaturated fatty acids are found in sunflower oil, corn oil, grapeseed oil and rapeseed oil. Consuming these oils helps to lower both HDL and LDL-cholesterol, thereby reducing total cholesterol levels. Vegetable polyunsaturated fatty acids also contribute to limiting platelet aggregation which cause clotting of the arteriothrombosis.

c) Animal polyunsaturated fatty acid consumption is recommended.

Eicosapentaenoic acid (EPA) and docosahexaenoic acid (DHA) are the two primary animal polyunsaturated fatty acids. They are derivatives of the alphalinolenic acid found in fish oils.

The Danish scientist, Dyerberg, observed that the Eskimos rarely suffer from cardiovascular disease. Is this an acquired or an inherited trait? Studies showed that

266

the Eskimos who left Greenland to start a new life in Canada or the United States soon became victims of cardiovascular disease. Therefore, it is not an ethnic characteristic but rather an acquired trait directly linked to the the Eskimos' rich fish diet in Greenland.

In 1985, a statistical study conducted over the course of 20 years was published in the "New England Journal of Medicine." It showed that the mortality rate due to cardiac diseases was 50% lower among people who consumed 1 oz (30 g) of fish per day.

It was later proven that these two fatty acids (EPA and DHA) produced three types of prostaglandins which diminish platelet aggregation. This phenomenon increases blood fluidity which reduces the risks of thrombosis. Furthermore, EPA and DHA lower blood pressure and act as vasodilators. They are also responsible for reducing LDL-cholesterol, triglyceride levels and, to a lesser degree, HDL-cholesterol level.

It is therefore clear that since fish fats lower the cholesterol level and reduce the risks of cardiovascular diseases, the fattier the fish, the better it is for the well-being of the body! Consumption of salmon, tuna, sardines, mackerel, anchovies and herring should thus be strongly encouraged.

NOTE: It is equally important to know that the fat content of fish varies widely depending on the season and the fishing location. Fish fat levels can vary from one percent to 64 percent. Mackerel contains 32% fat before spawning and 18% after. The amount for sardines varies from one percent to thirty-two percent.

d) Monounsaturated fatty acids

Oleic acid is the main monounsaturated fatty acid. It can be found in olive oil. It helps reduce the "bad cholesterol" (LDL-cholesterol) level and increases the "good cholesterol" (HDL-cholesterol) level, which is what is desired.

Therefore, it is highly recommended for use in olive oil salad dressings and in cooking. Many will be happy to learn that tuna fish seasoned with olive oil is truly a weapon against cholesterol.

If the LDL-cholesterol level decreases by 11% and the HDL-cholesterol level increases by 11%, the rate of myocardial infarction and coronary ischemia decreases by 35%!

4) Dietary fiber should be increased

The presence of fibers in the gastrointestinal (GI) tract improves fat metabolism.

a) Pectin

Three apples added to the daily diet (i.e. .28 oz or 18 g of fibers and .07 oz or 2 g of pectin) over a two month period will decrease the cholesterol level by approximately five percent. This reduction is significant in patients whose cholesterol level is higher than 6.20 mmol/l. The HDL-cholesterol level over this period of time decreases by 20% and LDL-cholesterol by 80%. The apolipoprotein B level decreases by 6.4% and the apolipoprotein A1 level decreases by 1%, resulting in an improvement in the ApoB/ApoA1 atherogenic ratio. Despite the consumption of 2.8 oz or 80 g of assimilable carbohydrates per day, the glycemic level decreases by 7% to 13%, thereby favoring triglyceride reduction.

b) Carob

In normal subjects, carob lowers the total cholesterol level by 11% and the LDL-cholesterol level by 10%. Among hypercholesterolemic cases, the total cholesterol level decreases by 17% and the LDL-cholesterol level by 19%.

c) Guar gum

- guar gum pasta: the Italians make a type of pasta with two types of flour: hard wheat and guar-gum. By consuming 3.5 oz (100 g) of this pasta with 2.8 oz (80 g) of parmesan cheese and 1.75 oz (50 g) of butter added, the total cholesterol level decreases by 10%. The result might have been even better if no parmesan cheese were ingested and if butter were replaced by vegetable margarine.
- guar gum flour: Tagliafero's experiment proved that 0.14 oz (4 g) of this flour added to the diet four times a day leads to a decrease in the LDL-cholesterol level and an increase in the HDL-cholesterol level.

In mmol/l	Control	Guar-gum	Standard Deviation
Total cholesterol	4.40 ± 1.10	4.40 ± 1.00	p 0.05
Apolipoprotein A1	2.30 ± .50	2.90 ± .80	p 0.01
LDL-cholesterol	3.20 ± .90	2.80 ± .70	p 0.01

d) Bran has no effect on cholesterol metabolism. It even tends to decrease the effect of pectin if the two are taken together.

5) Increase the intake of vitamins A and E, selenium and chromium

a) Vitamin E

LDL oxidation plays an important role in accumulation of cellular cholesterol. Vitamin E protects the LDL from oxidation and reduces its uptake by cellular macrophages by more than 20%.

Vitamin E is found in grain, in vegetable oils, and, in smaller quantities, in butter, green vegetables, eggs and liver.

b) Vitamin A

The anti-oxidizing action of vitamin E is reinforced by vitamin A, found mostly in fish, mammal livers, dairy products and egg yolk.

A provitamin A (or carotenoid) is found in vegetables (carrots, spinach, cabbage, oranges, apricots) and is transformed into vitamin A in the intestinal cells.

c) Selenium

This mineral reinforces the action of the vitamin E by acting on glutathione peroxidase to prevent the formation of free radicles and against excessive platelet aggregation. It is found in eggs, tuna, liver, red meat, garlic, beer yeast, wheat germ and whole grains.

d) Chromium

This mineral participates in the "glucose tolerance factor" which slows down

268

lipogenesis. It reduces synthesis of LDL-cholesterol and increases the formation of HDL-cholesterol.

It is found in large quantities in liver, kidneys, cheese, whole grains, beer yeast and black pepper.

6) Limit coffee consumption

Studies by Framingham, in the United States, and by Tromso, in Norway, have shown that when more than six cups of coffee are consumed daily, the total cholesterol level clearly increases and the HDL-cholesterol level decreases slightly. Although the exact cause for this effect is not known, it is certain that caffeine is not the cause of this negative effect. Decaffeinated coffee has the same effect.

7) A little wine is all right

Whereas distilled alcohols (whisky, for example) should be avoided, Dr. Masquelier has shown that the tannin in wine contains procyanidine, a substance that causes the cholesterol level to decrease.

Some observers have even noted an increase in HDL-cholesterol levels due to this substance, but it seems that only the HDL 3 components increases. The anti-atherogenic component is HDL 2.

Crete, where a large quantity of wine and olive oil are consumed, has the lowest rate of cardiovascular disease in Europe!

F) IMPROVE YOUR LIFESTYLE

1) Stress

In individuals under stress, there is an augmentation in the catecholamine level. This increase favors synthesis of the LDL-cholesterol precursors and decreases the HDL-cholesterol level. Exactly how and why this occurs has yet to be determined. Without knowing the precise reason for this phenomenon, we do know that an effective stress management or relaxation method is the key to avoiding such ill effects.

2) Smoking

Tobacco causes a decrease in the HDL-cholesterol level. It is important to stop smoking.

3) A sedentary lifestyle

A lack of physical activity is harmful. Exercise helps reduce the triglyceride level and increase the HDL-cholesterol level, particularly the HDL 2 fraction which is the most anti-atherogenic.

To obtain statistically significant results against cholesterol, it is important to practice a physical activity for at least twenty minutes three times a week. The best type of exercise is an endurance sport. Yet jogging six miles a week results in only a small decrease in the cholesterol level. In order to receive a sharp decrease in the total cholesterol level and an increase in the HDL-cholesterol level, it is necessary to run 36 miles a week; this is the minimum for a serious long-distance runner!

G) IN SUM, TO DECREASE YOUR CHOLESTEROL LEVEL, YOU MUST:

- lose weight if you are obese
- cut down on meat consumption (5 oz/day maximum)
- eat lean meats (lean beef)
- substitute poultry (without skin) for meat whenever possible
- avoid cold cuts and organ meats
- increase fish consumption (10 oz per week minimum)
- eat little or no butter (.35 oz per day maximum)
- limit cheese consumption
- drink skim milk and eat non-fat dairy products
- increase fiber consumption (fruits, cereals, vegetables)
- increase vegetable mono and polyunsaturated fatty acid consumption (olive, sunflower and rapeseed oil)
- make sure selenium, chromium, vitamin A & E intake is sufficient
- do not drink too much coffee
- if you feel the need, drink wine that is rich in tannin (1/2 bottle/day maximum)
- control stress level
- practice an endurance sport if you can
- quit smoking

BIBLIOGRAPHY

SPECIFICS ON CHOLESTEROL

BASDEVANT A., TRAYNARD P.Y.	*Hypercholestérolémie Symptômes* 1988 n° 12
BRUCKERT E.	*Les dyslipidémies Impact Médecin* ; Dossier du Praticien n° 20, 1989
LUC G., DOUSTE-BLAZY P., FRUCHART J.C.	*Le cholestérol, d'où vient-il ? Comment circule-t-il ? Où va-t-il ?* Rev. Prat. 1989, 39, 12, 1011-1017
POLONOWSKI J.	*Régulation de l'absorption intestinale du cholestérol* Cahiers Nutr. Diet. 1989, 1, 19-25

FATS AND CHOLESTEROL

Consensus	*Conference on lowering blood cholesterol to prevent heart disease* JAMA 1985, 253, 2080-2090
BETTERIDGE D.J.	*High density lipoprotein and coronary heart disease* Brit. Med. J. 15 Avril 1989, 974-975
DURAND G. *and al.*	*Effets comparés d'huiles végétales et d'huiles de poisson sur le cholestérol du rat.* Med et Nutr. 1985, XXI, N° 6, 391-406
DYERBERG J. *and al.*	*Eicosapentaenoic acid and prevention of thrombosis and atherosclerosis ?* Lancet 1978, 2, 117-119
ERNST E., LE MIGNON D.	*Les acides gras omega 3 et l'artériosclérose* CR de Ther. 1987, V, N° 56, 22-25

FIELD C.   *The influence of eggs upon plasma cholesterol levels* Nutr. Rev.1983, 41,
                            N° 9, 242-244
FOSSATI P.,   *Huiles de poisson, intérêt nutritionnel et prévention de l'athéromatose* N.P.N.
FERMONC.   Med. 1988, VIII, 1-7
DE GENNES J.L.,   *Correction thérapeutique des hyperlipidémies idiopathiques héréditaires. Bilan*
TURPING   *d'une consultation diététique standardisée* Nouv. Presse Med. 1973, 2,
TRFFERT J.   2457-2464
GRUNDY M.A.   *Comparison of monosatured fatty acids and carbohydrates for lowering*
                            plasma cholesterol N. Engl. J. Med. 1986, 314, 745-749
HAY C.R.M.   *Effect of fish oil on platelet kinetics in patients with ischaemic heart disease*
                            The Lancet 5 Juin 1982, 1269-1272
KRMHOUT D.,   *The inverse relation between fish consumption and 20 year mortality from*
BOSSCHIETER E.B.,   *coronary heart disease* New. Engl. J. Med. 1985, 312, 1205-1209
LEZENNE-
COULANDER C.
LEAF A., WEBER P.C.   *Cardiovascular effects of n-3 fatty acids* New Engl. J. Med. 1988, 318,
                            549-557
LEMARCHAL P.   *Les acides gras polyinsaturés en Omega 3* Cah. Nutr. Diet. 1985, XX,
                            2, 97-102
MARINIER E.   *Place des acides gras polyinsaturés de la famille n-3 dans le traitement*
                            des dyslipoprotéinémies Med. Dig. Nutr. 1986, 53, 14-16
MARWICK C.   *What to do about dietary satured fats ?* JAMA 1989, 262, 453
PHILLIPSON and al.   *Reduction of plasma lipids, lipoproteins and apoproteins by dietary fish*
                            oils in patients with hypertriglyceridemia New Engl. J. Med. 1985, 312,
                            1210-1216
PICLET G.   *Le poisson, aliment, composition, intérêt nutritionnel* Cah. Nutr. Diet.
                            1987, XXII, 317-336
THORNGREN M.   *Effects of 11 week increase in dietary eicosapentaenoïc acid on bleeding*
                            time, lipids and platelet aggregation Lancet 28 Nov. 1981, 1190-11
TURPIN G.   *Régimes et médicaments abaissant la cholestérolémie* Rev. du Prat. 1989,
                            39, 12, 1024-1029
VLES R.O.   *Les acides gras essentiels en physiologie cardio-vasculaire* Ann. Nutr. Alim.
                            1980, 34, 255-264
WOODCOCK B.E.   *Beneficial effect of fish oil on blood viscosity in peripheral vascular disease*
                            Br. Med. J. Vol. 288 du 25 février 1984, p. 592-594

ALIMENTARY FIBERS AND HYPERCHOLESTEROLEMIA

ANDERSON J.W.   *Dietary fiber, lipids and atherosclerosis* Am. J. Cardiol. 1987, 60, 17-22
GIRAULT A.   *Effets bénéfiques de la consommation de pommes sur le métabolisme*
                           lipidique chez l'homme. Entretiens de Bichat 28 Septembre 1988
LEMONNIER D.,   *Effet du son et de la pectine sur les lipides sériques du rat* Cah. Nutr.
DOUCHE C.,   Diet. 1983, XVIII, 2, 99
FLAMENT C.
RAUTUREAU J.,   *Effets des fibres alimentaires sur le métabolisme du cholestérol* Cah. Nutr.
COSTE T.,   Diet. 1983, XVIII, 2, 84-88
KARSENTI P.

271

SABLE-AMPLIS R.,   *Influence des fibres de pomme sur les taux d'esters de cholestérol du foi,*
SICART R., BARON A.   *de l'intestin et de l'aorte* Cah. Nutr. Diet. 1983, XVII, 297

TAGLIAFFERRO V.   *Moderate guar-gum addition to usual diet improves peripheral sensibility*
and al.   *to insulin and lipaemic profile in NIDDM* Diabète et Métabolisme 1985,
                          11, 380-385

TOGNARELLI M.   *Guar-pasta : a new diet for obese subjets B* Acta Diabet. Lat. 1986, 23,
                          77

TROWELL H.   *Dietary fiber and coronary heart disease* Europ. J. Clin. Biol. Res. 1972,
                          17, 345

VAHOUNY G.U.   *Dietary fiber, lipid metabolism and atherosclerosis* Fed. Proc. 1982, 41,
                          2801-2806

ZAVOLAL J.H.   *Effets hypolipémiques d'aliments contenant du caroube* Am. J. Clin. Nutr.
                          1983, 38, 285-294

VITAMINS, TRACE ELEMENTS AND HYPERCHOLESTEROLEMIA

1) Vitamine E

CAREW T.E.   *Antiatherogenic effect of probucol unrelated to its hypocholesterolemic effect*
                         P.N.A.S. USA June 1984, Vol. 84 p. 7725-7729

FRUCHART J.C.   *Influence de la qualité des LD sur leur métabolisme et leur athérogénicité*
                        (inédit)

JURGENS G.   *Modification of human serum LDL by oxydation* Chemistry and Physics
                        of lipids 1987, 45, 315-336

STREINBRECHER V.P.   *Modifications of LDL by endothelial cells involves lipid peroxydation*
                        P.N.A.S. USA June 1984, Vol. 81, 3883-3887

2) Selenium

LUOMA P.V.   *Serum selenium, gluthathione peroxidase, lipids, and human liver microsomal*
                        enzyme activity Biological Trace Element Research 1985, 8, 2, 113-121

MITCHINSON M.J.   *Possible role of deficiency of selenium and vitamin E in atherosclerosis* J.
                        Clin. Pathol. 1984, 37, 7, 837

SALONEN J.T.   *Serum fatty acids, apolipoproteins, selenium and vitamin antioxydants and*
                       risk of death from coronary artery disease Am. J. Cardiol. 1985, 56, 4,
                       226-231

3) Chromium

ABRAHAM A.S.   *The effect of chromiuon established atherosclerotic plaques in rabbits* Am.
                       J. Clin. Nutr. 1980, 33, 2294-2298

GORDON T.   *High density lipoprotein as a protective factor against coronary heart disease*
                       The Framingham study Am. J. Med. 1977, 62, 707

OFFENBACHER E.G.   *Effect of chromium-rich yeast on glucose tolerance a blood lipids in elderly*
                       subjects Diabetes 1980, 29, 919-925

COFFEE AND HYPERCHOLESTEROLEMIA

ARNESEN E.   *Coffee and serum cholesterol* Br. Med. J. 1984, 288, 1960
HERBERT P.N.   *Caffeine does not affect lipoprotein metabolism* Clin. res. 1987, 35, 578A
HILL C.   *Coffee consumption and cholesterol concentration* Letter to editor Br.
                       Med. J. 1985, 920, 1590

THELLE D.S.   *Coffee and cholesterol in epidemiological and experimental studies* Atherosclerosis 1987, 67, 97-103

THELLE D.S.   *The Tromso Heart Study. Does coffee raise serum cholesterol?* N. Engl. J. Med. 1983, 308, 1454-1457

IDEAL WEIGHT

When we measure ourselves, what exactly are we measuring? Usually, it is the total body weight, including bones, muscle, fat, organs, viscera, nerves and water. Fat makes up 15% of the total body mass in men and 22% in women.

Obesity is defined as excess body fat, surpassing average weight by at least 20%. We associate obesity with excess weight, even if the scale does not reveal the exact ratio of fat mass to active mass (e.g. muscles, organs). How can we measure the exact amount of fat in the body?

One way is to measure a fold of skin with a compass, but this is not a reliable method. Instead of using the weight charts strictly established by insurance companies, or the skin fold method, it is better to use the Lorenz formula (height in cm and weight in kg) in order to understand the concept of ideal weight:

Weight (men)   = (Height - 100) - 1/4 (Height - 150)

Weight (women) = (Height - 100) - 1/2 (Height - 150)

This formula does not, however, take into account age or the skeletal structure.

The Quetelet index or BMI (Body Mass Index)——weight/height (2)——is commonly used nowadays to define the relationship between weight and height squared.

BMI = Weight (kg)/Height^2 (m^2)

The average BMI for men is 20-25. For women it is 19-24. Any higher value, up to 30, signifies excess weight. If the value is higher than 30, the subject is considered obese. If the BMI is higher than 40, the case is medically alarming.

This definition is medical and not aesthetic but the BMI concept is useful because it is linked to the notion of fat-mass

The way fat is distributed determines the prognosis for obesity. This distribution is measured using the following ratio.

$$\frac{\text{waist measurement (at the navel)}}{\text{hip measurement (at fullest part)}}$$

It is generally 0.85 for men and 0.65 to 0.85 for women.

In android obesity, most fat is accumulated in the upper body (face, neck, abdomen above the navel). The ratio is always greater than 1.

Complications arrive early and are frequent: diabetes, hypercholesterolemia, high blood pressure, cardiovascular risks.

In gynecoid obesity, the fat mass is found essentially in the lower body (hips, buttocks, thighs, lower belly). This distribution is normal in the female body. The risks of complications are lower. The problem exists more from an aesthetic point of view than anything. The worst aspect of the problem is that this type of obesity may result in cellulitis.

Beyond the medical statistics, which try to describe scientifically what is more an aesthetic concern or a discomfort, the most important weight value is one at which the patient will feel the most comfortable. In sum, the goal should be a weight that gives the patient a sense of well-being.

This weight may sometimes be greater than the weight calculated by theoretical standards, but we really should not be concerned about this. If an obese person can reach this weight, then it is a more realistic goal than theoretical ideals established by doctors, which may even cause discouragement if the goal is too severe.

On the other hand, women are often overly influenced by media images. They should realize that a fantastic and unrealistic weight goal has no justification. Their bodies, fully equipped with reasonable regulatory systems, will prevent them from reaching such a goal.

The ideal——if it exists——should be carefully thought out by the obese person and if necessary, with the critical help of a doctor.

THE CALORIE THEORY

When food is placed in a calorimeter, the energy it contains can be calculated. For example: 3.5 oz of honey releases 290 calories, 3.5 oz of butter 750 calories, 3.5 oz of codfish 80 calories, and 3.5 oz pork 380 calories.
- .035 oz of protein release 4 calories
- .035 oz of carbohydrate release 4 calories
- .035 oz of fat release 9 calories
- .035 oz of alcohol release 7 calories

The term concept of "calories" is often misused. The word "calories" is actually a simplified version of the term kilocalories. And, if we really wanted to respect the international terms, we would count in kilojoules, where one kilocalorie is equal to 4.18 kilojoules.

The human body, to put it very simply, has too often been compared to a boiler: if intake is greater than the body's expenditures and not everything is "burned", the excess calories accumulate, and the subject gains weight. If, on the other hand, the calorie ration is inferior to the daily calorie requirement, the organism must, theoretically, draw upon its fat reserves and the subject should lose weight.

This reasoning ignores the human body's ability to regulate and adopt itself and denies the individual particularities that make each person unique!

Contrary to popular belief, an obese person is not necessarily someone who eats too much. In an obese population:
- only 15% over-eat (2,800 - 4,000 cal/day)
- 35% eat normally (2,000 - 2,700 cal/day)
- 50% eat little (less than 2,000 cal/day)

274

World class athletes are able to maintain a stable weight with caloric inputs ranging from 2,500 to 12,000 calories per day, according to the individual and the sport. The marathon runner, Alain Mimoun, maintained his weight and underwent difficult training on only 2,000 calories per day, whereas the cyclist, Jacques Anquetil, needed 6,000 calories to balance his diet and maintain a stable weight.

The differences in caloric intake are minimal among slim, normal, fat and obese individuals, as is proven by the studies of Doctors Bellisle and Roland-Cachera, who divided the studied subjects into five categories using the B.M.I. index (Weight/Height^2).

By examining the following graphs, it becomes evident that there is no correlation between daily calorie rations and corpulence. Obese and fat people do not automatically eat any more than slim and thin ones.

However, by classifying children according to their father's profession, it appears that among children with similar BMI indices, those whose fathers are blue collar workers eat more than those whose fathers are office workers or executives.

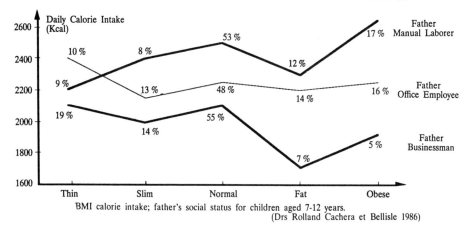

BMI calorie intake; father's social status for children aged 7-12 years.
(Drs Rolland Cachera et Bellisle 1986)

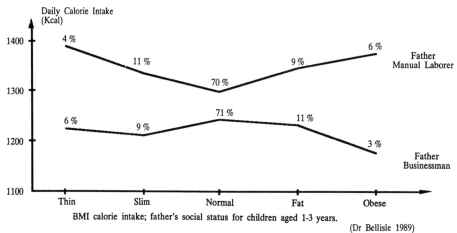

BMI calorie intake; father's social status for children aged 1-3 years.

(Dr Bellisle 1989)

275

Yet this data does not prevent most weight loss methods from being based upon a hypocaloric approach. The reasoning goes like this:

If the necessary daily ration for an adult is 2,500 calories and he is given a 2,000 calorie diet, a 500 calorie deficit results. His body is then forced to supplement the diet by drawing the missing 500 calories from the fat reserves, and the individual loses weight.

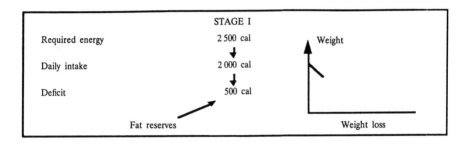

But, what actually occurs is the following: when the body is faced with this input deficit, it eventually adjusts the offer to the demand. That is to say, if it is given no more than 2,000 calories, it will function on only 2,000 calories.

Consequently, there is no longer an energy deficit. The fat reserves are no longer required and the weight stabilizes. The subject may believe that he has reached a plateau in his weight-loss and waits confidently.

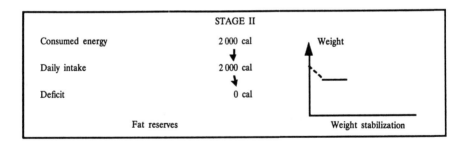

In this stage, the body "remembers" its previous frustrations. What if its daily ration were to be reduced again? Triggered by its survival instinct, the body decides to spend no more than 1,700 calories in order to save 300 calories in case new rationing happens. The 300 calorie surplus is stored away and the subject gains even more weight.

276

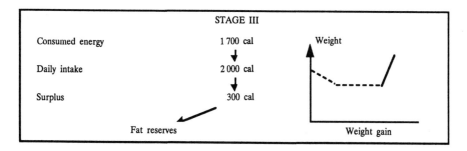

Worried by his new weight gain, the subject visits his doctor or nutritionist, who doubts the patient's story. The patient is suspected of having miscalculated his caloric intake or of having secretly binged on the side. In sum, the obese subject is assumed to be incapable of following directions, or even worse, a liar! To ensure the results, the doctor lowers the daily caloric ration and gives new advice, and the subject leaves with a 1,500 calorie diet as well as renewed hopes.

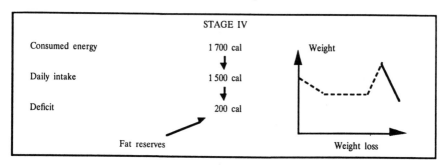

A few weeks later, we find that the patient's body, having functioned on 1,700 calories, is again taken by surprise, and further weight-loss occurs.

As we have seen already, the body is on guard for a decreased caloric intake. Subsequently, the regulatory system is triggered more quickly, and the weight-loss phase is shorter and not as noticeable. A new plateau has now been reached because the organism has readjusted to the imposed rationing.

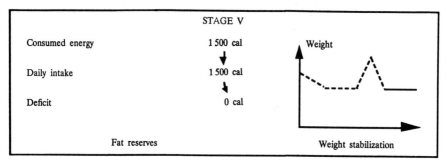

By this time, we know that the body's ancestral survival instinct has worked to build up reserves while consuming no more than 1,200 calories daily. Once again, the patient starts to gain weight.

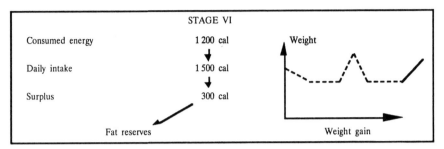

At this point, the patient now understands that weight-loss occurs if the food ration is continuously diminished. Using calorie tables, he calculates a 1,000 calorie diet for himself.

An ephemeral weight-loss phase follows once again, but is quickly halted when weight stabilization is attained. Weight gain occurs and the subject now exceeds his initial weight. The organism was on its guard and it quickly triggered its protective system. At the slightest calorie intake, it stored a maximum of surplus food.

Those accustomed to hypocaloric diets can bear witness that the slightest dietary mistake, "because it's the weekend", can make them gain four to five pounds within one or two days.

The obese patient thus watches his weight like bouncing a rubber ball. At the slightest lack of discipline, it goes bounding up.

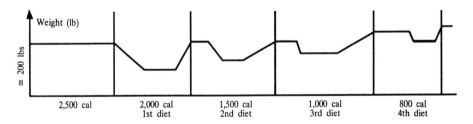

The Calvary of the Undernourished (by JP Ruasse)

Finally, the more the subject rations himself, the more his body tends to create reserves. Some individuals who weighed 154 lbs. for example, and who only had 10 lbs. to lose, found themselves weighing 158 lbs. at the end of the diet.

In the hypocaloric diet, the calorie ration must be continuously reduced in order for weight-loss to occur. But in the end, the less one eats, the more one gains weight!

278

Doctors are therefore confronted with a clientele, who, at the price of a severely controlled diet and enormous frustrations, manage to gain weight (or do not lose any) on an 800 calorie diet——not to mention the fact that the reduced intake leads to fatigue, low blood pressure and even depression. In addition, the patient risks becoming anorexic at any time. At this point, all they need to do is switch doctors, going from a nutritionalist to a psychiatrist!

Yet the sawtooth pattern of such diets that cause successive weight gain and weight-loss is well known, and has even been demonstrated in animals.

Professor Bronwell, of the University of Pennsylvania, studied this phenomenon on a population of rats alternated between high and low calorie diets: over the course of the first diet, the rats lost weight in 21 days and gained back the weight over a period of 46 days. Over the course of the second diet, the rats lost the same amount of weight over a 46 day period and regained everything in 14 days!

Later weight-loss is more difficult to achieve, and weight gain is more and more rapid. It has therefore been proven that the metabolism adapts itself to calorie reductions. Every caloric deficit can lower the metabolic expenditures by 50%, but every return to the norm, however brief, is accompanied by weight gain. The greater the difference between the diet and normal intake the quicker weight regain occurs.

Suffice it to say that it is not enough to follow a 1,500 calorie diet if the calories consumed are unbalanced. For example, a person who consumes a coke and a bologna sandwich on white bread has obviously missed the point. The diet must also include a proper balance of carbohydrates, fibers and minerals in order to have a positive effect on weight-loss.

BIBLIOGRAPHY

ASTIER-DUMAS M.   *Densité calorique, densité nutritionnelle, repères pour le choix des aliments* Med. Nutr. 1984, XX, 4, 229-234

BELLISLE F.   *Obesity and food intake in children : evidence for a role of metabolic and/ or behavioral daily rhythms* Appetite 1988, 11, 111-118

BROWNELL K.D.   *The effects of repeated cycles of weight-loss and regain in rats* Phys. Behavior 1986, 38, 459-464

HERAUD G.   *Densité nutritionnelle des aliments* Gaz. Med. FR. 1988, 95, 13, 39-42

LEIBEL R.J.   *Diminished energy requirements in reduced obese persons* Metabolism 1984, 33, 164-170

ROLLAND-CACHERA M.F., BELLISLEF   *No correlation between adiposity and food intake : why are working class children fatter ?* Am. J. Clin. Nutr. 1986, 44, 779-787

ROLAND-CACHERA M.F., DEHEEGER M.   *Adiposity and food intake in young children : the environmental challenge to individual susceptibility* Br. Med. J. 1988, 296, 1037-1038

RUASSE J.P.   *Des calories, pourquoi ? Combien ? Coll. L'indispensable en Nutrition 1987*

URASSE J.P.   *L'approche homéopathique du traitement des obésités* Paris 1988

SPITZER L., RODIN J.   *Human eating behavior : a critical review of study in normal weight and overweight individuals* Appetite 1981, 2, 293

LOUIS-SYLVESTRE J.   *Poids accordéon : de plus en plus difficile à perdre* Le Gén. 1989, 1087, 18-20

INSULIN

A) INTRODUCTION

Insulin is a polypeptidic hormone secreted by the islets of Langherans in the pancreas. It is the endocrine secretion of the pancreas. It maintains glycemia at around 5.5 mmol/l.

From a physiological point of view, it is the only substance responsible for glycoregulation in normal subjects. Catecholamines and glucagon only play this role in exceptional circumstances.

B) INSULIN SECRETION

There is a weak and continual basal secretion of insulin (2 to 20 microU/ml) which controls the secretion of hepatic glucose when the subject is in a fasting state or between meals. However, it is too weak to cause lipogenesis, i.e. the accumulation of fat reserves.

At the beginning of a meal there is a phase of insulin production in the head of the pancreas resulting in an instantaneous small secretion peak of low intensity, lasting only a few minutes. It is triggered by the mere sight of food or contact of the tongue's anterior taste buds with any substance. This response can be considered as a preparation for a meal.

The peak is rapidly followed by a drop which is then followed by a second peak in the post-prandial phase. Insulin secretion therefore depends on the extent of the glycemic increase. It favors intracellular penetration of glucose and its storage in the form of glycogen and triglycerides. This anabolising process, lipogenesis, occurs only when there are large amounts of circulating insulin.

C) REGULATING INSULIN SECRETION

1) **Glucose** is the substrate that stimulates the B-cells of the pancreas. But other carbohydrates have the same effect: galactose, fructose, mannose, ribose, xylitol and ribitol. Xylose and arabinose, on the other hand, have no such impact.

2) **Lipids:** certain intermediaries in fat metabolism such as ketonic substrates, butyrate, propionate and octanoate may favor insulin secretion. This has been proven in *in vitro* experiments but the concentrations found *in vivo* are physiologically insignificant.

Malaisse proved that a diet based on fats causes the plasmatic insulin level to decrease; but in order to avoid an atherogenic effect, it is necessary to limit the intake of saturated fats and instead favor consumption of mono and polyunsaturated fats.

3) **Protein:** amino acids, particularly leucine and arginine, can increase insulin secretion. But again, this phenomenon occurs at plasmatic concentrations that are never found in physiological conditions.

4) **Other factors favoring insulin secretion:**

- glucagon
- glucocorticoid
- cyclic AMP
- intestinal hormones (secretin, gastrin, entero-glucagon)
- estrogen
- thyroxin
- growth hormone

- stimulation of the Vagus nerve (X)
- stimulation of the B-receptors and inhibition of the alpha-receptors
- calcium, magnesium and potassium ions
- caffeine
- theophylline
- sulfonylureas

5) **Factors inhibiting insulin secretion**

- fasting state
- weight-loss
- hypoxia
- insulin
- glucosamine
- catecholamines (epinephrine, norepinephrine)
- inhibition of the Vagus nerve

- stimulation of the alpha-receptors and betablocking agents
- alloxan
- streptozotocine
- diazoxide
- phenethylbiguanide
- diuretic substances

D) HOW INSULIN WORKS

1) **On water metabolism:** favors water retention by causing sodium retention.

2) **On protein metabolism:** favors the intracellular penetration of amino acids.

3) **On carbohydrate metabolism:** triggers a drop in glycemia as a result of cellular absorption of glucose.

4) **On fat metabolism:** favors lipogenesis and consequently, the formation of fat reserves:
   - by causing excess glucose to be transformed into fatty acids,
   - by stimulating the lipoprotein lipase which allows circulating fatty acids to be stored as fat reserves in the form of triglycerides,
   - by increasing the volume of fat cells,
   - by inhibiting triglyceride lipase, which normally would be responsible for lipolysis,
   - and by neutralizing the lipolytic effect of cortisol and the catecholamines.

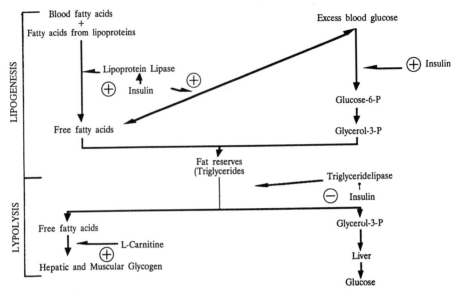

Source: Creff

In the cases of hyperinsulinism, the whole metabolism is geared toward lipogenesis. The fat reserves subsequently increase, and therefore, so does weight. This phenomenon is reinforced since lipolysis is impossible, as insulin inhibits the action of triglyceride lipase, which would normally cause the breakdown of fat reserves.

With the Montignac method, when we avoid carbohydrates with a high glycemic index, we eliminate hyperglycemic peaks. Consequently, insulin secretion decreases progressively. Once the insulin level is low enough (often less than 20 mU/ml), the lipogenesis system becomes physiologically impossible and it is "turned off" and lipolysis is "turned on." Hence, in the long term, weight-loss puts an end to insulin resistance. The phenomenon is, however, always reversible; this is what eventually ensures weight stability.

E) INSULIN AND OBESITY

Eating too many carbohydrates with a high glycemic index results in hyperglycemic peaks which induce high insulin secretion. At first, hyperinsulinism corrects hyperglycemia in the post-prandial phase. Then there is a decrease in glucose tolerance and glucose is inefficiently used peripherally. It takes a long time to penetrate the adipose, muscular and hepatic tissues. This is the insulin resistance stage: the insulin receptors are not as numerous, abnormalities in the post-receptors occur and the tyrosine kinase properties of the insulin receptors are altered.

As a result, in the second stage, the insulin is not correctly recognized by the gluco-dependent tissues which are not properly informed of the presence of insulin.

282

Since the sugar is slow to enter the tissues, the glycemic level remains high for too long and a second secretion of insulin occurs. This simply aggravates the hyperinsulinism.

In the third stage, insulin resistance affects the pancreas; there is a slow-down in the normal drop in insulin secretion, which further aggravates hyperinsulinism.

The question is whether or not hyperinsulinism and insulin resistance are a primitive abnormality or a consequence of obesity.

Clark studied both these hypotheses:

The Case of Primitive Abnormality:

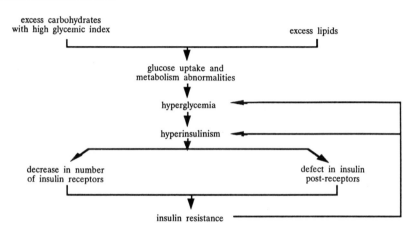

The Case for Secondary Abnormality:

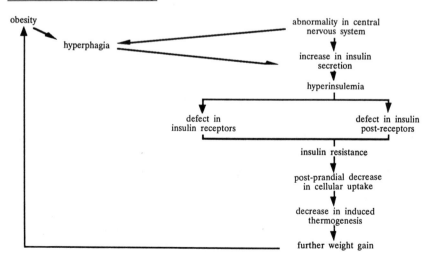

Hyperinsulinism most definitely plays an important role in obesity and insulin resistance. However, a secondary factor may be involved: the brown adipose tissue, specialized in heat generation, presents a number of abnormalities in obese persons. There is a decrease in thermogenesis which is normally induced by cold and by food consumption. This explains how weight increase is possible without hyperphagia.

F) THE MORBID DANGERS OF HYPERINSULINISM

It was long believed that hyperglycemia was more dangerous than hyperinsulinism. But, in fact, it is hyperinsulinism that increases the risk of arteriosclerosis with vascular, and specifically coronary incidents.

Hyperinsulinism is related to android obesity, periodic high blood pressure, hypertriglyceridemia, a decrease in the HDL-cholesterol level, hyperuricemia, excessive platelet hyperaggregation and sodium retention.

Moreover, hyperinsulinism plays a role in the alteration of the arterial walls because it facilitates the proliferation of smooth muscle cells and increases the LDL bonds to these cells.

Hyperinsulinism occurs when the blood insulin level is higher than 20mU/ml on an empty stomach or higher than 80mU/ml in the post-prandial phase.

BIBLIOGRAPHY

BASDEVANT A. *Influence de la distribution de la masse sur le risque vasculaire* La Presse Médicale 1987, 16, 4

CLARK M.G. *Obesity with insulin resistance. Experimental insights* Lancet, 1983, 2, 1236-1240

FROMAN L.A. *Effect of vagotomy and vagal stimulation on insulin secretion* Diabetes 1967, 16, 443-448

GROSS P. *De l'obésité au diabète* L'actualité diabétologique N° 13, p. 1-9

GUY-GRAND B. *Variation des acides gras libres plasmatiques au cours des hyperglycémies provoquées par voie orale* Journées de Diabétologie de l'Hôtel-Dieu 1968, p. 319

GUY-GRAND B. *Rôle éventuel du tissu adipeux dans l'insulino-résistance* Journées de Diabétologie de l'Hôtel-Dieu 1972, 81-92

JEANRENAUD B. *Dysfonctionnement du système nerveux. Obésité et résistance à l'insuline* M/S Médecine-Sciences 1987, 3, 403-410

JEANRENAUD B. *Insulin and obesity* Diabetologia, 1979, 17, 135-138

KOLTERMAN O.G. *Mechanisms of insulin resistance in human obesity. Evidence for receptor and post-receptor effects* J. Clin. Invest. 1980, 65, 1272-1284

LAMBERT A.E. *Enhancement by caffeine of glucagon-induced and tolbutamide-induced insulin release from isolated fœtal pancreatic tissue* Lancet, 1967, 8, 819-820

LAMBERT A.E.	*Organocultures de pancréas fœtal de rat : étude morphologique et libération d'insuline in vitro* Journées de Diabétologie de l'Hôtel-Dieu 1969, 115-129
LARSON B.	*Abdominal adipose ti ;ue distribution, obesity and risk of cardiovascular disease and death* Br. Med. J. 1984, 288, 1402-1404
LE MARCHAND-BRUSTEL Y.	*Résistance à l'insuline dans l'obésité* M/S Médecine-Sciences 1987, 3, 394-402
LINQUETTE C.	*Précis d'endocrinologie* Ed. Masson 1973, p. 658-666
LOUIS-SYLVESTRE J.	*La phase céphalique de sécrétion d'insuline* Diabète et métabolisme 1987, 13, 63-73
MARKS V.	*Action de différents stimuli sur l'insulinosécrétion humaine : influence du tractus gastro-intestinal* Journées de Diabétologie de l'Hôtel-Dieu 1969, 179-190
MARLISSE E.B.	*Système nerveux central et glycorégulation* Journées de Diabétologie de l'Hôtel-Dieu 1975, 7-21
MEYLAN M.	*Metabolic factors in insulin resistance in human obesity* Metabolism 1987, 36, 256-261
WOODS S.C.	*Interaction entre l'insulinosécrétion et le système nerveux central* Journées de Diabétologie de l'Hôtel-Dieu 1983

FUNCTIONAL HYPOGLYCEMIA

A) PHYSIOPATHOLOGY

In the morning on an empty stomach, the glycemic level is approximately 5.5 mmol/l. If the subject eats a balanced breakfast, the glycemic rate will increase to 7.7 mmol/l and, in response to the insulin's action, will drop to 5.5 mmol/l after two hours, and continue to decrease to 3.85 mmol/l during the third hour, before it again reverts to 5.5 mmol/l (see graph I).

However, if the subject consumes an excessive amount of carbohydrates with a high glycemic index (white bread, honey, jam, sugared coffee or tea, commercial fruit juices rich in saccharose) or drinks alcohol mixed with a sweet drink on an empty stomach, the result is a high glycemic peak after 20 minutes. At this point, the pancreas endocrine intervenes, reducing the glycemic rate, but the drop is often significant and can reach 2.48 mmol/l causing hypoglycemia (see graph II).

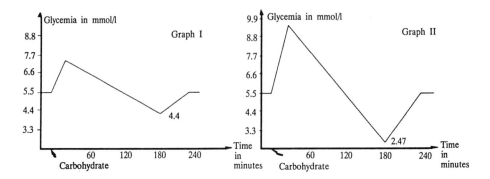

If the glycemic level drops drastically, the subject will experience a number of symptoms. These symptons include paleness, palpitations, perspiration, anxiety, shakes, sharp hunger pangs and other discomforts such as a loss of consciousness, which is the classic hypoglycemic symptom. Patients need to understand that if they are in a hypoglycemic state at 11:00 a.m., it is because they consumed an excessive amount of certain carbohydrates three hours earlier. Contrary to their belief that their condition is due to a lack of sugar, the real reason is that they have digested too many high-glycemia carbohydrates which then provoke severe hypoglycemia.

Usually, the glycemic level drops progressively, with more ordinary symptoms. This prevents the doctor from making an accurate diagnosis. Some of these symptoms are headaches, yawning, fatigue, irritability, aggressiveness, blurred vision, memory gaps, lack of concentration, dyslexia and chills. These symptoms are the patients' most common complaints and are often attributed to fatigue or to the beginnings of cerebral ischemia. They can, however, be signs of hypoglycemia. These signs then should not be overlooked or neglected. Functional cases of hypoglycemia are found in 19% of subjects of normal weight and in 31% of obese subjects.

It must be noted that some certain subjects may be victims of genuine hypoglycemia and yet do not show any symptoms. Others may complain of discomforts suggesting hypoglycemia which are not confirmed by blood sugar levels measured during the periods of malaise. Similarly, the glycemic level at which troubles appear varies: certain cases of hypoglycemia at 3.85 mmol/l are very badly tolerated whereas others are well tolerated at 2.47 mmol/l.

B) DIAGNOSIS

To confirm diagnosis of functional hypoglycemia, the clinical signs described above should be observed:
- the symptoms should appear when the subject has not eaten, a few hours after a meal or following physical exertion;
- they should disappear soon after consuming sugary foods.

286

It is important that hypoglycemia be biologically confirmed:
- orally provoked hyperglycemia is useful, but it can lead to false positive diagnoses;
- the tolerance test based on a standardized breakfast is more reliable;
- an increase of insulemia or plasmatic cortisol is an argument in favor of the diagnosis;
- but the ideal way to confirm it is to measure the glycemic level during periods of malaise by sampling a drop of blood from the finger and to dose the glucose level with a filleted automatic band analyzer. In fact, the only conclusive sign is a glycemic level below 2.75 mmol/l during the discomfort.

C) ETIOLOGY

Can certain mechanisms cause post-prandial functional hypoglycemia?

1) *Hyperinsulinism and insulin resistance* are common in the obese subject and facilitate secondary hypoglycemia. Hyperinsulinism is increased by coffee or alcohol absorption.

2) *Unsynchronized insulin secretion*: A delay in insulin secretion in relation to the glycemic peak. It is a sign of glucose intolerance. In this case, the patient runs the risk of becoming diabetic.

3) In rare cases, *insulin secretion is deactivated by auto-antibodies*: The resulting hyperglycemia provokes further insulin secretion. Then, the antigen-antibody complex acts like a veritable "insulin delayer" which will act late after the meal and cause hypoglycemia.

4) Sometimes, insulin secretion is quantitatively normal, but *insulin hypersensitivity* develops.

5) The release of insulin can be potentialized by an excessive release of gastro-enteric hormones: gastrin, entero-glucagon, gastric inhibitory peptides (GIP).

6) Insufficient *neoglycogenesis* can occur: upon awakening, the body produces 75% of its glucose comes from glycogen and 25% from neoglycogenesis. There are 5.40 oz (150 g) of glycogen in the muscles and 2.70 oz (75 g) of glycogen in the liver. There is considerably less circulating blood glucose, approximately .70 oz (20 g). The body consumes about .25 oz (7 g) of glucose per hour. It therefore has sufficient reserves for twelve hours. Neoglycogenesis functions more or less regularly depending on the dietary intake. When it functions poorly, this can cause hypoglycemia.

7) These phenomena are often related to an excessive vagal tonicity. It causes an acceleration of gastric emptying, a factor of hyperinsulinism. It provoked gastric hyperacidity, which leads to hypersensitivity of the pancreatic Beta cells. This results in exaggerated insulin secretion out of proportion with the glycemic level.

This vagotomy which occurs is often encountered in anxious subjects who tend to somatize, as is the case with spasmophilia. Indeed, some symptoms of hypoglycemia are also typical signs of panic. This is why it is important to establish a psychological profile of patients suffering from functional hypoglycemia.

D) TREATMENT

- The goal is to reduce the post-prandial hyperglycemic peak in order to limit insulin secretion and avoid secondary hypoglycemia.
- Dietary precautions should focus on breakfast .
- As the Montignac method suggests, carbohydrates with a high glycemic index (white bread, jam, honey, saccharose, sodas) should be eliminated from the diet.

Breakfast should be a high-protein and high-fat (preferably polyunsaturated fatty acids) meal. If necessary, its fiber content should be increased (e.g. with fruits). This reduces the post-prandial glycemic peak.

Coffee should not be drunk in excessive amounts. Caffeine increases insulin secretion. Also, avoid drinking alcohol on an empty stomach, especially if it is mixed with a sweet beverage (e.g. whiskey & coke, gin & tonic, vodka & orange juice).

These precautions are often sufficient, but it is sometimes recommended to snack between meals at 11:00 a.m. and at 4:00 p.m. Obese subjects must lose enough weight to make insulin resistance disappear and to correct hyperinsulinism. If nervous troubles occur, psychotherapy, yoga or relaxation will correct neurovegetative dystonia.

It is important to remember that post-prandial functional hypoglycemia also affects non-diabetic subjects and may be aggravated by some common prescription medications: aspirin, oxytetracycline, haloperidol, manganese, betablocking agents and destropropoxyphen-paracetamol.

On the other hand, medication is rarely necessary to treat hypoglycemia. Some form of drug may eventually be prescribed if carefully followed hygieno-dietetic health and dietary measures fail: oral antidiabetics, calcium gluconate, anticholinergics, anxiolytics and gastric dumping modifiers.

BIBLIOGRAPHY

CAHILL G.F.   *A non-editorial on non-hypoglycemia* N. Engl. J. Med. 1974, 291, 905-906

CATHELINEAU G.   *Effect of calcium infusion on post-reactive hypoglycemia* Horm. Meatb. Res. 1981, 13 ? 646-647

CHILES R.   *Excessive serum insulin response to oral glucose in obesity and mild diabetes* Diabetes 1970, 19, 458

CRAPO P.A.   *The effects of oral fructose, cucrose and glucose in subjects with reactive hypolgycemia* Diabetes care 1982, 5, 512-517

DORNER M.   *Les hypoglycémies fonctionnelles* Rev. Prat. 1972, 22, 25, 3427-3446

FAJANS S.S.   *Fasting hypoglycemia in adults* New Engl. J. Med. 1976, 294, 766-772

FARRYKANT M.   *The problem of fonctional hyperinsulinism or fonctional hypoglycemia attributed to nervous causes* Metabolism 1971, 20, 6, 428-434

FIELD J.B.   *Studies on the mechanisms of ethanol induced hypoglycemia* J. Clin. Inverst. 1963, 42, 497-506

FREINKEL N.   *Alcohol hypoglycemia* J. Clin. Invest. 1963, 42, 1112-1133

HARRIS S.   *Hyperinsulinism and dysinsulinism* J.A.M.A. 1924, 83, 729-733

288

HAUTECOUVER-TURE M.   *Les hypoglycémies fonctionnelles* Rev. Prat. 1985, 35, 31, 1901-1907

HOFELDT F.D.   *Reactive hypoglycemia* Metab. 1975, 24, 1193-1208

HOFELDT F.D.   *Are abnormalities in insulin secretion responsible for reactive hypoglycemia ?* Diabetes 1974, 23, 589-596

JENKINS D.J.A.   *Decrease in post-prandial insulin and glucose concentrations by guar and pectin* Ann. Intem. Med. 1977, 86, 20-23

JOHNSON D.D.   *Reactive hypoglycemia* J.A.M.A. 1980, 243, 1151-1155

JUNG Y.   *Reactive hypoglycemia in women* Diabetes 1971, 20, 428-434

LEFEBVRE P.   *Statement on post-prandial hypoglycemia* Diabetes cara 1988, 11, 439-440

LEFEBVRE P.   *Le syndrome d'hypoglycémie réactionnelle, mythe ou réalité ?* Journées Annuelles de l'Hôtel-Dieu 1983, 111-118

LEICHTER S.B.   *Alimentary hypoglycemia : a new appraisal* Amer. J. Nutr. 1979, 32, 2104-2114

LEV-RAN A.   *The diagnosis of post-prandial hypoglycemia* Diabetes 1981, 30, 996-999

LUBETZKI J.   *Physiopathologie des hypoglycémies* Rev. Prat. 1972, 22, 25, 3331-3347

LUYCKY A.S.   *Plasma insulin in reactive hypoglycemia* Diabetes 1971, 20, 435-442

MONNIER L.H.   *Restored synergistic entero-hormonal response after addition of dietary fiber to patients with impaired glucose tolerance and reactive hypoglycemia* Diab. Metab. 1982, 8, 217-222

O'KEEFE S.J.D.   *Lunch time gin and tonic : a cause of reactive hypoglycemia* Lancet 1977, 1, June 18, 1286-1288

PERRAULT M.   *Le régime de fond des hypoglycémies fonctionnelles de l'adulte* Rev. Prat. 1963, 13, 4025-4030

SENG G.   *Mécanismes et conséquences des hypoglycémies* Rev. Prat. 1985, 35, 31, 1859-1866

SERVICE J.F.   *Hypoglycemia and the post-prandial syndrome* New Engl. J. Med. 1989, 321, 1472

SUSSMAN K.E.   *Plasma insulin levels during reactive hypoglycemia* Diabetes 1966, 15, 1-14

TAMBURRANO G.   *Increased insulin sensitivity in patients with idiopathic reactive hypoglycemia* J. Clin. Endocr. Metab. 1989, 69, 885

TAYLOR S.I.   *Hypoglycemia associated with antibodies to the insulin receptor.* New Engl. J. Med. 1982, 307, 1422-1426

YALOW R.S.   *Dynamics of insulin secretion in hypoglycemia* Diabetes 1965, 14, 341-350

289

TECHNICAL APPENDIX II

by Professor Attilio Giacosa
Head of Nutrition at the National
Cancer Institute (Genoa, Italy)

BIOGRAPHY

Professor Attilio Giacosa was born in Neive, Italy in 1948. He graduated from the University of Turin in 1973 where he wrote his experimental thesis on the radio-immunological determination of gastrin in humans.

After spending two years in the Nutritional and Intestinal Unit at the General Hospital of Birmingham (England), he became a specialist in diseases of the digestive tract and digestive endoscopy.

Since 1976, he has collaborated with the Gastroenterology Department at the San Martino Hospital in Genoa, working in the field of digestive endoscopy and particularly clinical trials. He then went on to become a specialist in the science of nutrition at the University of Milan.

His studies are currently concentrated on the correlation between nutrition and cancer where his research is based on an experimental, epidemiological and clinical approach.

Professor Giacosa is a member of several medical societies, director of the unit on clinical nutrition at the National Institute for Cancer Research in Genoa and scientific coordinator of all European research for the ECP (European Organization for Cooperation in Cancer Prevention Studies).

In addition, his scientific activity is described in 270 papers and six monographies.

CLINICAL UTILIZATION OF DIETETIC FIBERS

In recent years, dietary habits in the industrialized countries have led to the overconsumption of meats, fats, dairy products and breads made with highly refined flour (to the detriment of dietary fiber content). Burkitt has shown that these new dietary habits favor many of today's illnesses (cardiovascular diseases and intestinal disorders).

The recent studies by Del Toma (1987) proved that meals rich in fiber can help control dysfunctions of carbohydrate and fat metabolism and contribute to weight-loss. One of the most important characteristics of the diverse dietary fibers is their degree of solubility in water:

- insoluble fibers (cellulose, hemicellulose, lignin) absorb water, increase the weight and volume of the bowels and reduce the risks of diseases related to intestinal transit, such as diverticulosis and colic cancers.

- soluble fibers (pectin, gum, mucilage) swell and form viscous solutions or gels in the digestive tube. This contributes to a certain feeling of fullness and reduces the intestinal absorption of carbohydrates and lipids.

Among these fibers, glucomannane and the Beta vulgaris fiber are the most useful:

The Beta vulgaris fiber:

These fibers are obtained from beets which contain 25% soluble fibers (pectin) and 75% insoluble fibers (cellulose 31%; hemicellulose 4.5%, lignin 2.5%). Professor Giacosa has shown their effectiveness against chronic constipation. In fact, there is only a 3.8% failure rate after one month of treatment. This result is obtained through the regulation of the bowel movement activity and the increase of the fecal volume. Fecal consistance is also modified, since the feces are soft in 69.3% of the cases.

The presence of soluble fibers means that beet fibers may also be prescribed for carbohydrate and fat metabolism problems. Beet fibers represent 77.82% of the total dry weight of the plant, which is more than the 40% of fibers found in bran.

Glucomannane:

Glucomannane is a derivative of the Amorpho Phallus Konjac plant family, grown in Japan. This fiber expands in water, absorbing 200 times its weight, and forms a viscous and gelatin-like mass. It reduces the absorption of some carbohydrates and lipids (See graphs I and II). In addition, it has proven to be effective in the treatment of obesity, as shown by the studies by Professor Giacosa (1989). If glucomannane (.14 oz or 4 g per day, taken three times before meals) is added to the diet, the subject loses 10.7 lbs. by the end of the month, whereas 7.26 lbs. are lost by control subjects taking a placebo. However, there is no difference whatsoever if the dose is reduced to .07 oz or 2 g per day.

	Average Weight	Weight at end of treatment	Difference
Glucomannane (4 g/day)	185 ± 10.3	174 ± 14.7	- 11
Placebo	183 ± 18.7	176 ± 16.7	- 7

Glucomannane is used today in the various dietary preparations, especially pasta, and together with guar gum. This pasta reduces the post-prandial hyperglycemic peak and considerably diminishes the pancreatic secretion (See graphs III and IV), and is thus useful for the obese and type II diabetics.

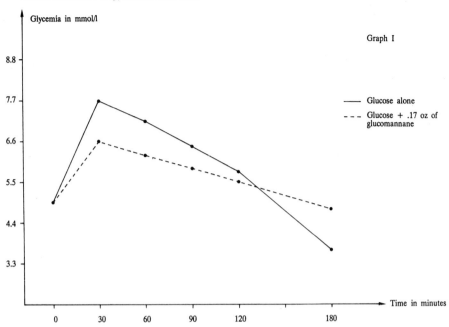

Glycemia in mmol/l

Graph I

Glucose alone

Glucose + .17 oz of
glucomannane

Time in minutes

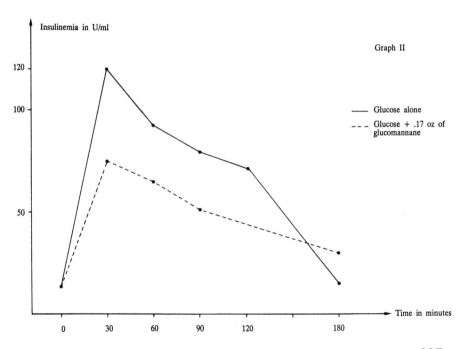

Insulinemia in U/ml

Graph II

Glucose alone

Glucose + .17 oz of
glucomannane

Time in minutes

297

Effects of the presence of fibers in pasta

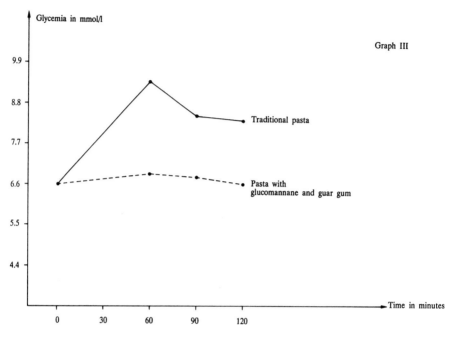

Glycemia in mmol/l

Graph III

9.9

8.8

Traditional pasta

7.7

6.6   Pasta with
             glucomannane and guar gum

5.5

4.4

                    Time in minutes

0   30   60   90   120

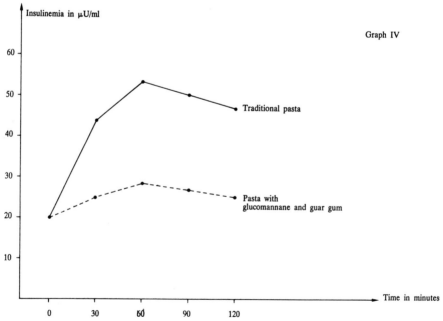

Insulinemia in µU/ml

Graph IV

60

50   Traditional pasta

40

30

20   Pasta with
                            glucomannane and guar gum

10

                    Time in minutes

0   30   60   90   120

Printed by R.R. Donnelley & Sons
May 1993

Data processing and typesetting: DL Graphique, Paris (France) - (033) 1-43.31.05.06